GW00504318

PASSPORT TO SUCCESS

PASSPORT TO SUCCESS

FROM MILKMAN TO MAYFAIR

PETER CRUDDAS

Biteback Publishing

First published in Great Britain in 2022 by
Biteback Publishing Ltd, London
Copyright © Peter Cruddas 2022

Peter Cruddas has asserted his right under the Copyright, Designs and Patents Act 1988
to be identified as the author of this work.

ISBN 978-1-78590-729-6

10 9 8 7 6 5 4 3 2 1

A CIP catalogue record for this book is available from the British Library.

Set in Adobe Caslon Pro

Printed and bound in Great Britain by
CPI Group (UK) Ltd, Croydon CR0 4YY

MIX
Paper from
responsible sources
FSC® C171272
FSC
www.fsc.org

To my darling wife Fiona. I would not be where I am today without your love and support for over thirty years. Together we have achieved so much, not least our two amazing children. As the best mother-in-law in the world would say, 'Two good heads.'

CONTENTS

ACKNOWLEDGEMENTS

I am grateful to so many people.

I have been married to Fiona for over thirty-four years. We have two beautiful and successful daughters together. One is a vascular surgeon; the other has just finished her business master's at a top London university. Fiona has been so supportive and loving over such a long period, and that has enabled me to be successful.

People assume that our daughters inherited their brains from me. They did not. Fiona is the academic brains of our family. When our children were growing up, she would help them with their maths and Latin homework. I would come in from a hard day's work, the children's homework would be done, and they would be bathed and ready for bed. All I had to do was pick them up, kiss them and say goodnight. When the children were young, Fiona did everything – she didn't want a nanny. She said, 'They are our children and we will look after them.'

When I started CMC Markets, a few years after I met Fiona, she suffered the highs and lows with me along the way. She understood how the business worked and I often discussed issues with her.

I've always confided in her and shared my worries. I consider my marriage to Fiona and our two children as my most successful achievements in life – more than my business achievements – and the platform for my success.

I am also grateful to my brother John, who I adore and who has been a terrific brother to me – always supportive and never jealous of my success. He has never asked for anything and is the most pleased when success comes my way. Also, my loving daughter Sarah and her husband Steve have always been supportive, and they have blessed me with three granddaughters, Molly, Lilly and Florence.

However, above all I must thank my mum, Lillian Francis Cruddas, née Grover.

She was not affectionate and loving. She only told me she loved me once, when she was dying of lung cancer, aged seventy-eight, at Colchester Hospital in 2001. But she was honest and fair, and without my mum's love and support I would not be where I am today. Thank you, Mum, I owe you so much.

All the proceeds of this book will be donated to the Peter Cruddas Foundation, helping young people achieve more.

INTRODUCTION

I am sitting in the drawing room of a Mayfair mansion, admiring its splendour. The house covers over 11,000 square feet and has seven floors, a lift and a roof garden. The agent's brochure described it as 'the best townhouse in the best location in Mayfair; a grand, double-fronted house with beautifully proportioned accommodation'.

Eustace Balfour, the Grosvenor Estate's architect in residence, designed the house in 1891. It is a handsome corner building of soft, red Suffolk brick with Portland stone dressings and wrought iron railings. It was previously occupied by a baronet, a knight, an earl and at least one lord, and here I am – Peter Cruddas, the son of a meat market porter and an office cleaner, brought up on a Hackney council estate and whose first job was a milkman.

The *Evening Standard* reported on 17 May 2016:

Leading City Brexit campaigner Peter Cruddas has splashed out on a £42 million Mayfair mansion ... The former Tory party co-treasurer ... paid cash for the seven-storey Victorian residence near Park Lane last month, according to property sources.

[His] new home is one of the most imposing properties in the central London neighbourhood that has become known as the Qatari Quarter, due to the large number of buyers from the emirate.

As well as the purchase price, Mr Cruddas, 62, faces a stamp duty bill of almost £5 million.

I am in a relaxed mood. I have just spent Christmas at Claridge's Hotel with my family, followed by a week skiing in St Moritz including a big New Year's Eve party at the Badrutt's Palace Hotel.

I left Shoreditch Comprehensive School in 1969 at the age of fifteen without any qualifications. My two brothers – John, who is six years older, and Stephen, my twin – ended up as taxi drivers. My dad, John (Jack) Cruddas, a Geordie from South Shields, was an alcoholic. He drank up to twenty-five pints of Guinness and a bottle of rum a day. Mum would get up at 5 a.m. to clean offices in the City and I would often help her out.

Sometimes I have to pinch myself when I think about where I have come from and what my life is today. It has been an epic journey from milkman to Mayfair – and along the way I was often asked to write a book, as so many friends and colleagues wanted to know how I turned a £10,000 company into a £1 billion business. I resisted for many years, but when the time felt right, I knew I wanted to tell the story myself, in my own words.

I decided against using a ghost-writer for this book, and the words you read now are all mine, apart from the quotes. Once I started writing, I could not stop: the words and thoughts kept flooding out. I wrote 90,000 words in ninety days and I enjoyed the experience very much.

I hope you enjoy reading it as much as I did writing it.

Chapter 1

GROWING UP

My name is Peter Andrew Cruddas. I was born on 30 September 1953 and I was raised on a Hackney council estate. I did not go to university, I left school at fifteen without any qualifications. In 1989 I founded CMC Markets with £10,000. At its peak, CMC was worth in excess of £1.5 billion. I did it without borrowing any money and without any outside investors. I not only created a billion-pound company, but at the same time, I invented an industry – online trading – when I launched Europe's first online retail trading platform in 1996.

This is the story of my journey from humble beginnings to billionaire status, dining with royals, attending the wedding of William and Kate at Westminster Abbey, having meetings with Prime Ministers at 10 Downing Street and a lot more besides. And to cap it all I am Lord Cruddas of Shoreditch, having been nominated for a peerage by the Prime Minister, Boris Johnson.

I was born at 5.50 p.m. on a Wednesday – ten minutes after my twin brother Stephen – at the Salvation Army Mothers' Hospital, Lower Clapton Road, east London. I had blond hair and blue eyes. Stephen had jet black hair and brown eyes.

Thinking back to my early childhood, I remember sitting in a pushchair eating a loaf of bread that my mother had bought and being pushed around the streets. We lived at 85 Bracklyn Court in Hoxton. With my other brother John, there were five of us in this two-bedroom, ground-floor council flat with no central heating.

Mum was a tough, hard-working lady who thought the world of her three boys. She brought all three of us up single-handed, getting in from her early morning cleaning job to get us our bowl of porridge and pack us off to school. I still love milky porridge to this day.

My dad used to work early at Smithfield's meat market and then in a pub, so he was never there, and he never bothered too much with us. So Mum had to do everything for us. She was our rock and another foundation for my success. But she was also very tough and wouldn't back off from anybody, man or woman.

I remember when I was about eleven years old, running home crying because a boy, five years older, had hit me. Her response was to kick me out of the door to go and hit the kid back. There was no sympathy, just anger that I hadn't defended myself. So I ran back and hit the kid to get even. Mum said, 'Well done, but don't you come home here if you haven't stood up for yourself.' I have done so ever since.

Thinking back, I realise that my mum may have had another motive for making me stand up for myself. I think she knew that one day there would be a major confrontation between myself and my dad. She was right.

My dad was useless as a father. He was in the army during the Second World War and found comfort in drink. I often joked that my dad is famous – he invented binge drinking. He kept still drinking more or less to the day he died. In later years he loved to go to the local pub in the hand-me-down clothes I gave him. He would often turn up in a Giorgio Armani Black Label suit with a smart shirt and tie that I had given him after I had upgraded to the current season's collection. I also gave him a pair of silver cufflinks to complete the look. Because he was so slim, due to heavy smoking and not eating, just drinking, he looked smart. I would say that he was the best-dressed alcoholic in Clacton.

When I was young, he contributed little to family life. We never went to a restaurant as a family. We had the occasional holiday in a caravan in Ramsgate and at a Warners Holiday camp in Great Yarmouth. We used to send boxed kippers, which was apparently the local speciality, to relatives. But my dad's idea of a family holiday was to drink all day and leave his wife and kids to get on with it. We barely knew his relatives as they lived in Newcastle.

Living with my dad was a nightmare. There were always arguments between him, Mum and my brothers and me. It was like living in a war zone and, as we all got older, I think Mum knew that one day there would be a stand-off.

It happened once between my dad and my older brother John. I don't remember too much about the incident, other than John rushing to the pub where my dad worked – The Fox in Paul Street, Finsbury – and punching him in the face. Soon after, John left home.

I have to laugh now, because another story springs to mind. One day there was a knock at the door of our council flat and some big bloke was asking for my dad.

Mum said, 'Why do you want to see him?'

The man said, 'Because your boy Peter just hit my son. I am not putting up with it. I am going to beat the shit out of your husband.'

My mum said, 'What's that have to do with my husband?'

'Nothing, but it will teach your son a lesson if I beat up his dad.' My dad was hiding in a back room in our flat and the man said, 'If he does not come out, I will come back with a shotgun.'

To that, my mum replied, 'Go on then, get your shotgun and I will be waiting here with a great big machete to hit you with.'

The man laughed and said, 'Alright, missus, fair enough, let's leave it then, but tell your son to leave my son alone,' and he went on his way. Once the coast was clear Dad resurfaced, but he avoided his usual pub for about a month.

The point is that Mum would stand up to anyone and everyone, she would not back down, and she instilled that in me.

I have few memories of my early years, but I do remember Saturday morning pictures at the Carlton Cinema on Essex Road, Islington, which was always a must. I saved every penny during the week so I could buy some Butterkist popcorn and a Kia-Ora fruit juice. I was around five or six years old.

Every October, Stephen and I used to go out collecting money for Bonfire Night fireworks, commonly known as 'Penny for the Guy'. One night in October 1958, my five-year-old self was sitting on New North Road at the bridge that passes over the Regent's Canal – it's still there today. We had our handmade Guy figure made from an old shirt, trousers and socks, all stuffed with newspaper, and a hand-painted face on some cardboard.

It must have been past our bedtime, because Stephen and I fell asleep next to our Guy. Mum was going frantic looking for us. Eventually, we were woken by passers-by who realised that we would otherwise have been there all night. When we got home, Mum calmed down and we went out again the next day to collect more money for fireworks. I still smile when I drive over that bridge on my way to the odd Arsenal football game.

It's amazing to think that as five-year-olds we were allowed out without supervision and we crossed the busy New North Road on our own. How times have changed.

I grew up in a household full of stories from my mum and dad about the war. Mum was sixteen when the war broke out and during the Blitz she often took her mother – my Nanny Grover – to Bank Underground Station from their home in Pitfield Street in Shoreditch while bombs were falling around them. She was not able to rush because Nanny was disabled and could not have kept up, and my mum was nearly killed more than once doing this. Ever since I was a baby, Nanny always used a walking stick supported by her elbow.

Mum worked in a munitions factory in Staines, Middlesex, where she helped assemble torpedoes. Often the women would chalk 'Bollocks to Hitler' on the completed torpedoes and send them on their way.

Mum always spoke highly of Sir Winston Churchill, who was a hero in our family. When Sir Winston died in January 1965, we had a day off school for the state funeral. My friend Eddie Hobbs and I jumped on a bus to Westminster to watch the procession. Eddie and I climbed up a lamp post as the horse-drawn carriage passed by. It was an amazing moment; I was eleven years old and yet I felt the need to go and see this amazing man's funeral. I am glad I did because it is a vivid memory that I will cherish all my life.

Another big memory from this period was England winning the World Cup in July 1966. What a day – I remember all the games and how great it was to see us win our first and, so far, our only World Cup. I watched it on TV and to this day I've felt the man of the match was Alan Ball. He was outstanding on the day, and he eventually played for Arsenal.

Around 1965, I joined the Boy Scouts with my oldest friends, the Hill brothers – John, Roy and William. William became a bit of a celebrity as he played drums with Labi Siffre, who had a string of hits in the 1970s. He also played in shows like *Hair* and *Jesus Christ Superstar*. I remember he took us for a spin in his new Vauxhall Ventora three litre, and it was fast. That was my first experience of fast cars, and I was determined to get one when I got older. Not a Vauxhall Ventora but a Jaguar XJS, a Ferrari and a few Bentley Turbos – I love fast, powerful cars. I have owned around eight Bentleys, a Ferrari and two Porsches. My current car is a Rolls-Royce Wraith Black Badge – an amazing car, which I love.

John Hill was my biggest friend as we were about the same age and we used to hang around a lot together. The Hills were considered the rich family in our block of flats because they had a corner shop just off Hoxton Market and they always seemed to have chocolate, sweets and pocket money. They often went on holiday to Spain; they had a cine camera and I have a short film of the four of us drinking some beer out of a cup we won in the Scouts. Their mum Dot was a superb pianist and often used to play and sing in their front room. They always had a Christmas party at their flat and they had lots of friends. To this day, we are all friends and John and I see each other two or three times a year, we have known each other for over sixty years.

Joining the Scouts changed my life. Often, when speaking to budding entrepreneurs at universities, I'm asked whether I would be as successful as I am today if I had gone to university. My response is I do not know. But I do know that if I had not been in the Scouts, I would not be where I am today.

I loved being in the Scouts. We met every Monday at the Hoxton Market Christian Mission, which John Hill tells me is a Greek restaurant now. It taught me life's basic skills, like cooking, sewing, teamwork, competition and caring for others. It got me out of an unhappy home life and gave me a break. I used to love camping at Gilwell Park, Chingford, and entering camping competitions, hiking around the Surrey Hills and earning all the badges. I learnt to be a team leader when I was made patrol leader of my pack at the 5th Shoreditch troop.

In July 1966, the borough selected me to represent the Scouts at a jamboree on Brownsea Island, Poole Harbour. I remember telling my parents I was going, and my dad said, 'No you are not, we cannot afford it.' However, 5th Shoreditch Scouts paid for it, so I still went. I remember fishing off the harbour wall and catching a small fish. It was an exciting moment.

Thirty years later, I would see that same pier wall that I sat on as a boy when I was test-driving a Sunseeker 52-foot motorboat. We cruised right by the spot where I had been fishing, and it brought a lump to my throat. It had been an amazing journey, but I still remembered that day I caught my first fish as a small boy. I pointed it out to Fiona and the girls, and they could tell I was emotional – so emotional that I bought the bloody boat, which cost me a fortune.

These lifelong memories from the Scouts are the reason I eventually started a charitable foundation. I initially wanted to give to charities that helped young people from disadvantaged backgrounds. I wanted to help others who had a similar upbringing to me and support organisations that provide a safety net for young people, help them see a different way of life, give them hope and direction, and help those without a stable home life to cope.

I often advise university students that if you ever make it big, give to charity. It is the moral thing to do, but you also meet more top businesspeople through charity than you do through business.

It is a great way to network and you are meeting like-minded, caring people. I once had dinner with Bill and Melinda Gates in London and I have had tea with the Prince of Wales at Clarence House. I was a trustee of the Prince's Trust and chairman of Youth United, a charity that Prince Charles asked me to set up. Through this work, he invited me and Fiona to Prince William's wedding at Westminster Abbey. If you watch the footage on YouTube, you can see me in the front row as William and Kate pass us by. Prince Charles nodded to me as he walked by. I also had dinner with the Queen and Prince Philip at a private dining room in Windsor Castle for ten people. I have to confess I was feeding the Corgis under the table with scraps off my plate.

I remember in 2011 attending the launch of the National Citizen Service (NCS) at 10 Downing Street with the Prime Minister, David Cameron, where I was a guest of honour because I had been a founding donor, giving £50,000. This was the day after I had tea with Prince Charles. Prince Charles said the Prime Minister had been to see him about the NCS to update him on progress. He told me that he thought it was an interesting project and wondered if I was going to get involved, to which I responded, 'Too late, sir, I am already a founder donor.'

At the NCS launch, I was speaking to David Cameron, who was thanking me for my support. Then he mentioned that he had spoken to Prince Charles and wondered if the NCS could link up with the Prince's Trust to attract more young people. The PM knew I was a trustee of the Prince's Trust.

My response was, 'Yes, I know, Prime Minister; His Highness told me you had been in to see him and we both think it is a good idea.' Cameron looked shocked: here I was informing the Prime

Minister that the future King of England had told me about their meeting!

He may have wondered who the hell I was to mix in such high circles. There was no breaching of confidentiality or protocol, just a passing comment from Prince Charles that came up in conversation over coffee at No. 10. I could not help marvelling that this boy off a Hackney council estate was having this type of conversation at 10 Downing Street. It felt like a seminal moment in my life and a reflection of how far I had come from my humble beginnings.

Chapter 2

THE WILL TO WIN

My twin brother Stephen and I started at Thomas Fairchild School, Napier Grove, London N1 in September 1958, which was a few minutes' walk from our council flat at 85 Bracklyn Court, Wimbourne Street. Apparently, this area is now a trendy part of Shoreditch and Hoxton and many private buyers have bought council flats there, but in my day, it was a shithole.

Our flat was on the ground floor, next door to my mum's disabled mother. Mum looked after Nanny every day and we often had our meals with her. She was a widow, a lovely old lady but she had no qualms about hitting us with her walking stick if we got too noisy.

Mum would be out every morning cleaning offices, so we had to get ourselves up and ready for school. Once dressed, we had to pop next door to Nanny's for our breakfast of toast and a big mug of milky tea with four teaspoons of sugar.

However, I had one other task. Mum told me I had to put Nanny's bloomers (knickers) on the end of her walking stick every morning so she could put them on under her dress and apron. Nanny could not bend over due to her disability, so she used to hook her bloomers on the end of her stick and somehow yank them up. I was never allowed to watch this. My role was to hook the bloomers on the stick and turn my back. Nanny had perfected it to a fine art and she never missed a leg. Once her bloomers were on, she could prepare our breakfast and the world could go on.

Bracklyn Court was a typical brown-brick council estate, but it had a nice, green grass area where I could kick a football. I became a good footballer, playing for a few amateur teams and might have had a decent career in the game but I was worried about being seriously injured, as football in the 1970s was rough.

I once received a nasty ankle injury playing for Edgware Town and was off work for two weeks. I could barely walk. The guy dived in feet first deliberately and almost broke my ankle. As I hobbled off, he told me he had been looking to nobble me all game and 'got me good and proper'. I guess he did that because he thought I was a decent player. If I was useless, he would have had no need to do it unless he just fancied a punch-up. At that time, I already had my own house and I was worried about paying the mortgage and missing work, so I stopped playing at a higher level at twenty-two.

I also did not enjoy amateur football because there were too many nasty comments and nasty people who were just looking for a fight, or to kick you off the pitch. Mostly, they were failed professional players who lacked the skill to make it at a higher level, so they survived on kicking people who could play a bit. All I wanted to do was enjoy the game and win – but it was not worth the risk.

Edgware Town was quite a long way away from where I lived in Ilford and so I had a run-out for Walthamstow Avenue. However, that did not last long as it seemed you needed to be a big drinker to get anywhere. As I grew up with an alcoholic father, I have always been a moderate drinker and have seldom been in a pub over the last thirty years. Even to this day, it brings back too many bad memories.

I left amateur football and played centre half for Brunswick

Albion, a Sunday football team in the North London League. This was great fun as I played with my two brothers and we went a whole season undefeated. Stephen was goalkeeper and John was centre forward.

One game at Hackney Marshes was a top-of-the-table clash. It was a close game. The ball came out to the edge of the penalty box and I let rip with my left foot (I am right-footed). The ball flew into the net from about 30 yards – it was a thunderbolt and the goalkeeper did not stand a chance.

This was memorable because it won us the game, but also watching on the side of the pitch was Alan Hudson, the Chelsea and England midfield player. He just happened to be there watching some matches. As I ran towards him to celebrate, he shouted, 'Great goal, mate.' It was a bonus to the best goal I ever scored, as it was acknowledged by an England international.

John and Stephen both say that I was an excellent player who should have tried to become professional. However, when you leave school at fifteen, you have to hit the ground running earning a living and you have no time to take chances. I was also going home and giving all my wages to Mum, who depended on me.

I liked Thomas Fairchild School. We had a headmistress called Miss Perkins and a deputy headmaster called Mr Pedley. They prided themselves on never having administered the cane to anybody in over five years – although one or two of us came close.

Stephen, myself and another boy called Alan Rowham were the cleverest kids in the school. Stephen was excellent at maths and went on to a grammar school, getting three maths A-levels – pure, applied and combined. Alan could not be bothered too much even though he was clever, and he ended up a scaffolder.

I then went to Shoreditch Comprehensive School, on Falkirk

Street, just off Hoxton Market. This might be a posh area now but one night during the winter when it was dark, I was chased through Hoxton Market by two kids with a sword who wanted to shove it where the sun doesn't shine. That night I realised I could have been Olympic champion at sprinting from a standing start. Boy, I have never moved so fast. I was eleven years old, it was frightening, and after that, I made sure I never went out after dark – not around Hoxton anyway. Thankfully, they never caught me. Otherwise, you might not be reading this book.

To this day, I feel disappointment and upset about Shoreditch Comprehensive School. It was a decent enough school but there were so many people. We had thirty-plus to a class and although I was in the top class we had to move from classroom to classroom for lessons. With over 1,000 pupils at the school, it was like coming out of a football stadium to change lessons.

I wanted to go to a grammar school because I wanted to go to university. I was clearly bright enough but my mum wanted me to work as soon as possible and I was told that I could not go to a grammar school, as I would have to stay on until I was eighteen. To rub salt in the wound, Stephen was allowed to go to a grammar school – Parmiter's, in Bethnal Green – presumably because he was perceived to be cleverer than I was. That might have been true, but I am the one with the Mayfair mansion.

Stephen was probably academically smarter than me, but I was an all-rounder. I was good at everything including sport. I tended to be player of the year or school captain at nearly every sport in which I took part. Playing for Thomas Fairchild, we got to our first cup final in over twenty years but lost poorly four-nil in the final to Burbage College, who had many big lads playing for them. Even today, I am a three-handicap golfer and a half-decent skier.

I also had a winner's instinct. If I came up against opponents better than me, I figured out a way to win.

One incident springs to mind. It was a freezing January day in 1966 and the school coaches parked up at Hackney Marshes for two or three classes to have their compulsory sports afternoon. There were loads of us piled up in three coaches.

Unfortunately, the grounds were covered in a foot of snow and the football pitches were all closed. So Mr Reynolds, our sports teacher, said, 'Right, lads, kit on and run around the whole track for a cross-country run.' That was around five miles to run, which did not go down too well, but off we set, freezing cold in our football boots and kit.

It did not take long for my football teammates and me to get ahead of the no-hopers and soon there were about ten of us ahead of the pack. We carried on running but slowed down a bit once we were well clear. I said, 'Lads, no need to kill ourselves as we'll have to wait for the others when we get to the finish and stand around getting cold, so let's just trot along and pace ourselves.'

With about 500 yards to go, I said, 'Look, lads, we're all in the same football team and mates, let's link arms and cross the line together. This is not a real race; we should be playing football and we're only running around this frozen wasteland because the teachers couldn't be bothered to take us back to school. They're probably having a nice cup of tea in the warm while we are flogging ourselves to death out here.

'I'll give the word about 100 yards to go so we can link arms and cross the line together as a team.'

So we all linked arms. But I made sure I was on the end, and with the winning line in sight I broke away and sprinted across the line to glorious applause from Mr Reynolds.

'Well done, Cruddas, that's ten house points for you, the rest of you get changed and get on the coach.'

The lads were angry but I just said, 'Well, I decided to go for it at the last minute.' Poor buggers never stood a chance.

The will to win was ingrained. Another time, when I was living in Monaco, I was invited to play golf with three professionals at a nearby golf club, Royal Mougins, near Cannes. This time I knew I would have to play well to win, and I was determined they would not beat me. I am sure they were not in competition mode, but I was. The three of them shot seventy-six, seventy-seven and seventy-eight, but I shot seventy-five and beat them all off scratch.

There was another professional I played with now and again, called Stefano Maio. In one year, we played three times and each time he got a hole in one. Three holes in one, in one year, at three different holes on the same course. I didn't beat this guy – he was a great player.

The professional at Royal Mougins Golf Club is David Berry, an Englishman who married a beautiful French girl, Sophie. I met my match in him, as I have never beaten him off scratch. He is a superb player and he once shot twenty-eight on the front nine and ten under par at Royal Mougins.

There were more stories around my sporting ability and finding a way to win. However, what made it more enjoyable was that I was better at sport than my twin brother Stephen was.

Chapter 3

THE BOY KEEPS COMING
BACK FOR MORE

Stephen and I used to play tennis on a Saturday morning on hard courts in a park off Pitfield Street. They are still there today although one of them is now a basketball court.

We hired the court and would spend an hour whacking balls at each other. I always won and never held back in telling Stephen that I kicked his arse. Rightly, Stephen didn't take too kindly to being called useless. I also wound him up no end asking him if he knew anybody that could play tennis to give me a decent game.

As twins, Stephen and I would argue about everything. On the sports field, he just never knew when he was beaten, poor sod. He was a sucker for punishment. I remember one tennis match: as usual, I was winning and he hit a good shot, but it was clearly out and I called it out. He was not having any of it because he thought he had a chance of beating me. After all, I was only winning the match five games to love and forty-love up in the final game. When he turned around and bent over to pick up a ball, at that moment I fired another at him that hit him square in the crack of his arse.

I could not have hit a better shot if I tried but he went ballistic and fired a ball back at me. When this missed by about 40 feet, which was good for him, he threw his racket at me and started chasing me around the court, yelling what he was going to do to me. As I was a better sportsman than him he never caught me, thank God, and after a couple of weeks he calmed down. But boy, he could get angry and I was not a calming influence. I always used to say, 'Don't worry about it, you can try and beat me at another sport to even things up.'

So in sports, to his credit, he kept coming back for more. One time we were playing end-to-end football behind our flats. At the age of six, we all moved to 14 Vince Court, Brunswick Place. The flats are still there today, behind the fire station in Great Eastern Street, just off the Old Street roundabout. As usual, I was beating him and I was getting bored. When he hit a wayward shot towards my goal, the ball disappeared behind some garages. I went after the ball, got it and hid behind a wall. I could hear him saying, 'I know what you're doing – you're hiding, waiting for me to come and find you,' but I said nothing.

After a few minutes, he could not resist and had to see where I was. As he approached, I could hear his footsteps and when I thought he was near enough I reappeared and lobbed the ball over his head and into an empty goal.

He was furious but I was lying on the ground laughing. However, I had to get up quickly because he came charging towards me ready to kick the shit out of me. Ah, brotherly love. I ran off with my sides splitting. I just loved winding him up, especially because he never knew when he was beaten.

On the rare occasions when he caught me, I perfected an arm lock technique to stop him hitting me – pinning his arm behind his back, using my arm to lock behind his neck. I would hold him in that position until he calmed down, which was usually three or four minutes. No matter how hard he tried, he could not break out of the arm lock. I learnt it from watching Les Kellett, a wrestler who was on the TV every Saturday afternoon.

Stephen also liked to kick, and I nullified this by putting my foot across his shin so the harder he kicked the more it hurt him and not me.

Once I had perfected all these techniques, I was free to wind him up even more. To make matters worse, I also sang various tunes to taunt him, and I learnt to squawk like a bird – that drove him crazy. Often, I would squawk, 'Just because you're losing nah-nah-nah-nah.' I taught all my children the squawk over the years. Unfortunately, when I had my teeth straightened, I could no longer squawk but I had perfected it over forty years and my kids loved it. Well, I think they did.

Stephen married his childhood sweetheart Susan Robinson. They were married for forty-five years and have three children. But unfortunately, Susan died of cancer in 2020 at the young age of sixty-seven. Stephen never went on to university, which was a shame, as he was bright enough. My mum was also disappoint-ed because she felt that when Stephen met Susan, he lost interest in school and just wanted to get married and settle down. By this time, she realised that she had sent the wrong son to grammar school because she could see that I was a harder worker with more ambition.

I have always regretted missing out on the university experience, having wanted to go since I was at primary school, but I was denied the opportunity as my family couldn't afford it. So it was a proud moment when I was awarded a doctorate from Loughborough University and an even prouder moment when I was awarded a full master's degree from Oxford University. This was possible as

I am a fellow of Harris Manchester College and a member of the governing body. Receiving these educational awards alongside my peerage meant so much to me and my family. Mum would be very proud.

Stephen ended up being a quantity surveyor. His party piece would be to say, 'I know how many O-levels I have – one for every month of the year. I know how many A-levels I have – one for every season of the year.' He used to like winding me up over the school he went to and the qualifications he had. Who can blame him as he suffered years of abuse from me on the sports field and I was always the first to point out his shortcomings. Later Stephen moved from being a surveyor to being a black cab driver as my older brother John was doing this job and making more money than Stephen.

Chapter 4

THE SADDEST DAY
OF MY LIFE

Stephen was close to our mum. He was holding her hand when she died, and I felt he was lucky to have been with her at that time. He deserved to be with her as she was probably closer to him than I was, although Mum was also close to John. She loved us all equally but John and Stephen spent more time with her, primarily because I was living in Monaco. But I am grateful that Stephen was with her when she died. John arrived at the hospital less than an hour later.

Mum's death was sudden in a way. She clearly had symptoms of lung cancer, coughing up blood and feeling breathless, but she never told us about any of this. She did once say that she was coughing up blood, but this was because she had burnt the back of her throat eating a hot roast potato and she would be fine. I wish I had paid more attention to this at the time but whenever I pushed Mum on it she said, 'Stop fussing, there is nothing wrong, I'm fine.'

Mum started smoking when she was eighteen and stopped when she was seventy. But she was also smoking my dad's cigarettes passively. He could easily get through three packs a day along with the bottle of rum and twenty-five pints of Guinness.

Mum went into hospital in October 2001 when her breathing

became bad and within a few weeks, she was dead. She just ignored it too long for doctors to be able to do anything for her. She said, 'You don't want to go to the doctor at my age as you never know what they will find.' I am the complete opposite because of this. I have a top-to-bottom check-up every year.

I remember spending an entire evening with Mum in the hospital – just her and me. She knew she was in deep trouble, although still not letting us know the full extent of her illness and her concerns. She was always trying to be tough and show the world that she could stand up to anything.

That evening, we had a nice time together talking about old times and we exchanged some loving words. This was the night she told me she loved me, and it meant a lot but it did not change anything, I just said, 'I know, Mum, and I've always known.'

I knew she loved me, but she wasn't able to tell me. We also spoke a bit about why I wasn't allowed to go to grammar school and she admitted that she held me back because she wanted me to work and bring in some money. Times were desperate and she felt bad about not sending me to the school I wanted to go to. But I played it down due to her illness, joking, 'Thank God you didn't send me to grammar school otherwise I might not be where I am today.'

We laughed a lot that night. I sat on her bed, held her hand, and told her that she had been an amazing mum to all three of her sons and that none of us would have changed anything.

We joked about her organ playing. Mum used to play 'Spanish Eyes' on her electric organ with background music. No matter how hard she tried, it was awful and whenever I hear 'Spanish Eyes' now I smile. It reminds me so much of her and the funny times we had listening to her play it. She thought she was good but, on this night, we laughed about her organ playing and how it sent my dad to an early grave.

This was the last time I saw my mum alive. Although I was not there at her death – I could not get to the hospital in time – I cherish the last moments we had together. Being honest with each other, declaring our love for each other and saying thank you for all that we had done for each other.

I rarely visit Mum's grave. She was cremated at Weeley Crematorium near Clacton and there is a small plaque with her name on it next to a bush we planted. I feel that where her ashes were scattered is a cold place and I do not feel her presence when I go there. Stephen and John visit every year but I have many memories of my mum that I will cherish and I know she is up there watching over me. Also because of our last night together, I feel we parted on loving terms and said everything we needed to say to each other.

I bought Mum a bungalow in Clacton. She liked it there and she chose to live there, and she was near to her sister, my Aunt Jean. Mum lived with my dad until he died in January 1990 of cancer of the oesophagus.

Mum and I shared lots of times together when I took on many of the household responsibilities when I lived at home with her. Before I got married, I helped Mum with bills and dealing with the council. I even talked to her about divorcing my dad and what it would have meant for the family and whether she would be able to keep the council flat we lived in.

When I was young and way before I was married, Mum leant on me a lot to help her if times were tough, financially and emotionally. We had a great and loving bond.

Chapter 5

THE FASTEST VACUUM
CLEANER IN THE EAST

My first full-time job, at fifteen, was with Western Union, the telegram and payments company. After I got through my probation period, I was put on the shift system. One shift involved two weeks of nights that started at 4 p.m. and ended at 6 a.m. the next day, fourteen hours non-stop. I would work this shift Monday, Wednesday and Friday the first week, and Tuesday and Thursday the following week. It was a long shift but at least you got plenty of days off to relax in between.

If work was quiet, the supervisor would let people on the night shift go home early and the first people to be invited to leave early were those on the fourteen-hour shift. Once I was offered the chance to leave at 3 a.m. because it was quiet and the big rush from the previous night was over. But I refused, as I wanted to meet my mum at 6 a.m. to help her with her cleaning.

On another occasion, we met up around Liverpool Street as Western Union's offices were in Great Winchester Street, just off London Wall behind the Deutsche Bank building. We walked over to the offices that are above Boots the Opticians in Bishopsgate – the branch opposite Heron Tower on the corner of Camomile Street. Mum and I cleaned the offices. I emptied the bins and did the hoovering while she went around dusting. This was around August 1969. I had just started the night shift with Western Union and I was nearly sixteen years old.

She was so grateful for this support and help even if I was tired after my fourteen-hour shift. It created a bond between us because this was the first time Mum had been truly supported by a man. Her father had died when she was a child and my dad was a liability, not an asset. But I helped her and at the end of the week, I gave her all my wages from Western Union.

I loved helping my mum. She deserved all the help she could get. She was married to an abusive alcoholic; she was looking after her own mum; and she was getting up early every day to clean offices. I thought it was the least I could do.

I often pass that branch of Boots in Bishopsgate and look up at the offices I used to clean and smile. But I also feel sad because that was where Mum and I worked together and had the odd laugh when she was still alive.

I cleaned many other offices around Finsbury Circus and Moorgate. I helped my mum for about three years until Western Union made me redundant when I was eighteen. One office I used to clean was 2 London Wall Buildings, where, ironically, twenty-one years later I would start my own company.

Chapter 6

I WAS MADE AN OFFER
THAT MUM COULD REFUSE

My first job was as a milkman. I was just fifteen years old, still at school, just, and madly in love with my first girlfriend, Susan Hunt. Susan was an arts student at Goldsmiths College and a bit of a lefty so it was never going to work, but for a time we thought we would be married with kids. Ah, the optimism of youth.

Susan's brother-in-law John Smith worked for Express Dairies. He offered me a job helping him deliver milk while he was collecting the money from customers over the weekends, his busy period. I usually worked Saturday and Sunday mornings, rising at 5 a.m. to meet John at Express Dairies at 6 a.m. at the back of Paul Street, Finsbury, east London. I loved the job and did it for around six months until I got a full-time job.

Mum always made it clear to my brothers and me that we were expected to go to work as early as possible and bring home some money. Her plan would have worked perfectly if we had all been halfwits but John, Stephen and I were all clever. Stephen got his three A-levels and today I am a member of Mensa with an IQ of 155.

John was a bit unlucky as he contracted rheumatic fever at

fourteen and missed a crucial year of schooling at home recovering. He went to work at Smithfield Meat Market at fifteen because he was so far behind the other boys. He did have home tutoring but, without the day-to-day bustle of school, he lost interest. Thankfully, he got through the illness.

When I got to fifteen, Mum said it was time for me to work. In Easter 1969, I left Shoreditch Comprehensive, picked up the *Evening Standard* and got an interview with Western Union to become a teleprinter operator. It was a random job search, but it would have major repercussions for my future career. It gave me a skill that I could use to get into banking and ultimately the financial markets.

I learnt to type and started on the night shift at Western Union, typing telegrams and sending them on ticker tape all around the world. Today, I can touch-type over eighty words a minute. It's a great skill to have and I used it to write (type) this book.

However, before I started at Western Union, I got a message to call my old biology teacher. Dr Baker had previously been a doctor working in Harley Street. He used to tell us he looked after Ginger Rogers. We didn't know who the hell he was talking about, but when I told my mum, she said Ginger Rogers was a big movie star, the famous dance partner of Fred Astaire.

Anyway, I called Dr Baker. He asked me why I had left school and I said my mum told me to and I needed to earn some money. He asked me how much I was earning, which was seven pounds and eight shillings. I was shocked and flabbergasted when he offered me a job in the school's biology department as a laboratory assistant on the same money. His condition was that I would stay on to take my O- and A-levels while working part-time in his department. Dr Baker made it clear that I was one of his and the school's brightest pupils. He said I was A-level material and it would be a waste to leave school early.

I was over the moon at the offer. I was going to be paid to go to school and I could not wait to tell my mum. I thought Mum would be happy, but she wasn't. She said that I had left school, I had a job and I should just get on with it. So, I called Dr Baker back, told him I could not accept the offer and thanked him. Then I took up the job at Western Union.

Though Dr Baker was a successful and wealthy Harley Street doctor, when he retired early, he decided to teach poor kids to give something back to society. I found out that two of my classmates became doctors and he paid for all their medical fees and education. I wasn't sure how the school would have paid me to stay on, but I suspect the money would have come out of Dr Baker's own pocket. I will never know.

He was a great man who wanted to help me because he saw potential. I do not regret refusing his offer because I do not know where it would have led me. But I wish I could have thanked him for his confidence and belief in me.

Chapter 7

THE LONG-AWAITED
CONFRONTATION

As soon as I started work, it gave me a sense of control over my own life and destiny. I was earning money, and I was contributing to the household by paying for my keep. I had a girlfriend and I bought my first car, a peacock blue Vauxhall Viva. Not exactly a Ventora like William Hill's but my pride and joy.

I also had respect from my employers, who gave me good wage rises because they saw me as a hard worker and good at my job. I was very skilful at typing and sending long messages without error for hours on end and my colleagues liked me. Things felt like they were moving in the right direction – except at home, which was still like a war zone.

Now I was one of the breadwinners at home, I started to stand up to my dad more. I felt compelled to help my mum and not sit back and take the shit that my dad dished out daily.

As a schoolchild, I felt my dad was still the man of the house and that, because of his volatile temper and his addiction to alcohol, we all feared him. But as I got older, he continued to drink and smoke and became weaker.

Then in the autumn of 1970, when I was seventeen years old, there was a major confrontation between my dad and myself. One afternoon, after he had his nap in the chair by the fireplace, I confronted him for hitting my mum. I told him to leave her alone and I said that if he hit her again, then he would have me to deal with.

I was 6 foot and skinny but a fit and sporting young man who had been in a few scraps already. But I had never confronted a man.

My dad's reaction was 'Oh yeah? What you going to fucking do about it?' and as he rose to confront me, I smashed him full in the face and splattered his nose with an explosion of blood that went everywhere.

It broke his nose instantly – I heard it break. I knocked him spark out and he fell back into the chair. My mum was screaming. As he lay there groaning, I bent over him and said, 'If you lay one more finger on Mum the next time will be your last.'

My dad lay in the chair for about thirty minutes as he recovered, holding a tea towel to his face as the blood poured out. I stayed in the room with my mum, as I was concerned he would blame her for what had happened.

Then Mum told him to go to the hospital, which he did, and I didn't see him until the next day. When I did see him, his eyes were black and blue, and he had a support plaster and plate across his nose. He looked like he had done a few rounds with Muhammad Ali.

He was in no fit state to be confrontational. But he must have had a few brandies to give him strength because he said, 'You only got me because I was in the chair getting up.'

I said, 'Well, if you want to have a go now, then go for it. But this time, I won't stop with one punch. I'll make sure you are well and truly hammered.'

He backed off and left the room and he never laid another finger on my mum, nor confronted me again. The power had shifted in the house and I was in charge. I was bringing in money, my dad was in fear of me and I felt great because, for the first time, I could protect my mum. My dad knew that if he tried anything, he would have me to contend with and even if he got in a few punches, he knew he would come off worst. He knew I would not back down.

I remember this whole scene as if it were yesterday. I have often described it as the best and worst event in my life because even though I had little respect for my dad he was still my dad and I didn't want to be fighting with him. It was horrible, but at least Mum could relax a bit knowing that if he ever touched her, I would sort him out and he was in for a good pasting.

Looking back many years later, I think Mum knew that one day I would have to confront my dad and that is why she always pushed me hard to stand up for myself and never back down. I am grateful she did because I carried that toughness into my business career.

Chapter 8

MY BIG BREAK

Life at Western Union was tough. It was a good company, but it knew how to work its staff hard. We had to clock in and out daily to make sure we did the hours.

There was a massive floor of teleprinters and telex machines and there were rows of us typing out messages all day and night. In those days, most of the typing was done on heavy metal tape machines without a screen. When you typed the messages, it punched holes in a ticker tape.

As well as learning to type, I had to learn to read the holes in the ticker tape to see if I had made any mistakes. I can still do it today, although there is no use for it.

Western Union was a good first job because it made me realise that, if I worked hard, I would get recognition and more money. Like the Boy Scouts, it gave structure to my life and a purpose.

One afternoon on the late shift (2 p.m. to 10 p.m.) I was teamed up with an ex-military person who was lazy. We took turns every thirty minutes, typing messages then switching to tear off messages that came in through the receiving teleprinter. When a message came in, we checked it for spelling mistakes and checked the word count in the preamble of the message. Then we had to put it in the conveyor belt to be distributed to the telephone or post department so it could be sent off to the recipient.

Receiving messages was the easy part of the job because it wasn't always busy and there was no typing involved, just reading the messages as they came through, time-stamping them and sending them on their way. It was meant to be a contrast: typing non-stop for thirty minutes then relaxing for thirty minutes ready for the next typing stint.

On one shift, whenever it was my turn to type messages there was always a backlog of messages to be sent, left by the ex-military person. Whereas I could send one message a minute, he would send a message every five minutes. So I said to him, 'Look, you sit there receiving messages and I will send them because it's too much hard work to catch up with your slow work.'

He said, 'Let me give you some advice: slow down and stop making me look like a lazy bastard.'

I said, 'Well, there is an alternative. You could work a bit harder and then you will stop making yourself look like a lazy bastard.'

Anyway, I stayed typing the messages and let him sit back and relax. It made life easy for him, but it meant there was never a backlog of his work that I had to catch up on. On this day, I cleared the backlog and I got the supervisor to give me another machine, which he put next to mine so I could help the bloke sitting beside me, who was sending messages to another location.

The person next to me wasn't lazy, he was just inundated with work and so I helped him out. I was flat out for three hours typing and sending messages from two terminals and I helped clear a massive backlog of messages in record time.

Following that day, I was given the best wage rise of anybody in the company. I got double the amount and I was destined for great things.

However, unfortunately, at the age of eighteen, the company made me redundant along with a third of the workforce. This was actually a blessing in disguise because I ended up being a telex operator in a bank dealing room, which set me on my path to becoming a trader and subsequently setting up my own company.

Since I started work in 1969, I have always been able to make money one way or another. Starting at Western Union was the beginning of making decent money. In those first years, whatever I earned I handed over to Mum on a Friday evening along with my payslip. She would hand me back pocket money to live on for the week. As I was living under her roof, I thought this was fair.

One day, after I had qualified as a full-blown teleprinter operator, I did my first bit of overtime at Western Union and they put me on the wrong overtime rate. Instead of receiving double, I got something like four times the hourly rate.

Call me old-fashioned, but I decided to keep my head down and do as much overtime as possible. I was raking it in and I wondered how long it would last. After about four months, an old manager called Mr Nancarrow called me over for a word in my ear.

I knew what was coming. He said, 'Have you noticed your wages have been very high lately?'

I surprised him with my answer, 'Yes, Mr Nancarrow, I have noticed that but that's because I have been working hard and doing lots of overtime and the overtime rate is higher than the normal rate. I was going to ask you for more overtime tonight. I love earning that extra money, as I want to buy my mum a washing machine, as she has to wash everything by hand. I am also helping to pay for my brother to stay on at school.'

I thought, 'I will have this bloke in tears at any moment.'

However, he looked at me, smiled and said, 'Don't get smart

with me, Sonny Jim. Now be off with you and next time you do overtime, you will be on normal rate. You cheeky little bastard.'

I cut back on my overtime after this. They only noticed it after they had to give me holiday pay. I knew I should have worked my holidays.

I left Western Union at eighteen with one skill, the ability to type very fast. I got a job at International Marine Banking, 40 Basinghall Street, in the telex department.

I had to demonstrate my typing skills to the head of the telex department, Paul Beatty. Paul was a smart person who had me up a ladder fitting a weatherboard at his house in Sidcup after he tried to sell it. Anyway, at the interview I was horrified to see they had the latest telex machines with screens and four-bank keyboards – not a ticker tape in sight. I had trained on a three-bank keyboard with all the numbers on the top row. The new machines had the numbers separately, which sounds easier, and it made sense that telex machines and typewriters should have the same keyboards, but I was not used to it.

I was nervous, as I was a speed typist, often typing faster than I could read the text as the fingers get into a rhythm, but I thought, 'Well, typing is typing so it shouldn't be that difficult.'

Paul told me to have a warm-up first to get used to the four-bank keys. So, I started typing 'now is the time for all good men to come to the aid of the party', which thankfully was all letters and no figures. But the test was a complete disaster as I kept forgetting that the figures were on separate keys – my test results were a mess.

However, Paul was an ex-Western Union man. He knew that I had been well trained, and he gave me the job based on my warm-up, not on the actual test. Phew – that was a close call because International Marine Banking was to be my big break.

Chapter 9

A NEW ROAD OPENS

International Marine Banking was an offshoot of Marine Midland Bank, which was eventually bought by HSBC. It was a small subsidiary bank. Working in the telex department involved sending messages on behalf of the director and manager, but also the dealers would ask me to call up various banks around Europe to ask for their deposit and foreign exchange rates. It was exciting stuff, fast-moving and sometimes hectic.

As the bank's dealing room expanded, we ripped up the carpet to reveal a concrete floor. I was bought a chair on castors so I could whizz up and down the different machines typing and closing out deals. Eventually, I worked full-time in the dealing room as a dealer's assistant, calling up banks on the telex machines, tying up deals and even buying and selling on behalf of the dealers.

That is how I got into financial trading, but I was still a dealer's assistant working the telex machines.

The foreign exchange manager was John Brodie, a real-life David Niven-type character with a pencil-thin moustache who took me under his wing. The chief dealer was Doug Lowings, a struggling artist who gave up trying to make money from art and got a proper job. I once visited Doug's house in Winchmore Hill after he tried to flog me his Morris Marina. Very nice and probably worth a fortune today – the house, not the car.

Doug and Mr Brodie had both worked at Lloyds and Bolsa Bank and came to International Marine as a team. There were some smart dealers there but unfortunately, the bank got into financial trouble, primarily lending money to South American companies that defaulted on the loans. Soon Marine Midland had to bail us out.

After the bailout, International Marine was basically a shell company, but the owners wanted to keep its merchant banking licence and also use it to offset costs and tax losses. Mr Brodie was due to retire so he took over International Marine as the responsible officer to keep it going until the bank decided what they wanted to do with the licence – Marine Midland only had a commercial banking licence. Therefore, there was value in keeping International Marine going in the hope they could sell it for the licence or use it themselves later.

The good news for me was that International Marine needed to keep operating so Mr Brodie took me on as one of its two official dealers, which was a major step up from being a dealer's assistant. It was a big move for me as it meant I could be classed as a dealer going forwards and that opened up better job opportunities. Mr Brodie was a good and decent man and he gave me my big break as a dealer. He did not have to do this but he saw potential in me and he promoted me.

He also taught me so much about banking and trading. He even offered to lend me money to buy a car when my old car blew up. He was a father figure to me and a loving family man to his wife and twin daughters. Unfortunately, Mr Brodie died shortly after he retired but I worked with him for two years as his dealer and I was extremely grateful to him and the knowledge and expertise he gave me. He even used to take me on lunches at other banks and introduce me to their heads. That was way above my pay grade.

As soon as Mr Brodie retired, I started looking around for a dealing job and I ended up at the Iranian Bank Sepah, trading currency pairs such as dollar/Deutschmark. This was a good time to be working for an Iranian bank as the Shah of Iran was still in power. We had many trading lines with US banks and there was lots of trade between Iran and the rest of the world. Often, we had to cover forward currency exposures as letters of credit matured.

It was a great job with a good bunch of people. But once the Shah was deposed, the bank lost most of its trading lines and banking relationships. So, in 1982, I moved to a Middle East futures broker in London called SCF Finance, which was run and owned by the Chalabi family from Iraq, who were also the owners of Jordan's Petra Bank.

SCF was a small broker but it was a great training ground for my future creation of CMC Markets. Hussein Chalabi was running it when I arrived, but he did not seem totally focused. He had a beautiful American wife and outside interests including a fantastic villa in Marbella, playing tennis and generally doing other things for the family.

Hussein was intelligent, having graduated from Columbia University, New York, with a PhD, and we had some great conversations. I could never generalise with Hussein: if I used terms like 'Well, everybody is saying this', he would pin me down and say, 'Who's "everybody"? Give me their names.' So, I always had to be careful when speaking to him. He was very sharp, and he certainly sharpened me up. I liked him a lot and he had great confidence in me.

Hussein liked the contrast between us. He was rich, well-educated and diverse and I was straight off a council estate and comprehensive school and into work at fifteen. I often joked with him that leaving school at fifteen was a big mistake – I should have left at fourteen because I wasted a year. Hussein loved the British sense of humour and I was always ready to rough him up with my sense of humour and many East End expressions.

Hussein and I often discussed different business opportunities like options trading and futures trading. He was amazed that I could answer something without going through some long series of mathematical equations to work it out. He often said to me, 'You always come up with the right answer. You do not know how to calculate it, but you know instinctively what it should be.'

For example, Hussein was trading his own personal account using the company's money, which was fine. Every morning, he would spend a few hours plotting his buy and sell orders for the day in his chart book. To him, trading was a science and he felt he could calculate when to buy and sell using maths and charts. He was one of the early adopters of technical analysis. However, he had to make good any losses.

While Hussein was trading his own account, I was also trading for the company and servicing our clients' trading futures. By the end of the first year, I had not used a single chart or slide rule and I made $1 million for the company, while Hussein lost $300,000.

I used to make money by following trends in the market and pouncing on a movement that I felt would happen if the markets were lagging. I also sought to exploit price inefficiencies by arbitraging between cash and future prices, running future legs of a contract and financing them on the overnight financing market, in other words using futures to lend money at a high rate and borrow it at a low rate. This meant being 'short future', so I could gain the price differential between the cash and the future positions. This helped to produce profits by taking advantage of cheaper short-term borrowing rates.

This is what we call classic 'market making'. With a solid client base, it meant I could add value and earn more than just commission income from futures. The best time to make money was when the US markets were closed and I could quote futures prices off the cash price and make on the future points differentials.

I also used to speculate with the company's money, with its permission. Once, in December 1988, Soviet president Mikhail Gorbachev gave a speech at the United Nations and we were all watching it live from the dealing room. Gorbachev talked about reducing military spending in Russia and reining back on big military projects. He was handing an olive branch to the rest of the world and I thought this would be good for the US dollar. Their budget deficit would reduce over time, as they would not have to keep spending on the military to keep up with the Russians.

As I watched the speech, I started to buy dollars in the most liquid currency pair – dollar/Deutschmark. By the end of Gorbachev's speech, I had made $150,000 in about twenty minutes.

The next day, I marched into Hussein's office and asked him how his trading was going, knowing I had made money and he had lost. Poor Hussein said he had been hit on futures and lost money. I told him gleefully what I had made.

It wasn't because I wanted him to feel bad, but I felt that here was a highly educated man with a PhD and I was out-performing him. I got great delight in feeling that I could compete with an Ivy League graduate.

To be fair, Hussein never made me feel inferior; he was always respectful and decent towards me. It was more about how I felt and the fact that I had been denied going to grammar school and university. There was always this nagging feeling of wanting to prove myself and the more educated the person was, the more I enjoyed competing against them. Hussein was really an academic who once told me that he took exams because he could, and it was fun. He liked studying, getting degrees and passing exams with flying colours as it was a mark of his intelligence.

The *coup de grâce* came a few days later when Hussein asked me to trade his personal account as he had lost $300,000 and with it his confidence. I agreed immediately and within a year, I had made $2.3 million – $300,000 for Hussein and $2 million for the company, out of which I got a very nice bonus. This bonus was the security I needed to start my own company, CMC Markets.

I enjoyed our conversations, especially when he spoke about the old days in Iraq. He once told me that in the mid-1950s his family had the chance to buy either Dolphin Square or a farm in Iraq. I cannot remember the exact sums involved but £5 million springs to mind. This was a lot of money in the 1950s and a reflection of how successful the family was.

Unfortunately, his family passed on Dolphin Square and decided to buy the land as they were farmers by lineage. This made them the biggest farmers in the Middle East with one million acres of land. Whether this story is true or not I do not know but a few years later, all their land was nationalised by Saddam Hussein and they had to flee the country. He said they made a bad decision. I thought, that's putting it mildly.

Chapter 10

THE BANKSY OF TRADING

Being an academic, Hussein loved figures and numbers and was a natural at technical analysis. In the mid-1980s, technical analysis was starting to catch on, especially as the futures markets were becoming more mature and volumes were increasing. There was more volatility and the options markets were beginning to gain traction.

In the mid-1980s, before the advent of electronic data and exchanges, charts had to be updated by hand every day. Every Monday morning, a chart book would arrive from McGraw Hill in Chicago with the last week's prices printed and updated, so you only had to update charts one week at a time or daily as movements happened.

Hussein would plot the current week's movements by hand and spend hours analysing the charts to try to work out which way the financial markets would go. When the new book arrived, he handed me his old book and I updated it until the following week when we repeated the process.

For about a year, we tried to work out price patterns and which way the markets would move. I even studied charts at home to try to understand them better. We would compare notes and price patterns with the aim of advising clients and positioning SCF Finance the right way in the financial markets.

Hussein was convinced that making money was all in the charts, and for a time I believed him, although I always remained sceptical. I went along with it because it meant working closely with the managing director and I felt that if an intelligent man like Hussein believed it, then I should not ignore it and I might learn something. Therefore, I kept an open mind.

However, that all changed on 19 October 1987, so-called Black Monday, when the Dow Jones Index dropped over 20 per cent in one day and the world's stock markets followed suit. It was a bloodbath.

While the crash was going on, Hussein was in his office, head down, plotting the charts. He was oblivious to the mayhem that was going on in his dealing room as we tried to get clients out of losing positions.

By the end of the week, we were all exhausted – except Hussein, who had been shut up in his office trying to make sense of the mayhem through mathematics and slide rules. Because it had been so busy, I did not have time to update my own chart book. But I thought, 'No problem, Hussein will hand me his on Monday when he gets his latest edition from Chicago.'

When he handed me his chart book on the Monday, he had attached two extra pages to the bottom of the Dow Jones page to show its rapid drop. He could not fit the complete price movement on one page – the range was too extreme for his chart. It was almost like a Banksy work of art with the two pages dangling below and flapping around as he brought the book to me.

We all burst out laughing, as the chart book looked ridiculous. I said to Hussein, 'Well, did you make money out of the market collapse? Because surely it was all in the charts and you saw it coming.' Hussein looked sheepish and said no but this was a new beginning and he would get it right next time.

In front of him, I took his hand-updated chart book, threw it in the bin and said, 'That's what I think of your charts. They are not worth the paper they're written on, let alone the extra pages. It is a complete joke. If you cannot see an extreme movement like this coming from your charts, then what's the point?'

That was the last time I ever bothered to follow charts. I am sure many readers swear by technical analysis, but I am an old-school market maker, which means I provide buy/sell prices for clients to trade on and my job is to provide liquidity around different market products. I quote a buy and a sell price in a financial instrument or commodity, hoping to make a profit on the bid–offer spread or through running risk around a client trade.

As such, I am not looking for where the markets will be in the next few days or weeks. I want to know where they will be in the next few seconds so I can manage my risk book, which means I am market making with minimum risk and maximum profit. Price movements and predictions are for clients, not for market makers, and I prefer to be a market maker than a market taker.

Black Monday was an important lesson for me. Here was Hussein, a highly intelligent man, with a fantastic education and a rich and powerful family behind him. His family had founded an Iraqi bank and were top financiers. They had created a path for him through the highest educational institutions. Yet I was making more money out of trading than he was and running a trading room that generated millions for the shareholders.

It doesn't matter how intelligent you are and how much money you have, that does not give you a passport to success. Hussein was using his intelligence to trade the financial markets using technical analysis and I was trading the financial markets based on gut feel and fundamental analysis. More importantly, I was making more money for the company through market making to our clients; it would prove to be a seminal moment in the future of my career and the creation of CMC Markets.

To me, it was obvious that trading the financial markets for one's own gain can be rewarding and satisfying but market making produces consistent profits without taking on all the risk. Let the clients do the trades and make money from managing the risk as trades come and go.

This approach would form the basis of CMC Markets and the path to my future success, but more about that later.

Chapter 11

SCARIEST BUSINESS
TRIP EVER!

The Chalabi family owned various financial institutions around the world as well as SCF Finance in London. After a few years working for them, in 1981 they asked me to travel to Amman, Jordan, to help them establish a dealing room in Petra Bank, their family-owned retail bank.

I was in Jordan for about a month and I helped establish their treasury and risk management desk, primarily to advise them on how to manage their foreign currency risk. This was mainly generated through their customer Visa card business.

When I arrived in Amman, the existing staff were effectively speculating around the different currency transactions that were being generated by the bank's customers from overseas trips. At the end of each month, the customer would have, say, a French franc balance on their Visa card, from a trip to France, which had to be settled through their Jordanian dinar account. The bank would have to sell the client the francs to pay off the deficit on their Visa card by debiting the client's dinar account. A simple foreign exchange transaction between the bank and the client. Nothing complicated about it at all.

However, Petra Bank staff were trying to make more money from the bank's currency exposures. They were systematically selling the clients the francs but not covering the transactions in the underlying currency markets. They just left a lot of the bank's currency exposures unhedged. They tried to offset customer balances against each other, but it was all one-sided business because when customers travelled they were just using their card to make foreign currency purchases. These were Jordanian residents, with a Jordanian dinar bank account, making foreign currency transactions. Unhedged currency exposures created volatility around the bank's earnings as the bank was not locking in guaranteed profits from the very wide currency spreads, it was charging clients.

The first thing I told the incumbent team was to lock in guaranteed profits. The Visa card currency transactions were not to be speculated with, as they needed to be locked in profits. I explained they were guaranteed profits on all the different currency balances that accumulate at the end of each month. I told them that they should not jeopardise this golden profit opportunity. If they wanted to speculate on currency movements for the bank, they should open a separate account with another bank and trade the markets that way. I got the head of the Chalabi family, Dr Ahmad, who was running the bank, to give these instructions and I laid down very clear guidelines on what should be done. Dr Ahmad agreed with me and supported my decision.

At the same time, we changed some of the staff and we recruited a new head of trading, Ali Sarraf, who was instructed on day one to operate the business in this way.

It proved to be a great success because in the first full year of the changes the bank made around $20 million through the management of their Visa card foreign exchange risk. It sounded a simple exercise, but it needed a lot of organisation and a clear view on what needed to be done. Also getting the right staff was not easy but Ali Sarraf did a good job and managed things very well. Another team that set up a currency speculation unit lost money and the unit eventually closed down.

I continued to advise the bank from London and I helped by going out there once or twice a year, primarily to keep an eye on things and to support Ali and the team.

Obviously, the Chalabi family were very happy with my efforts and following this successful trip the family asked me to help them in other locations around the world. Apart from Jordan, I worked for them in Geneva, Egypt and Washington, DC. This all went well until one day they asked me to visit their Beirut bank, which was called Middle East Banking Co. (MEBCO).

I knew that they would ask me to make a trip to Beirut as they had been sounding me out a few months beforehand and they were trying to reassure me that everything was fine. This was the early 1980s and the first wave of hostage-taking in Beirut had not really happened but the country was volatile and there was plenty going on to make me think long and hard about the trip. However, I liked and respected the Chalabi family, I trusted them, and they had always been supportive and kind to me. I also thought that I could do a good job for them and help them with their bank and make it more profitable. Just like I had done in Jordan.

The plan was to fly into Beirut for a week and then immediately fly out again. They assured me that they would take good care of me. So I took the chance and I said I would do it. In April 1982, I took a Middle East Airlines (MEA) plane to Beirut full of worry and trepidation. It turned out to be an eventful trip.

MEA was at the time practically the only airline flying directly to Beirut from London as British Airways refused to do so because of the troubles. The first thing I noticed on the plane was somebody had written in black marker pen 'Ali was here' right next to my seat and on the panel that housed the window. I instantly thought, this does not bode well, and it put me on edge right from the beginning. I thought, if the airline could not clean its planes properly, what about the engine maintenance? It made me think I was flying into a volatile country on a second-rate airline. This was nothing like the BA planes I was used to in business and first class.

It was a small moment but it made me feel uneasy. I was already concerned about the trip anyway and this got it off to a nervous start. However, to be fair the flight was fine and the aircraft was in fact very safe. But there was worse to come.

In the car journey from the airport to the hotel I could see there were shelled-out buildings and rubble. However, people were going about their business and if you looked beyond the rubble and destruction you could see how beautiful Beirut was. It was like a major city on the sea and it reminded me a lot of Nice. Even their second language was French.

I stayed at the Summerland Hotel, which was right on the beach, and it was in pristine condition. I believe today it is a Kempinski Hotel. Once I unpacked, the head of MEBCO Bank, Samir Balaghi, took me to dinner and then afterwards we went to the nightclub in my hotel, which was run by a manager who also sold life insurance during the day. It did make me laugh.

I said to him, 'Why do you need to run a nightclub? Because surely you are making enough money through life insurance.' He responded that people do not really bother with life insurance in Beirut, as the premiums are so high so you might as well save the money and leave it instead in your will. He said that the problem with a war zone is that nobody wants to spend any money on insurance and other things like property. They prefer to have a good time and enjoy themselves because tomorrow could be their last day.

I said to Samir, 'Bloody hell, this sounds very dodgy.'

He said, 'Ah, forget that guy, he is full of shit. He just wants you to spend money in his club and to have a good time.'

Samir's explanation did not help and I felt uneasy. I had in the back of my mind that a bomb could go off any minute. A shell from across the Green Line.

The Green Line was a line of demarcation in Beirut during the Lebanese Civil War from 1975 to 1990. It separated the mainly Muslim factions in predominantly Muslim west Beirut from the predominantly Christian east Beirut controlled by the Lebanese.

I did not stay long in the nightclub because all I wanted to do was go to my room and give myself time to think. I had only been in the country for a few hours but I was already beginning to think that the trip was a big mistake.

That night as I lay in my bed I could hear gunshots in the distance between factions firing at each other across the Green Line. I thought to myself, what am I doing here? It was the first time I had ever been near any kind of conflict and this was scary stuff. However, there was little I could do in the middle of the night. I was safer staying in my hotel room rather than trying to get out. Anyway, even if I wanted to run away where could I go? I lay there all night listening to the gunshots, which were probably a few miles away but during the quiet of the night their sound travelled far.

The following morning I was ready to pack my bags and leave town but Samir turned up early and we had breakfast together. He reassured me that it was normal and most of the conflict was just posturing and firing into thin air to keep the other side at bay. He said very few people were shot along the Green Line. Anyway, he said, 'We have lots to do at the bank this morning and for lunch, we are going to have a nice juicy steak right on the Green Line. You will see for yourself how safe it is. You will see that it is all noise and nothing to worry about.' I just hoped he was right because I was nervous.

I also realised that I was in MEBCO's hands and if I did want to leave the country they would need to organise me a flight and get me safely to the airport. I had the feeling that without their help I would be trapped in the country.

Over breakfast, I asked Samir what would happen if they closed the airport.

'Ah,' he said, 'do not worry, we will get a fast boat and make the trip to Cyprus. It is about a five-hour boat journey but it is what everybody does if there is trouble. Do not worry,' he said again, 'there are plenty of ways to get out of the country. Anyway, you are British with a British passport so you are safe here.'

This did reassure me a bit, because the head of the Chalabi family had said the same before I left London. Therefore, I thought I would go to the bank, get on with things and get out of Beirut as soon as possible. I had only been there for a day and I thought, if I could go to the bank and check things out then I could make some excuses and get out of the country quickly.

As soon as I got to the bank, I was shocked. There were bullet holes everywhere on the outside of the building. Samir said they were from a couple of years back, were part of various battles, and were from crossfire. They were not directed at the bank so there was nothing to worry about. However, when I got inside the bank there were holes in the walls of the offices where stray bullets had made their way through the windows. It was a bit worrying but I had a plan so I just got my head down and got on with things.

After a morning at the bank, we drove to the Green Line and you could hear the odd gunshot, but it was not as bad as the night before. Samir showed me (from a distance) where people were firing from and some of the buildings that had been hit. There were gunshot marks on buildings everywhere.

As we walked to the restaurant, having got out of the taxi because the driver would not go any further as he said it was too dangerous, we passed a parked car. All four doors were wide open and inside there were four men, each with a sub-machine gun on his lap, smoking and relaxing.

They did not like the look of me, I could tell, because here was a white European near to the Green Line and seeing their faces. Samir said, 'Don't worry, they will think you are Israeli, and they won't touch you. They are lying low now because only a few months back an Israeli officer was killed by mistake and all hell broke loose.'

I said to Samir sarcastically, 'That's a relief, because I didn't like the way they looked at me. Anyway, they did not mean to kill the poor Israeli person, it was just an accident, so that's alright then.'

He said, 'Do not look at them, just keep walking,' which was exactly my plan. They did look very scary people who were not to be messed with and they had some serious guns on their laps. I was sweating when we walked by and it wasn't because it was 25 degrees outside.

When we got to the restaurant, I asked Samir what those people were up to. He said they were getting ready for the next shift on the Green Line. They would take over early afternoon but they had to be ready for anything. At any time, the other side could attack the Green Line so they had to be prepared to defend themselves against anything.

I said to him, 'I thought you said it was safe around here.'

He replied, 'Don't worry, we will get plenty of time to run away and get away from any trouble.'

Samir was right about the steak, it was nice, but all I could do was poke it around my plate because I was getting more and more on edge.

That night I spent at a local beach restaurant along the coast with some staff and clients of the bank. We had a delicious meal of fresh fish. I hadn't really eaten for a couple of days so the food went down easily and it was one of the best meals I have ever had.

The evening took the tone of each person talking about their near-death experiences in Beirut. They all seemed to have a second passport so they could leave the country quickly. The night was quiet and I slept quite well despite the odd gunfire shot. The following morning I went to the bank and did not leave all day.

In the early evening, I was ready to leave the bank to go back to the hotel. Samir said, 'Hang on a bit, I want you to meet some clients of the bank.' Then three men turned up with guns and a couple of handheld grenade launchers, which were all packed away in bags. They got them out one by one and laid them out on the bank's counter as if they were at a jumble sale unpacking their goods.

The clients were in a good mood and they could see that I was just a businessman. So they invited me to handle a few of the weapons, which I did. However, I had never handled guns before and they laughed as I held the guns as if they were made of jelly. I was seriously worried that the grenade launcher would go off accidentally and kill us all.

Then they said, 'Do not go, we are going to watch a video from British television. It is all about Beirut and what is happening here. Let us all watch it together.' Samir had to drive me back to the hotel and he wanted to watch it so I stayed with them and we watched the video in one of the side offices. To be clear, this was a documentary made by a British television company and it was about real-life events and real dead bodies and explosions in Beirut.

I cannot explain how surreal and unnerving the whole experience was. Here was a television programme showing bombs going off and gunfights in the centre of Beirut, and here I was in the centre of Beirut. It was clear that this was a trouble hotspot and I was sitting right in the middle of it.

Sitting there watching the video I made up my mind there and then that I was going to leave the next day whether the bank liked it or not. I had had enough and I wanted out. It was not my fight and I should not have been there.

Once the video had finished, the clients brought out a bottle of Scotch and started drinking. That was when I got up and said I had to go and Samir drove me back to the hotel. I could not get out of the bank quickly enough.

On the drive back to the hotel I told Samir that I had an urgent message from home and that I had to leave the next day and would he take me to the airport. I planned to get on the first flight out of Beirut. I did not care where it was going. Samir tried to talk me out of it and said that everything was fine and if things escalated, he could get me out. Nevertheless, I said I had to leave and I was not going to change my mind. It was in the car back to the hotel that he told me he had applied for Canadian citizenship and he himself would be leaving Beirut in a couple of months. He said his wife and children were already in Canada and he was just waiting for his visa and then he would be off.

I said, 'If it is so safe here and you are confident of getting me out, why are you leaving and why did you send your wife and children out of the country?'

He said, 'Fair enough. You are right.' He apologised about the clients in the bank and he said that was wrong and the whole situation could have got out of hand with their drinking. We did the right thing to leave. He said, 'I will pick you up tomorrow first thing and take you to the airport and at the same time, I will arrange your flight.'

The next day we left for the airport around 9 a.m. I remember the drive very clearly; there were many people looking into the car. Wondering what a white man was doing in their neighbourhood. It was a beautiful sunny day and the drive was slow but we eventually got to the airport where I felt safe. I was in the full glare of the public with lots of police and military people around.

Samir parked and took me to a place outside the main terminal and told me to wait there. I am not sure where he was but he was gone for about an hour and I was getting worried. I just wanted to be checked in and get on the plane.

When he got back I asked where he had been and he said, 'Oh, nowhere, just sorting out your flight and your smooth exit. It is all taken care of and no worries.' The next thing I knew was he took me through passport control in one minute flat. Then walked right out to the plane with me and waved goodbye as I got on. A soldier accompanied him and they were both standing on the tarmac waving to me.

Once I was on the plane, I sat back in my seat and felt an enormous amount of relief and guilt. I kept thinking that I might have over-reacted, and I should have stayed a bit longer. I felt a bit of disloyalty towards the Chalabi family, who were good to me and I know would not have put me in harm's way. However, it was a volatile country, things could escalate quickly, and nobody could control an outbreak of violence.

I really liked Beirut; it had the potential to be a beautiful place once all the fighting had stopped. It was often described as the Paris of the Middle East and I could see why. In addition, the bank was doing well, there was a lot of potential for them, and I knew I could help them. For a split second, I thought about getting off the plane and staying but that did not last for long. I sat back in my seat, fell asleep and woke up in London. Thank God. That was an experience I never wanted to repeat.

When I got back into the office the following week, the Chalabi family were laughing at me because they said I was always safe. But they understood why I wanted to leave. They also knew about the incident in the bank with the clients and the video on Beirut.

They said, 'We could understand why you felt nervous,' and they thanked me for going there and trying to help.

Maybe they were right, maybe I was safe, but I was not prepared to take the chance. I told them that I would go back another time and be more relaxed about it. But they knew I didn't mean it and I never went back.

Chapter 12

THE FOUNDATIONS FOR
GOING IT ALONE

I had been working in the financial markets since the age of twenty-one. By 1989, at thirty-six, I was ready to start my own company. I did not see a gap in the market for anything in particular and I did not have a flash of inspiration to start a company to tap into something that I thought could work. I just felt that I had been working for other people for twenty years and it was time to start out on my own. I had always felt slightly uncomfortable working for other people because it meant that I was not fully in control of my own destiny. I was an employee not an employer.

I registered my first company in December 1989 with £10,000 paid-up share capital. It was not a lot of money but I needed a UK company and so I registered it with two shareholders, myself with 70 per cent and my wife Fiona with 30 per cent.

I included Fiona as a shareholder because she was so supportive of me starting my own company. I figured if it all went wrong and we had to sell our house and car to survive, she was taking on some of that risk. Therefore, if there was an upside to the business, she should share in that as well. Fiona and I have been a team since we got married so it was a natural thing to do.

Initially, I called it Currency Management Consultants. I did not have a clear plan of what I wanted to do. I just knew I did not want to pick up from where I left off at SCF Finance; I wanted to try new things.

By then, Fiona and I had one daughter with another one on the way. We lived in a beautiful detached house with four acres of land and some outbuildings. We had no mortgage and some savings, and I drove a Mercedes 500 SEC coupé with my own personalised number plate.

Working in the City had been lucrative because I always stayed focused and invested any bonuses in property. I did not gamble, drink or go nightclubbing and I never did drugs apart from a few puffs of 'wacky baccy' when I was seventeen. I rarely went out for long lunches and I just worked hard because I loved working and learning new things. Working also gave me a structure to my life before I met Fiona. That carried on after we met, but with marriage to an intelligent, beautiful woman I felt more empowered and confident.

A few years after starting the company I realised why I loved being my own boss. I realised all those years ago, that when I hit my dad it gave me control of the household. It meant that my dad could not hurt my mum anymore, either physically or emotionally, because he would have me to deal with. That moment, however nasty for me emotionally, meant that I was in charge. I loved being in charge at home because it meant that I could protect my mum, which I did until the day she died.

Now I had my own company, I loved the feeling of being in control of my destiny. I did not depend on others to pay me a salary and I could control my own affairs and financial future. It meant that I could make the decisions and protect my income, thus protecting my family and our future. I loved that feeling and still do today.

Who knows why people are successful, because many things drive people on. If you become successful in business, you are classed as a clever and far-sighted entrepreneur, but that description does not account for people's background and upbringing. Success has many foundations, and, for me, it was built on being in control of my own destiny, underpinned by a loving wife and family.

Being off your head on drink or drugs or having a gambling addiction means you are not in control of your life and destiny. Events or substances control you. My adrenalin rush comes from being successful and creating and making things happen, then enjoying the rewards.

When my dad was drunk, he was useless. He did not even know his own name and he often had to be carried home after a family party or event. I found it embarrassing because it reflected on my mum more than my dad and my mum did not deserve to be treated in such a way. It was disrespectful to her and to her children, but that never stopped my dad. He just could not stop himself from drinking too much. Family Christmas lunches were spoilt, as he was always home late from the pub, always drunk and unable to enjoy one meal a year with his wife and kids. Christmas lunch always ended up in an argument as my mum begged him to be home by a certain time as dinner would be ready.

I have often wondered why my mum and dad did not divorce. My mum would say that it was my dad's name on the rent book, and she would have to be the one to leave. My dad always used to say, 'If you don't like it then fuck off because I am not leaving this flat and the rent book is in my name.' He also used to say, 'You can leave the twins here and I will get someone to look after them.' He was cruel and uncaring, and he knew my mum would never abandon her boys. It would have been hard for her to walk away as she had nowhere to go. So, she just got on with it and did the best she could. However, it was not an easy life for her or for us.

Also, it just was not the thing in those days to get divorced. There was only one kid in my class with divorced parents and we looked on him as an outcast. He used to be bullied for it because there was stigma attached to it and my mum did not want that for her boys.

By the time we three boys had grown up and left home, my dad's drinking had slowed down. He could not drink so much as he had had two thirds of his stomach removed and he was weak and frail. Instead, he used to take nips of spirits like rum. Mum and Dad got on better then. They had been at war for so long and they were both tired of years of conflict, so they just settled down. However, my dad had been out of control for much of his life and we as his family had been on the receiving end. That was not the life I wanted for my wife and kids and myself.

But one thing I have learnt in business is that you cannot control everybody and everything all the time – especially in financial services, where you depend on so many people to keep you compliant. If you want to be successful and expand – we now have eleven offices worldwide and around 800 people – you have to delegate well. Creating software and trading platforms is not my skill set, so I depend on developers and clever IT people. I have learnt to employ good people and let them get on with the job. The control is seeing what they can produce and then blending their endeavours and my ideas to make a successful company.

Another aspect of being successful was the adulation and praise I got from doing something well. It sounds attention-seeking and, in the early days, it probably was. However, growing up in an unloving household with dysfunctional parents, any praise I got was very welcome because I was not getting that at home.

In 1989, on the day I left SCF Finance, I went to work as normal, but I was back home by noon and Fiona said, 'What are you doing home?'

I told her I had resigned, because the job was going nowhere. I said Hussein had lost interest and I wanted to make a change before I got too old. I had not discussed it with her beforehand, but she knew I was not happy and I wanted to start my own company.

Her response was, 'Well, get on with it then, if it does not work out at least you tried and we will get by one way or another.' She was not concerned about losing everything that we already had, she just backed me all the way. Wow – what a woman. The best!

So I got on with it. Initially, I started a consultancy and wrote to various companies to see if I could advise them on how to manage their foreign exchange forward exposures. I rented a serviced office in London Wall. I made sure I got up every morning at six and put on a suit, shaved and commuted like the rest of the world. I wanted to feel like I was working and doing a normal day's work even if there was no income.

I also felt that by looking the part, people would think that I had a successful business even if I was just meeting people like the sales reps from Reuters or some photocopier company. It was all about perception: if you dress smart, you look successful even if you are not. However, if you dress like a tramp you look unsuccessful even if you are doing well. It is probably a dated view now, but back then for me it was all about working in the City and enjoying the cut and thrust of City life.

I could have worked out of the spare bedroom, but I needed to keep myself disciplined and focused and I wanted to be in the City to feel the vibe and see what was going on.

Chapter 13

STICK TO WHAT YOU KNOW

In the first two weeks of Currency Management Consultants' existence, I must have sent out over 100 letters to various companies that I found in Yellow Pages. I wrote to Christie's, Rolls-Royce, Jaguar, the European Tour Golf Association – any major international company I thought might have currency exposure.

I received a handful of replies with only one company wanting to see me. However, that company was Rolls-Royce. They asked me to ring and make an appointment, which I did. The appointment was eight weeks in the future, but I had my first bite and I was counting down the days until I could jump on a train and head to Derby to meet their finance people.

Then about two weeks before the appointment, they cancelled and asked me to make another appointment. So, there I was a few months into starting a consultancy, earning no money and getting almost zero response from any company I wrote to. I thought, 'Fair enough, let's try something different.'

I decided to get back into brokerage and the market-making business. It was an easy decision because that was all I knew, apart from working a telex machine. In those days, you only needed to be regulated if you dealt in futures. Therefore, to keep costs down and to keep it simple, I decided to make Currency Management Consultants a forex brokerage and currency market maker.

However, before I got started, in June 1990, I took Fiona and the children on holiday to St Raphael in the south of France. We hired an apartment that was about 300 yards from the car park. Every morning, on our way to the beach, I had to load up the car with nappies, pushchair, baby milk bottles and baby food, and it always took me two trips. I felt like a Sherpa, but it was one of the best holidays I ever had, even compared to five-star hotel holidays in Barbados or St Moritz or chartering a private yacht. It was just magical to be with the children so young and Fiona on the beach. Also, the 1990 World Cup was on and after dinner in the apartment every night, we would watch the football together with the kids falling asleep in our arms. It was a wonderful family holiday and one I will always remember.

I knew when I got back to London, I would have to ramp things up as I had my own company that was going nowhere. I was determined to make it work and so I would be working extremely hard and probably never be so relaxed again.

When I got back to the serviced office in July 1990, I was ready to go. I started to tap into some of my old SCF clients. However, the SCF business was going backwards when I left. It was small and most of the business was through contacts of the Chalabi family. I tried to buy SCF Finance off the Chalabis, but they kept it for other reasons, and I think eventually they dissolved it so they could access the remaining cash.

CMC at first was naturally small as I only had a few clients, but at least there was some business and income. However, this all changed a few weeks later when, on 2 August 1990, Saddam

Hussein invaded Kuwait and all hell broke loose in the financial markets.

I no longer had to start looking for business. Business came looking for me as many Middle Eastern clients, including banks and brokers, lost their currency trading lines with American banks. Because of the Gulf War, they needed new trading lines. I was independent and British, and I could use my relationships to secure trading lines with other brokers like Shearson Lehman Brothers, Merrill Lynch and Rothschild Bank. Middle East clients traded with me and I would hedge their trades with my banks and brokers. I acted as an intermediary, either as a broker or as a market maker. Business boomed and I started to make some decent money.

Once the Gulf War was over, things settled down. However, I retained the clients, as I was their insurance policy if things flared up again. Between 1990 and 1996, the company was making around £1 million a year profit before tax. I was drawing a good salary and bonus and I bought my first Bentley Turbo as a company car. As Fiona and I owned 100 per cent of the business, it effectively meant that was our income for the year, although we kept most of the profits in the company and lived on my salary and bonus.

For about six months when I started the company, I did not draw a salary but then I joined the payroll along with the team and I was driving a nice company car. It was a good living, but it was a boutique type of business and I had about twenty-five people working for me in 1994. We had moved offices to Old Jewry in the City, having had a short-term lease at Winchester House, London Wall – just in front of the old Western Union building. Things were going well; I was having two or three family holidays a year and I had started paying the staff and myself good bonuses. We also got a full futures licence and became regulated by the Association of Futures Brokers and Dealers (AFBD), the regulator at the time.

Then, in 1994, I started to read about the internet and the 'information superhighway'. I thought, 'Wow, this could be interesting.'

Chapter 14

THE WORLD GOES ONLINE

When I first read about the internet, I understood its power immediately. I knew that it could do the same as what I was doing when I was sending telegrams for Western Union from London to our office in Syracuse, New York electronically. At Western Union, I could see that a telegram could be transmitted across the Atlantic in seconds and delivered to the recipient at their home or office, within an hour, even on the other side of the world. However, in this case, it would be from people to people, not company to company.

My first thoughts were, 'Wow, with the internet a message could be sent person to person, so why would anybody need to send a telegram via a company?' It was as clear as day to me because of my experience at Western Union.

I felt that the stars were aligning because I also thought, 'Why not try to get clients to deal with their broker over the internet and not over the phone or telex machine?' Not everybody had a telex machine at home, and I saw the internet as combining the telephone and telex machine. For me it was a complete no-brainer – a eureka moment.

In addition, I thought clients could deal more quickly, more transparently, with a record of their trades. And processing trades automatically via the internet platform meant you could trade more efficiently with clients, which offered the company scale.

To get going, I started looking around for somebody who could develop the technology. I knew it was possible because Western Union had a massive network of private wire connections that stretched across the Atlantic and somebody must have created the technology for that. I needed someone that could do the same but across a public network. The concept was the same because a network is a network, whether it is private or public. It is no different to making a business call or a private call on a telephone, it is still a call.

As I understood it at the time, the internet worked by allowing independent companies to tap into anybody's networks – primarily the telephone companies' – and use the cables under the sea to transmit their own messages. It allowed private networks to become public networks. The World Wide Web was the gateway for people to access these networks.

Eventually, I met someone called Chris Ferri. He is a super-smart software person who was looking for his next big project and he was as excited about the internet as I was. Chris had worked with a team of software engineers, writing telecommunications software for phone companies that linked telephone callers to voicemail boxes and call diversion technology. This was the person I needed, and Chris quickly got to work for me as a contractor. Unfortunately, he didn't last long as he was a New Zealander and after about six months decided he wanted to go home. However, he did not leave me in the lurch; he introduced me to Terry Johnston, another super-smart guy who had worked with Chris in the past. Terry was a Man United supporter, but hey, nobody's perfect.

Terry, like Chris, is a genius and once we agreed terms, he got on with the job. Terry brought in lots of smart young people and built a good team of around eight developers and programmers. He even plucked people out of university before they finished their courses to work on our project.

After about eighteen months, I remember a seminal moment in early 1996 when Terry connected two computers and we sent a message from one to the other across the internet. He declared, 'You just sent a message across a public network from one computer to another.' A person-to-person message. I nearly cried in disbelief because I knew this small step would be the gateway to bigger and better things for my company.

However, it was not all plain sailing. Terry and his team of contractors were eating into our profits as the costs of building a new internet trading platform got higher and higher. So much so that in September 1996 there was a knock on my door and in walked my two fellow directors – finance director Ajay Pabari and company secretary Tom Greenwood – and somebody I had worked with at SCF Finance who helped me to register CMC Markets as a start-up private company.

They looked serious and they let me have it. They said, 'This internet project has been going for nearly two years. It's not working, and we should cut our losses and close it down. CMC is a nice business, making a good profit every year, and you are spending most of the profits on this crazy internet idea. It's time to knock it on the head, scrap the whole project and stick to the way we have always worked.'

They did not like the developers turning up at lunchtime, staying until midnight and ordering takeaway pizzas because there was always a mess in the mornings when we started work. They said, 'The developers are untidy and scruffy, they don't wear suits and they don't mix with the rest of the staff. They are outsiders, costing us a fortune, and so far, nothing is working. It is time to get rid of them all.'

In addition, most of the other employees, mainly dealers, felt that the internet threatened their jobs and would eventually replace them. The dealers felt that if they were not speaking to clients on the phone and doing the trades, they would one day be replaced by computers and their days were numbered.

Out of twenty-five people who worked at CMC, I was the only one who believed in the internet and how it was going to transform the business. Of course, the developers believed in it, but they were being paid as contractors. If it did not work, they could just get another job.

With Tom and Ajay sitting in front of me, I felt isolated, but I had this tremendous belief and excitement that the internet would work. I had seen it working at Western Union, even though it was not across a public network, and I knew that the developers just needed a bit more time. They were making progress, but it was slow, primarily because this had not been done before. I explained to Ajay and Tom that they were wrong; it was going to work and we should stick with it.

That moment lives with me to this day because I felt that was when I became an entrepreneur. That was the day I stuck to my beliefs and my vision against everybody in the company. At that moment, my company and my credibility were on the line. But I was tough enough to stand firm and I thought, at the worst, we could write off a year's profits and go back to where we were before.

I was an experienced risk-taker, mainly through my dealing and market-making days, and I could assess risk quickly. I knew the downside. I did not know the upside, but I thought it was worth pushing on because it could be phenomenal.

Today, it is easy to see the benefits of the internet and there is hardly a company without an internet connection or website. However, in 1996, most companies did not even have web pages, let alone an online trading platform. At moments like this, when I stood alone and with the whole company against me, I realised my tough upbringing at Mum's hands stood me in good stead and helped me cope with the challenges of business. I was tailor-made to run a company and I loved the challenges and uncertainties because I had this inner toughness to stand by what I believed in.

It is a point I feel obliged to pass on to others. I once gave a talk to a classroom of students at Westminster School, a very good fee-paying private school. I said to the whole class, 'When you leave this school, you will be at a disadvantage compared to me when I left school.' I told them about how I was brought up. But I said, 'If any of you has a problem, you can pick up the phone to your mum, dad, nan or grandad and they will help you. I had no one to call; no one could help me. So, I was on my own and this made me strong and independent.' It meant that I had to learn to do things for myself at a much younger age. I had to learn how to make my own decisions and drive myself and my career forward.

I explained that life is not just about education and having money. Sometimes, having a supportive family can put you at a disadvantage to people like me, who had to create success without advice and support from my family.

This was a complete contrast to the way I treated my own children as I have always tried to support and help them as much as I can, and I paid for them to have private education. However, I was just trying to help these kids understand that somewhere amidst the fog of life you have to be on your own fighting for what you believe in and making your own success. That is what made me successful.

My mum once said to me, 'Peter, if I have a problem, I know I can call you and you will sort it out for me. I am lucky to have you. However, I feel for you, as if you have a problem, they are million-pound problems and only you can solve them.' It was a stark reminder of the level I was operating at and it emphasised that I was alone with any problem that arose. Of course, Fiona was always there to support me, but we are talking about large financial problems and I was the only one who could deal with them.

Back at CMC Markets, heads were down. I was avoiding Tom and Ajay and putting lots of pressure on Terry to deliver something. Then the moment came on 20 October 1996 when we did our first trade on the internet between a client and ourselves. We had created the first retail platform for clients to trade across the internet.

Effectively, I invented online trading.

I cannot prove it; I just know nobody had an internet platform at that time. We were the first. My vision and dreams came true that day because it was like sending a Western Union telegram across the world electronically but now I could do it with financial transactions, directly with my clients, and I owned the company.

Other banks and brokers were saying that the internet would never work for trading because clients need to deal real-time. But my answer was that nothing is real-time in trading, as there is always a time lapse, even just a millisecond, whether you are trading on Reuters or Bloomberg or on the telephone. You just presume it is real-time because you cannot see the delay. It is just too fast for the brain to measure. I argued that real-time is what we perceive to be real-time when, in fact, it is not.

In addition, my logic was that the internet would improve as things did at Western Union, because every month we seemed to get faster networks. New machines were invented regularly, for example, screens superseded the old metal ticker tape machines, and the three-bank keyboards were replaced by four-bank ones with lots more features to eliminate typing errors. (We also had one of the first fax machines in Britain, which burnt letters into some horrible-smelling paper, which in the 1960s was innovative.) Therefore, in time the internet would do the same. I thought once it gripped people it would expand exponentially.

I also assumed that the internet would become more powerful as it would one day operate like a private wire network, just like we had at Western Union. It would only be a matter of time before trading and financial transactions online became accepted. At Western Union in the 1960s, we transferred money around the world, from one office to another, by sending a money mandate. Why not do the same for currencies and shares? It all seemed logical to me. It was just a matter of getting the software to work.

The internet also brought scale. Today we transact 99 per cent of our trades on the internet and around 70 per cent of that is done on mobile phones and devices. Less than 1 per cent of trades are done by telephone conversation. If we executed trades the way we did in 1996, before the internet, we would need more than 3,000 people. Today we have around 800 people.

However, it's not all about trading. Today, it is possible for a client to find our company and services via a Google search; open an account; fund the account; trade; withdraw money; and never speak to us. A client can be on holiday in New Zealand, click 'buy' or 'sell', and that trade will be routed via our Sydney or London dealing room and executed in milliseconds. If our Sydney dealing room is closed, it will be routed automatically to our London dealing room. Talk about scale and efficiency – nothing compares to the internet.

This scale is also good for clients because they have never before traded on lower commissions and tighter spreads, nor had more choice and transparency around their transactions. The internet has improved profits for companies through scale, which has driven down the costs of trading for retail clients. CMC and other online companies have opened the world's financial markets to the masses.

One reason CMC Markets was successful pre-internet was the wide spreads that banks had to charge to clear small transactions like foreign exchange. Whether the transaction size was £10,000 or £10 million, the cost of clearing and settling the transaction was the same. We had a competitive advantage because we could clear trades more cheaply than banks because our overheads were much lower. However, once we got online, we could really push our transaction costs down. In addition, with the creation of financial spread betting and contracts for difference (CFD) products, we could also make financial trading less costly in terms of capital gains tax (CGT) and stamp duty.

Client funds are segregated and protected in a client trust account, allowing them to trade all the world's major financial markets from one platform and one account. With no CGT and stamp duty, and mobile and internet trading on the lowest costs, what's not to like from a retail client's perspective?

Business was booming and I was fully vindicated in launching an internet trading platform despite the early reservations of staff and directors. It might seem an easy decision today but in 1996, it was revolutionary. The internet was still in its infancy and not many people believed it would catch on.

Chapter 15

TRADING CATCHES ON
TO THE INTERNET

In 1996, there was little or no electronic pricing coming from exchanges or banks. Exchanges were open outcry with manual clearing. There was some electronic functionality, but this was across private wire networks.

Therefore, with our first online platform, we had to update prices with a mouse manually, clicking up and down the prices depending on what we were quoting at the time. Dealers would watch the markets on a Reuters terminal or listen through voice broker commentary and click our prices up and down manually. Waiting for clients to buy or sell at any time.

It was not sophisticated, but it worked and soon word spread that you could trade online with Currency Management Corporation. (I changed 'Consultants' to 'Corporation' when we went into market making and broking. Later we became CMC Markets when we added more products like shares, commodities and indices.)

We were up and running by October 1996 and it did not take long for clients around the world to start trading online via our platform. For me, it was just like the old days sending telegrams at Western Union and dealing on the telex machines at International

Marine Banking, only this time the transactions were for my own company.

I loved it and, because this time it was across a public network, not private wires and telex machines, the world was our oyster. These were very exciting times as I could see the future and it was all about the internet and online trading.

In October 1997, the business was expanding. We had to move out of our nice offices in Old Jewry, as we needed more space for the increasing number of staff we were employing. I bought a beautiful old Victorian mansion in Hertford town centre called Bayley Hall, which was 5 miles from my house in Much Hadham, Hertfordshire. It meant I didn't have to commute, and I could work outside London for the first time ever. It also meant I had more time to concentrate on the business and more time to spend with Fiona and the girls. I could also slip in the odd round of golf in the summer before going to the office.

I was in my mid-forties and I had been working non-stop for thirty years, so I felt I could improve my life by cutting out some of the stress of commuting. Delays on the trains annoyed me as they could mean the difference between seeing my kids before they went to bed or not. So, moving out of the City nearer to my home was a lifestyle choice, but I also felt that if I had more time to concentrate on the business, that would be beneficial.

At that time, the developers working on the trading platform project wanted to branch out, work for themselves and create other platforms for other institutions. That was fine by me. I had a great platform, which I had paid handsomely for. However, the developers did not quite see it that way. Their logic was that they owned all the intellectual property of the software, even though I had been paying them generously to develop it on behalf of CMC.

Effectively, I felt that the intellectual property belonged to me as I had paid for it. They felt it belonged to them. There was a bit of a standoff. However, this was early days in the development of the internet and lots of new stuff was evolving. I also felt that CMC could continue to work with Terry Johnston and his team. They had delivered our first platform and they were good at their jobs. I said to Terry and his team that they could own all the intellectual property – but we should put it into a new company that they controlled but which I owned shares in. It was a compromise and we agreed to this.

Terry thought, as the lead developer behind the technology, that he deserved to have the controlling share of the newly formed company, called Information-Internet or, as I called it, 'Information in the Neck'. Eventually we agreed after Terry realised that I had a legal claim over the intellectual property. I was generous, especially as I thought Terry could still work for CMC through Information-Internet, so I settled for 25 per cent of the new company. Terry had around 55 per cent and his senior developers shared the rest.

Terry and his team found offices for the new company in City Road and they moved there in late 1997, at the same time as I was moving CMC Markets to Bayley Hall. The two companies effectively split and went their own ways and I thought that was the last I would see of the developers, at least on a daily basis.

At the same time as the move, I decided to make some changes to staff at CMC. I had felt for a while that some of the dealers were not applying themselves to the new internet platform, they just did not believe in it, and most seemed threatened by it. A year after the launch of our internet platform was time enough for existing staff to see the potential – if they did not see it then, they never would.

Some people just cannot handle change and most of those who had been working for me for five years were not so keen on the company's new path. They wanted things to carry on the same as before. They thought the internet would ultimately replace them but, whatever the reason, I needed fresh blood and people who believed in the internet and its future power.

I had learnt quickly in business that if you have people who do not share the vision from the start, they will not do so in the future. Usually the right thing to do is to put them out of their misery and replace them with people who do share that vision. Let them follow their own career paths and do what they believe in.

CMC was still a private company and I figured it was my money on the line. If I got it wrong, it would cost me so I had to do what I thought was right. I did it when Ajay and Tom told me to cut my losses over the money I had invested in the internet. It was time to do it again. This time with some key staff.

As the owner, I always have to concentrate on what is right for the company no matter how hard the decision. If you cannot make tough decisions, you will not survive running your own company for long. Furthermore, I felt that if I did not make the necessary changes, the business would not move forward, and we would miss a great opportunity. It is hard enough running a business with people who are behind you, let alone with people who are not.

Over the years, I have made many tough decisions at CMC Markets and this was one of the toughest. I had to replace five senior people who had been with me more or less from the beginning and helped me build the business. It was a ruthless act and I did not enjoy it one bit. It was upsetting and hard. I had to dismiss those people myself, as we were too small to employ a full-time HR person. However, it was not personal, and all the people involved had been given a fair chance to learn something new and be at the start of something special.

One morning in September 1997, I called in each dealer, one by one, to tell them that their services were no longer required. I told them I needed fresh blood that embraced the internet and its full potential. I said I needed people who believed in the direction of the company and who would help me develop the business. Most of them were not surprised and they were given ample financial notice to thank them for their efforts.

At the same time, Tom Greenwood, my company secretary, retired. Tom was the first employee of CMC outside of myself. I always kept in touch with him over the years and we would have lunch together every year with his wife Elizabeth. Tom died on 19 December 2020 aged ninety-two and I attended his funeral – virtually, because of Covid lockdown restrictions.

Tom once told me that I saved his life. When he retired, I kept him on the company's private medical scheme; it was my idea to do this. In his seventies Tom was diagnosed with a serious medical condition and was referred to see a consultant twelve weeks later. Tom told me he used the company's private scheme and instead he saw a consultant within a few weeks. He had an emergency operation and lived another twenty years. The consultant told Tom that if he had waited for his twelve-week appointment he would have died before he made it. Tom was a great man and I am proud to call him a dear friend.

The dealers were good at their jobs with nice families and mortgages, but I felt compelled to act. The situation had gone on too long. I liked all of them, but they could not get over the barrier of the internet and its perceived threat to them. Years later, when I bumped into two of them, they said they were amazed at how well the internet had done for CMC Markets, they did not realise it at the time, and they wished they had understood it better.

People have often thrown at me that I was in the right place at the right time because the internet helped me so much. Well, here were five people who were in the right place and time and they did not see what a great position they were in. Even with it staring them in the face and me banging on about it. The words 'horse' and 'water' spring to mind. Still, they all did well for themselves after they left me and two of them started their own fund management business and became best performers.

Unfortunately, a few years after leaving me, one of my top traders, who had a good job elsewhere, died suddenly. It was a sad moment and I was invited to his funeral. He was a nice person with a young family. We were together once on a trip to New York and we enjoyed our time together. He even told me the night he was going to propose to his girlfriend. So sad and upsetting for everybody that knew him because he was a top person.

I tell my staff now that change is good. You should be open to change, be part of and embrace it, as it will only make your job or your career better. Never worry about losing your job because if you adopt a defensive mentality you will lose your job anyway.

If things are changing, it means the company is progressing and investing for the future, which is better than the opposite. If you become part of that change, you will have a better chance of keeping your job and learning something new at the same time. Even if change causes you to lose your job, by learning something new, you will have a better chance of securing another job.

In late 1997, we were a smaller team because of the redundancies but I brought in some school leavers and two people who were barely twenty years old. I needed young blood that would come in with an open mind and be willing to learn the company's technology and internet strategy. Although we were stretched staff-wise, it was an exciting time as the young team felt that being internet-based made the company dynamic and cutting-edge.

One of the new recruits, David Fineberg, is still with me today, twenty-five years after first starting as a nineteen-year-old, and is now deputy CEO. David embraced the internet and our trading platform. He has grown and developed with the company, which is exactly what I was looking for in 1997. Today he is a board member of a public listed company and my number two.

Once we arrived at Bayley Hall, the team settled in and the business started to expand. At that time, we were still only offering forex trading on our platform. However, with more time on my hands, because I was not commuting, I started to expand the business by adding other products.

Chapter 16

ANOTHER DAY,
ANOTHER PRODUCT

Around the late 1990s, I started to read about a new product that major banks had developed for pension funds. They were called contracts for difference (CFDs).

In the UK, there is a stamp duty tax of 0.5 per cent when you buy physical shares. If you are a major pension fund investing in billions of pounds' worth of shares, this can increase your costs dramatically, reducing the value of your pension fund and undermining its management performance. Transaction costs including taxes reduce the size of the pension pot and ultimately the pension paid out to its workers. The CFDs were created to help pension funds reduce their costs.

Using the new CFD product, a pension fund can buy shares on behalf of the fund and avoid paying stamp duty. Because the pension fund has effectively bought a derivative of a share and not the physical share there is no stamp duty payable. The share transaction is merely a financial agreement between the pension fund and the bank, without delivery of the physical share. The bank then buys the physical shares in the underlying market to cover the transaction but issues a CFD contract to the pension fund. Because the bank is a registered market maker, exchange member or clearer, it is exempt from stamp duty.

CFDs have been around since the 1960s and 1970s in the form of index futures or exchange traded funds (ETF). There are other ways to avoid stamp duty by investing in ETFs or buying a basket of shares through an index. The banks just applied the same concept across individual shares and other financial products.

The pension fund still receives dividends on its CFD. In addition, corporate actions are be applied to the CFD (share) product. However, the pension fund does not have any voting rights for the company it has bought share CFDs in, because it never actually owns physical shares in the company. It owns a mirror derivative product in the form of a CFD. This is fine because the pension funds are just looking for good investment performance, not to take over a company. If you want to take over a company, you have to own the physical shares in that company – although some clever people can use CFDs as leverage to build a long-term position in a target company then convert them to physical shares when they initiate the takeover.

CFDs are widely traded financial products around the world, mainly on exchanges as futures contracts. Effectively a CFD is merely a settlement term with a net cash payment upon expiry or when you close the trade. The settlement is the difference between where you bought the product and where you sold the product, which represents a profit or a loss. There is no physical delivery of the product you have bought or sold, just the cash difference.

CFD products far outnumber physical delivery-type products. For example, the FTSE 100 futures contract traded on exchange is a CFD. Because, when the contract expires, you cannot own one hundredth of a share. The FTSE 100 futures contract is a weighted compilation of the UK's top 100 companies, traded as a basket or index. Upon expiration, the product is net cash settled as opposed to delivery of shares in those 100 companies.

Other examples of CFD products are trackers, ETFs, baskets and various indices like the Dax and Nasdaq. All are CFD contracts, even if traded on an exchange as futures contracts.

In 1999, I was thinking about how to add more (CFD) products to our internet trading platform. So far, it was only used for trading foreign exchange. I spoke to the developers and they said they would have to rebuild the existing platform, which would take at least two years as it was only built to trade foreign exchange.

However, I had a better idea. I asked the developers: what if we configured the platform to think a CFD is a forex transaction? After all, if you execute a forex trade you buy, say, US dollars and sell sterling. You are buying one currency and selling another. If you buy British Airways shares, you are buying one thing (shares) and selling another thing (sterling). I said we could configure the platform to make it execute a share trade as if it was a forex trade. It sounds simple. It was not, but that is how we launched CFDs and thousands more products across our platform in 2000, right at the top of the dot-com craze.

It was perfect timing.

Being a forex market maker by trade, I felt the way to make money on any financial product including CFDs was by managing the trade flows and then the risk. Just like the way we handled forex risk. This is in contrast to stockbrokers, who make their money from brokerage, by buying shares through exchanges or from market makers on behalf of their clients and collecting a fee for doing so. They do not manage the risk, indeed they are not allowed to as part of their licence; they execute trades on behalf of their clients. They match up a buyer and a seller and charge commission for the privilege. They are the intermediaries. As a market maker, we are the counterparty to the client, meaning clients buy and sell directly with us. Market makers have bigger capital requirements and higher capital ratio requirements.

Market making is the art of quoting a buy/sell price to a client on shares, say, then selling to the client directly and looking for a way to hedge the shares in the underlying market; or running the risk of not covering the position in the underlying market. This is called a short position by the market maker.

Sometimes to mitigate risk, you can do a sector hedge: for example, if one client buys British Airways shares and another client sells easyJet shares, you then manage the exposure as a sector risk. Because you are long and short airline stocks at the same time.

Often a market maker will sell something they do not yet own (going short). They just have to make sure they do own it before the trade is settled. It is all about managing the risk of the underlying product, providing liquidity to clients to buy and sell, then settling or clearing any outstanding transactions. It is like writing a cheque before being paid, but knowing the cheque will clear because your salary will be paid into your bank account before the cheque is presented.

I saw CFDs as a way to reach a wider trading audience by offering a wider range of products from one platform. We already had a distribution network through our existing client base trading foreign exchange. However, foreign exchange was not a wide-reaching enough product; it only appealed to a limited section of clients. The real action was in stocks and shares.

I remembered the Black Monday crash in 1987 and working for SCF Finance. While the world's stock markets were crashing around us, we were trading foreign exchange, bullion and future currencies but no share business because the company did not offer a share service. It was surreal as the world's financial markets were in meltdown and yet it was a normal day in our foreign exchange dealing room. We saw a bit of action on precious metals and currency futures but primarily all the action was in the world's stock markets.

I saw CFDs as a generic financial product that allowed clients to trade, from one account, any product they wanted. We just had to add all the world's different financial products as CFDs and then clients could trade anything and everything. Eventually we added over 10,000 different financial (CFD) products and asset classes to the platform and we were the market maker, not a broker, to our clients on all those products.

Chapter 17

THE ART OF RISK
MANAGEMENT

The art of risk management is to aggregate and offset as much of your client trade flows (buy/sell orders) as possible, to minimise your hedging costs. You do this by internalising trades of buyers and sellers of the same products to try to earn the price spreads and neutralise your risk book. Any residual (risk) balance can then be hedged in the underlying markets.

However, frequently, clients trade at different times, and there is a mismatch of buyers and sellers of the same products throughout the day. In this case, you manage risk around the trade time differences. The issue here is that you never know if you will get the opposite trade later in the day. This is more difficult during volatile market conditions. Nirvana for a market maker would be clients buying and selling at exactly the same time, which means the market maker has no risk to manage and they just collect the difference in the buy and sell prices, the spread.

When managing risk, you can hedge using index futures to offset individual client share trades. This is to avoid execution costs of individual share trades on exchanges, keeping costs to a minimum. It is all about aggregation and managing flows and settlement throughout the day. It is not about taking on the clients' trades but balancing your books and using different financial instruments to keep your own hedging costs lower than the clients' trading costs. Aggregation and portfolio hedging are typical ways to reduce hedging costs.

There is no point in a market maker taking a view on whether the markets will go up or down. They are not looking to second-guess the stock market movements. They are looking to keep hedging costs to a minimum, especially as their risk book is changing constantly as clients keep buying and selling throughout the day.

I was excited about the prospect of launching CFDs on our Market Maker platform. However, I needed scale to maximise profits and minimise losses. The more trade flows a market maker gets, the more they can aggregate and mitigate risk.

Even though CMC are market makers, we must reflect and mirror the underlying market price. Therefore, if today somebody wants to trade Facebook shares, we have to offer the latest Facebook share price. We cannot make up our own price above the underlying market price. In other words, we cannot skim the client. Otherwise, clients might as well trade physical shares and pay the stamp duty and commission – it must be worth their while to trade with us.

When I started CMC Markets, my first eureka moment was launching the first internet trading platform. Adding all product CFDs to the platform alongside foreign exchange was the second eureka moment and, in many ways, more exciting. To me, online trading was inevitable once I learnt about the internet because I had seen wire transfers at Western Union, and I knew it would work. However, to lunch a generic financial product in the form of CFDs to add to our internet platform was truly exciting.

The problem was that we already had very good foreign exchange flows, as we were an online forex trading company. If we launched share CFDs and other products it would take time to build flows and get the scale we needed to mitigate and manage the trade flow risk.

We needed scale as quickly as possible. I had to come up with a plan to hit the ground running on day one, which is when I thought of commission-free share trading. This was the first time commission-free share trading had been offered in the UK and it proved to be explosive.

Chapter 18

THERE'S NO SUCH THING
AS A FREE LUNCH

The plan was to be a market maker of all the new CFD products and make the bulk of our income through risk management, not brokerage or commissions.

It was market practice to charge a commission on shares, primarily because it was a stockbroker's market and they needed to earn their income. However, for our forex service we were not charging commissions to our clients. So, I thought, why not make shares commission-free as well?

Early 2000 was the height of the first dot-com boom. There was the fear of missing the next big dot-com stock and there was a big appetite from clients to buy technology shares. I wanted to find a name for the service that fitted in with the technology craze that was emerging. Names such as lastminute.com were popular. I needed a catchy name to attract clients, so I came up with deal4free.com.

To say it was a game changer puts it mildly. Now, clients could log onto the platform and trade around 10,000 global financial products, all from one account. They could leverage their positions (trade on margin); go long or short; and trade gold, oil, shares or the Dax index – whatever they wanted – all from one account and all commission-free.

Before the launch of deal4free and CFDs, we were opening around 500 forex accounts a month. When we launched deal4free, we were opening that amount in a day!

In 2000, I remember walking through the reception area at Bayley Hall and there were piles of envelopes ready to be sent out to clients with account opening forms – there were no online applications in those days – and CD-ROMs ready for the clients to download our platform technology onto their computer. The receptionists were swamped, but I immediately got developers to create a web page so that clients could type in their own addresses and personal details. We could then print off labels and stick them on the envelopes. It saved us lots of time, which removed some of the pressure, but we were still inundated with account opening applications.

The launch was a great success, and alongside the deal4free brand, I came up with some catchy marketing phrases. I remember sitting by the pool at the Hôtel du Cap in Antibes in the summer of 2000 and writing lots of these straplines. I will not bore the reader with too many of them but here is just a flavour of the deal-4free straplines I created:

1. There's no such thing as a free lunch but there is free share trading.
2. Du pain, du vin, do shares – commission-free French share trading. (I stole that from the Boursin cheese advert, and it is my favourite.)
3. Houston, we don't have a problem – commission-free US share trading. (From *Apollo 13*, the Tom Hanks film.)
4. There's no such thing as a free pizza but there is commission-free Italian share trading.
5. Will the last broker left please switch off the lights.

There were so many more, I just kept reeling them off as I sat by the pool. Oh happy days, to be creating so many exciting things. I was coming up with fixes for technology, developing new products and creating marketing campaigns. I loved it, but more importantly the company was expanding and developing and my actions of 1997 with the staff changes felt vindicated.

It was about this time that I realised how much I loved working for myself and running my own company. It gave me a sense of being creative and innovative and being in control of my life and my destiny. I had a beautiful wife and children; I was staying at the Hôtel du Cap; and for the first time in my life, I felt truly happy inside and out.

Chapter 19

BUILDING ON SUCCESS

2000 was our first year of offering contracts for difference. In that year, we made more money on CFDs than we had in the previous five years trading just foreign exchange. The company was transformed, the internet had arrived, CFDs were established and we were flying.

Just as in 1990, when Saddam Hussein invaded Kuwait, we were lucky in the sense that in 2000 we had the dot-com craze. That meant many clients were buying and selling tech stocks and, with so much volatility in stock markets, it was a market maker's dream. Clients kept trading and we just kept managing risk and making money.

However, from a client point of view, there were turbulent times ahead as the dot-com bubble was about to burst.

Wikipedia describes the dot-com bubble as 'a historic economic bubble and period of excessive speculation mainly in the United States, a period of extreme growth in the use and adaptation of the internet'. This volatile period was very profitable for the company and, in a way, I was lucky there was so much volatility around for a market-making business. However, if I hadn't created a company and an internet trading platform and launched CFDs to the retail market these events would just have been news items for me to read about and I would probably be making money for somebody else, not myself.

When I created CMC in 1989, a few people said to me, 'No point in starting a foreign exchange company, because eventually there will be one currency in Europe, and nobody will need to do forex deals anymore.' I ignored that advice and I am glad I did.

I was also once told that I was lucky because I found something that I was good at. My response was, 'So what am I good at?'

'Trading.'

I replied, 'I am good at running a company because, when I learnt trading, there was no such thing as the internet, mobile phones and CFDs.'

There are plenty of times when a market maker loses money. For example, a client may buy some shares from us and in the few seconds it takes to click 'buy' the market could easily move higher and the client will have bought shares at less than the current market price. That means potentially a loss for a market maker – it happens all the time. Alternatively, the market can move in your favour in the split second between quoting a price and the client clicking the button.

When I talk about making money, I mean net or overall. Remember, we are not a broker covering deals on an exchange and charging commissions for execution and clearance without any risk. We make our money from aggregating client flows and from risk management. Every day, market makers work on averages, netting off as much as they can and offsetting losses against profits. Coming out net ahead at the end of the day, week, month and year is all that counts.

Being a market maker enabled CMC Markets to expand its business because it meant we could compete on pricing with exchanges. We could add all major financial products onto one platform using CFDs and we could operate commission-free because we were making money from risk management. In addition, we could settle trades directly with the client, not through a third-party clearer, creating more cost reductions, which we could pass onto clients in the form of (again) commission-free trading and competitive trading spreads.

Over the years, a few exchanges have launched individual share CFDs but they have never succeeded because clients want to trade everything from one account. For clients, it is about choice and flexibility, not necessarily trading on an exchange with limited products and trading hours. We are open twenty-four hours a day across all of the world's financial markets.

After our CFD launch, we started to open offices overseas and we took our platform and products as far afield as we could. Our first overseas office was in Sydney, our second was in Frankfurt. Soon we were opening offices all around the world.

The internet gave us distribution and scale. It meant we could deal with other people on the other side of the world without having an office in that country. However, people like to deal with local companies and local people, and they like to trade in their local currency. Importantly, they want to see their money in a local bank. They also want to come in and kick the tyres and meet the people, to see if you are a real company with real people. It also helps to employ locals with the local accent. In addition, clients want you to be regulated by their country's regulator. It can in some cases give them more protection. It is more about perception rather than solid commercial reasons because logically there is no reason to have an office on the other side of the world if you can access those clients online.

However, in 2000, it was still early days for the internet and financial trading. Google was still a private company and search engines were just starting up. If you asked somebody what SEO (search engine optimisation) was in 2000, they would probably have no idea. We felt we needed a strong client support programme as clients were also just discovering the internet and its power. We wanted educational programmes to teach clients how to trade the financial markets and to use our platform. Therefore, we ran lots of local seminars, and later webinars, in our offices to support and educate clients.

In addition, we created practice, or demonstration, trading accounts with make-believe money so clients could 'trade' on our platform without risking their own money before they funded for real. The demo platform offered real prices from the underlying markets so clients could assess their abilities before they parted with their cash.

By now, the Market Maker platform was becoming more than just a front end to buy and sell financial products. We started loading it with information such as real-time charting, news, market research and market depth pricing. As the internet matured and got faster, our platform developed into a sophisticated trading front end for clients to research stocks and shares, commodities and all major financial products. Effectively, we were creating a middle tier of financial trading for retail clients.

I often described what we were doing as opening the world's financial markets to the masses so they could trade on the same prices as Goldman Sachs. We were transforming the way retail clients executed trades and their appetite was enormous. Who can blame them? Suddenly they could access all the latest financial products and overseas markets with the click of a mouse or from their mobile phone.

Why shouldn't ordinary working people be able to trade shares in companies such as Apple, Facebook, Alibaba, Google and Amazon? Being a market marker, we could facilitate all levels of retail client trading. Also, through the introduction of leverage, clients could buy and sell shares by putting a small deposit with us. The deposit size changed from product to product but, in most cases, clients could buy and sell over twenty times the size of their cash deposit.

So, if a client wanted to buy, say, $100,000 worth of BHP shares in Australia they could deposit a fraction of the amount needed – in this case, from $5,000. They could also leverage, or scale up, their trading by borrowing money to increase their trade size. This was riskier as their losses, as well as profits, would be reflected on the size of their position, not the size of their cash deposit. If a client deposited £1,000 and bought £100,000 worth of gold, their profit and loss would be based on the £100,000 position. If the price of gold fell more than 1 per cent, they would lose all their deposit and we would automatically close their position in gold. If the gold market fell rapidly by 2 per cent, we would close the position and the client would owe us an additional £1,000. This is why there are risk warnings on financial products, for example, you can lose more than your initial deposit. CFD trading is not fixed-odds trading, you use a small deposit to trade a larger position. Great if you are making money. Not so great if you are losing.

As CMC Markets expanded around the world, we needed to explain to clients how leverage combined with the platform and market volatility worked. We were not obliged to do this by any regulators and we still aren't. But we invested in building enormous educational programmes. In the early 2000s, we even had weekend boot camps to give clients a crash course in trading. Usually, we charged for these boot camps but if you funded your account and traded, we would refund you the costs.

Back then, there was so much news about dot-com businesses and amazing stories about how they opened overnight and became worth vast fortunes. Retail clients wanted a slice of the action. They thought, it's OK buying the odd British Gas share in a government sell-off and making a few hundred quid, but some of these dot-com companies were making their owners and investors millions and they wanted in big time. If they wanted to trade online, they usually found deal4free.com quickly.

By the end of 2000, CMC was in good shape and the team were happy. The young recruits had bedded in nicely. They were learning the CMC way and they were very supportive of technology and the internet in general.

Over the previous five years or so, we had launched the first online trading platform for retail clients. We had loaded it with thousands of new products using CFDs to appeal to a wider audience. We had plans for the office in Sydney with Frankfurt on the horizon. We had become regulated, getting our futures licence from the AFBD, and we were making more money than we had ever made.

However, technology was moving fast. Mobile phones were becoming the rage and broadband internet was on its way. Firms like

Dixons were launching Freeserve, making it free to connect to the internet.

I knew we needed to keep investing in technology to stay ahead of the game. But I had a nagging worry that commercially we could be challenged. I woke up one morning in December 2000 and I knew what I needed to do. It would be another game changer – eureka moment number three.

Chapter 20

ROLLING OUT
A NEW PRODUCT

I realised we had to get into the next phase of internet trading – spread betting. This eureka moment was not as exciting as launching the first internet trading platform, or loading it up with CFDs, but it was just as important.

Financial spread betting is unique to the UK's financial markets. You can spread trade overseas, but it does not have the same tax benefits as spread betting in the UK.

If you spread bet on a financial product, as opposed to buying, say, physical shares, there is no stamp duty and, more importantly, no capital gains tax (CGT). This is because, if you spread bet, you never own the underlying product. This is the same as a CFD, but with a spread bet you are merely betting on the price going up or down. You are not buying, you are betting.

A CFD is a financial product but a spread bet, back then, was considered a form of gambling. It was regulated by the Gambling Commission and gambling profits were generally CGT free. Bizarrely, if you wanted a spread bet licence you had to apply to the local magistrates' court, which I did personally a few times in Hertford Town Hall.

Because spread betting is a betting product, to trade (or bet) you do not buy shares, you bet a sum of money per point that the market will go up or down. It's a great product because any profits are tax free and generally you do not have to declare your winnings to HMRC.

The UK government charges a betting levy, which every spread bet firm pays monthly. The government likes this system of collecting taxes indirectly. It's more like a transaction tax. It makes complete sense to tax gambling this way, primarily because more clients lose money gambling or trading than make it but the government collects revenue in the form of a levy regardless of whether clients win or lose.

Spread betting in financial products was already available. But it was not online, it was generally done over the phone.

I knew that when it did go online it would be a major threat to our CFD business. I saw spread betting as trading with all the benefits of CFDs, such as no stamp duty, and with leverage. But with one big difference – your profits are tax free. I surmised that clients would abandon CFD trading and spread bet instead, because of the tax benefits, once spread betting came online with our competitors. All it needed was for the existing spread bet companies to get their act together and our CFD business would be under threat, so I needed to get a move on and I already had a master plan.

We launched a spread betting service in June 2001 once we got our licence from the Gambling Commission. Whether a client spread bets or trades CFDs, we can aggregate the risk side of both of those products together. This is because, if a client trades, say, Vodafone shares either as a spread bet or as a CFD, they still get the underlying Vodafone price and we still manage the risk the same way.

We could use our existing platform, technology and risk management teams to launch spread betting and manage the pricing and risk in the same way. This opened another avenue to generate flows and drive scale through to the dealers and our risk book of business.

But this was not the master plan. In the run-up to the launch, while we were applying for our gambling licence and building a spread bet platform, I was thinking of a way to position our spread bet service in the market to gain scale and flows. I needed another angle, just as I did with deal4free.com.

In early 2000, there were two main spread bet competitors. They were building internet platforms and would compete with us on technology, in due course, but I wasn't too concerned about that. I thought we could get an advantage over them through the product itself.

The competition was very expensive to deal with because their trading spreads were wide. Also, they tended to trade futures products to push the settlement of the trade to a future date. This meant building in the financing costs to the cash price, then quoting their customers a three-month future delivery price. They also added their own commissions and spreads, which made the futures price very expensive, because it was all added onto the trading price. Because of all these added costs, the spread bet price looked very expensive and different to the underlying market spot price that appears on Bloomberg and other financial terminals.

Our competitors quoted futures prices because clients wanted time for their investment or trade to make money. But I thought there were better ways of doing this, which would reflect more of the underlying market price. Because of the discrepancy in the price they were quoting compared to the spot price, I thought their products were not appealing to ordinary retail clients. The spread bet price was so much higher that it was almost cheaper to do a physical or futures transaction instead.

My master plan was to come up with the rolling cash spread bet. I wanted our spread bet prices to be the same as the underlying market prices on Bloomberg and the exchanges. So, if the Vodafone share price on the London Stock Exchange was, say, £151.25, I wanted our spread bet price to be the same.

Quoting a cash spot price and not a futures price meant there were no financing costs built into the trading price and no commissions, hidden or otherwise. As with deal4free.com, we were not going to charge any commissions to spread bet on shares. The spread bet trade could be carried forward every night as an unsettled bet. This meant the client could keep the trade open indefinitely. They would be charged overnight financing on their open trade if they carried it over to the next day. But this would be reflected in a debit to their cash account and not built into the price they traded at.

I thought our rolling cash spread bet offering was compelling for clients. More importantly, our competitors could not match it overnight because they didn't have the platform or infrastructure to change what they already had. And to make life harder for them, I trademarked the phrase 'rolling cash spread bet'. This blocked competitors from using the term, although not the product because that is generic, and I couldn't trademark that.

Trademarking 'rolling cash spread bet' doesn't make much difference today as competitors call it 'daily cash' or something similar. I just did it to slow people down and make them come up with their own name. We did serve an injunction on at least one competitor, but I saw this aggressive stance as all good sporting fun and improving the industry.

I was also thinking about what competitive advantages we had apart from technology and product. A platform loaded with CFDs underpinned by deal4free gave us great traction, scale, brand and lots of business. But I realised that another factor was my background and market-making experience. It was a real advantage to have market making underpinning the business.

Back in 2000, I was approached by a team that worked for GNI, a broker that was eventually bought by Man Group. The team wanted to move to CMC, to broker CFDs to clients, save the client's 50 basis points (0.5 per cent) on stamp duty but charge them half of that back as commission, which was a high commission. The GNI team argued that by saving them 50 basis points, the clients would be prepared to pay 25 basis points commission. This might have been true, but it was alien to my thinking as a market maker.

They had a great product, but they were brokers collecting commissions. They were just trying to split the stamp duty cost savings among themselves because they wanted a large slice of the commissions they generated. This would have worked for a while, but I knew that an on-exchange, commission-driven model was doomed because the transparency of the internet and the scale and efficiencies it brought to financial markets meant commissions were shrinking, not growing.

It wasn't rocket science. Our foreign exchange business was already lowering trading costs for retail clients because the internet made it so much cheaper to execute and clear trades. I told the GNI guys that I wouldn't be offering them a job and I wished them well.

However, I realised after speaking to them that we had a massive competitive advantage being a market maker. It underpinned everything we had achieved to date because it meant we could offer commission-free trading, a free trading platform, and free charts, news and analysis, because we made our money from risk management and managing client trade flows. This was a very hard business model to compete with.

Clients generally do not give a damn whether they trade on exchange or off exchange, they just want the latest price and they want to make money. I thought market making would be key to launching spread betting, and I was right.

Before we launched our spread betting platform, I needed another killer strapline that would gain people's attention and have the same impact as deal4free. Having registered 'rolling cash spread betting' as a trademark, I wanted to ramp up the pressure on competitors even more.

The strapline I came up with was 'compare the spread'. I wanted potential spread bet clients to see how much they would save in costs with us compared to the other spread betting firms. From a client's point of view, it was a no-brainer as we were so much cheaper.

But I took it further, sometimes comparing our spreads to competitor spreads in print and pushing them in front of clients so they could see their choices. I was not the most popular person in the spread bet industry. But I was not in business to be popular, I was in business to innovate, make money and keep pushing the boundaries. I loved pushing boundaries and still do.

It was an aggressive move. It caught the competition on the back foot and our business boomed. As with the deal4free launch, the girls in reception were buried with account opening applications. Today, all spread bet firms operate the way we did when we launched in 2001. All offer daily rolling cash products and over 90 per cent of spread bet business is done on cash pricing, not forward pricing. All the main firms offer commission-free spread bet share trading on the underlying market cash price. All spread bet firms aggregate flows and manage risk through market making.

Rolling cash spread betting, with competitive pricing, commission-free trading and online platforms, has made the spread bet industry more widely appealing and more profitable for all competitors. It has also benefitted clients by driving down spreads and costs so they can trade and save on stamp duty and CGT.

If you want to speculate or bet on financial markets today and you are a UK resident, why would you trade any other way? Anything else is more expensive, and that still stands today.

Chapter 21

PASTURES NEW FOR THE CRUDDAS FAMILY

By mid-2001, CMC had an amazing platform offering foreign exchange, CFDs and spread betting and the business and profits were rolling in. Deal4free and 'Compare the spread' were flying. We were establishing offices all around the world and we launched our business-to-business proposition, albeit on a small scale, offering white label and sales trader services. And the Cruddas family was living in Monaco.

Fiona and I had always dreamt of living in Cannes in the south of France. When Fiona was young her family travelled the world with her father's job in the British army. She is one of three children; all are British but born in different locations. Fiona was born in Paris.

When Fiona and her siblings were younger, her parents would drive down to the south of France for family holidays. Fiona knew the area well and she has always loved it there, as do I. We had some fantastic holidays there with our own children. I remember swimming out to the bathing platform opposite the Carlton Hotel, Cannes, with a rope tied to my waist, towing a plastic dinghy containing the girls behind me. We would often sing 'All aboard, Cap Ferrat'. By the end of the holiday, we were taking on passengers and I lost nearly a stone.

At first, the plan was to live in Cannes, but we liked the International School in Monaco. It had smaller class sizes and offered the International Baccalaureate, which is what the girls eventually took and passed with flying colours.

I still paid UK taxes even though I was living in Monaco. But at least I didn't have to pay French taxes, which I would have if we lived in Cannes. We were tax exiles from France rather than the UK.

UK law at the time stated that if you lived overseas but derived income from the UK, you had to pay UK income tax on your UK earnings. I am not a tax expert, but I knew that, because I was a major shareholder and a director of CMC, I did not qualify for complete non-residency. I didn't mind, because we always knew we would come back to the UK and we moved to Monaco more for lifestyle than for tax purposes.

Also, I didn't want to change my domicile. I saw recently that I was in the top fifty taxpayers in the UK, which is fine by me. When we listed CMC in 2016, we were back in the UK as resident and domiciled, on a pay-as-you-earn (PAYE) payroll. Fiona and I paid the full capital gains tax on the shares we sold at the initial public offering (IPO). The total amount we paid in that tax year was nearly £50 million.

Paying your taxes gives you the freedom to travel anywhere you want and it means you can sleep at night. Also, when it comes to financial planning for your children, you know you are not passing any legacy tax issues on to them. For me, it's the only way to live. It leaves you completely free to concentrate on business without double accounting, hiding bank accounts and playing silly buggers with HMRC, who in my experience are smarter than any businessperson or accountant when it comes to taxation. They have seen it all before and heard all the excuses.

In 2001, I was forty-eight years old. I had been working for thirty-three years, which was 70 per cent of my life, and spent twelve of those years working for myself. I had left school at fifteen and did the night shift on Christmas Day at the age of sixteen at Western Union. I had done stressful jobs as a market maker in banks and brokers and then for my own company.

I had worked hard supporting my family, including my parents by buying them a bungalow and a car and supplementing their pension by paying their bills. Often you read of traders burning out in their forties. I didn't feel burnt out, but I didn't feel like I could run the London Marathon either, even though I was fit.

I also thought that I deserved to improve my lifestyle, having achieved so much and supported so many through family and business. I wanted to live in a warmer climate and, as an ardent golfer, I always enjoyed playing overseas in warm weather. I also felt that it would be better to try living overseas now rather than when the girls had grown up. I thought they would benefit from living overseas by learning a language and having a different lifestyle. It didn't take us long to make the decision and Monaco seemed like a glamorous location and not far from Cannes and London.

CMC Markets was in great shape, making money and developing business, and I felt that I could ease off a little and enjoy the sunshine. Instead of going to a local restaurant in Hertfordshire for Sunday lunch, we could pop along to the Carlton Hotel in Cannes, where we had spent many a nice holiday together. It all seemed to make sense at the time – why not enjoy the trappings of our success?

My plan was to cut back to a two- or three-day working week and spend the rest of the time in Monaco enjoying the sunshine and spending more time with my family. I would commute to

CMC's offices in England, leaving on Tuesday and returning on Thursday. I still needed to stay involved with the business and carry on doing what I was doing. I was not retiring, just living in Monaco.

It was not difficult to check and answer emails every day; the internet had liberated the business and it had liberated me. I didn't need to be in the office every day – I could monitor things remotely – and it was easy to speak to staff as we all had mobile phones.

It was business as usual and it worked for a short while. But there is nothing like being outside your comfort zone to make you realise what your comfort zone is.

CMC Markets had given me a platform to be innovative and successful and to demonstrate to the world that I was a good businessman and that going to a comprehensive school did not hold me back. Being good at business seemed to make up for not being allowed to go to grammar school and university. Creating my own company was a way to show the world that I was smart and could still succeed, despite not having any qualifications.

Running my own business was not just about passion for success and riches, it was about doing something much more than that and it still is. It provided a structure to my life that I didn't have when I was growing up. It reversed many of my early disappointments and rejections. CMC Markets also changed my personal life, by allowing me to support myself and my family, not depend on others, and be in control of my destiny.

This was all fine while I was running it in England. But the moment I handed the company to others by moving overseas and I stopped being in the office each day, the dynamics changed for me and for the company.

We are all products of our upbringing. Somewhere in the fog of life, people manage to achieve things, but often you can trace that drive to achieve back to when you were young – things that happened to you that inspired you to go forwards and do something with your life. That moment for me and the real turning point in my life as a young man was the day I stood up to my dad and punched his lights out. That gave me control over what was happening at home, which meant I could protect my mum, and life at home calmed down. It was almost as if my mum and dad wanted somebody to stand between them and stop the nonsense between them. They now had someone to step in if things got out of hand, especially as neither of them would back down. More importantly, my dad now had boundaries.

That feeling of control stayed with me all my life. It gave me respect at home from my parents and made me feel that you can change things. It was respect with control – respect for my mother who worked so hard to bring us all up and respect for my father as he had been in the army during the war.

With hindsight, it was a peacekeeping role because, I think, deep down my mum and dad wanted a life together. My mum had a hard life but having children was her greatest joy and she was very proud of all her boys equally. I think she was grateful to my dad that they had children together.

Once I started work, I was not looking for the same control in my business life. I was happy to do a fair day's work and get my salary. However, I often wondered why people paid me to work for them.

It was a bizarre feeling. I always worked hard and did a good day's work. But at that time, I always thought that deep down I was inferior because I was often surrounded by people from different backgrounds with private education and university degrees. I used to think that the only way to break out of that feeling was to be successful at my job and prove to anybody that I was as good as them. I suppose I was trying to prove myself constantly.

By 2001, I had achieved so much, and everything was going well. Then, amazingly, I took myself out of that life and moved to a different country. I am sure there is some psychological assessment that could be done here. I will leave the reader to make of it what they want, but it felt like my life was moving forwards. Living in the south of France felt like a step up. I suppose it was, but it came with consequences.

I have always wanted to keep pushing myself to the next level. Often as a trader, I would increase trading positions and increase risk levels as the markets moved in my direction. I knew that the markets don't always go your way, so when they do you have to keep pushing to gain maximum profits. It was an instinct that grew with me over the years and one that I still have today.

When I was living in Monaco and outside daily contact with the company, I believe the vision and the passion that had been part of CMC's DNA from day one was missing. The business lacked inspiration, leadership and focus. It stopped moving forwards because of my move to Monaco.

At first, it was difficult to see this change because profits kept coming in and we kept signing up more clients. In Monaco, I would get up early, walk the kids to school with Fiona, then have a coffee before I began my day. Instead of commuting from Hertfordshire to London I was spending that time with the family and doing it in the sunshine.

Naïvely I thought I could run the office from afar and I did for a while. However, when I lived in the UK and I was in the office daily I could influence thinking, steer the company and do what I thought was right. My DNA was all over CMC Markets.

I kept myself busy and occupied by using Monaco as a hub to travel to our different offices. I oversaw the expansion of our overseas offices, including making a number of acquisitions. We bought Shorcan Brokers in Toronto and turned that into our Canada office. We bought Digital Look in the UK, Red Monitor in Vienna and Andrew West Stockbroking in Sydney. We opened offices in Beijing, Singapore, Stockholm, Oslo, Vienna, Madrid, Milan and Edinburgh.

I was not exactly sitting on my backside sipping champagne and putting on the sun cream. I was very busy, even though I was not working in the company every day. But I was not busy in the areas of the business that needed me most, which was right at the heart, making day-to-day decisions, coming up with new ideas and innovations, pushing the boundaries, and leading from the front.

My time in Monaco was a major mistake from a business viewpoint. I may have saved a bit in tax, but this was a false economy. By living overseas, I took my eye off the daily running of the business and replaced that by concentrating more on the bigger picture.

Costs and overheads started getting out of control. Staff numbers had gone from about 700 in 2001 to over 1,600 in 2008 and rising. Our technology was becoming dated and it was harder to release new products and trading systems like mobile phone trading. So, we kept bringing in more and more people to try and get things delivered.

We were effectively developing ourselves into a technology corner as we tried constantly to add bits onto a trading platform that was conceived and developed in 1994 and released in 1996. We were now five years into the 2000s and technology had moved on.

The company was still making good profits, but we were storing up problems for the future. If we carried on that way, we were heading for major problems.

What also concerned me was that the competition was catching up and, in some cases, overtaking us. The main reason was that our trading platform was becoming dated. We struggled to get it to work across web pages. It still had to be downloaded from a CD-ROM, so clients couldn't get it to work through their company firewalls. We had a forty-person product development team that couldn't get anything delivered.

Even more alarming was that, in the wider market, client trading spreads were becoming more competitive while our overheads were rising.

For me, it was obvious that the golden years that had started in 2001 were ending. In that period, which ran through to 2008, spreads were wider, interest rates were higher – creating more finance income from clients' leverage – and there was a lot less competition. Little did we know that the global economic crisis was just around the corner.

The retail market was expanding with more and more retail clients trading. But increasing competition was squeezing trading spreads. Because of our dated systems, it was getting harder to improve profit margins through technology. Clients were also demanding more products like real-time charts and better pricing and it was becoming impossible for us to keep upgrading our dated platform.

Also, there was a price war and clients were getting more competitive terms from different providers to induce them to open an account. Commission-free trading on shares was the norm by this time and one company even offered spread-free (no bid/offer spread) trading. Suddenly, we were being beaten at our own game.

The worry for me was that our platform and technology were struggling to deliver scale, making it hard to remain competitive.

Also, the platform was slowing down, and pricing efficiency was getting compromised.

So, while in Monaco, I could see that we were heading for a difficult period. I tried to influence things, but people got used to me not being in the office and my voice was being heard less or, worse, being ignored. The senior management team had got used to having things their own way and doing what they thought was right. They had all done well out of the company, so they were not as hungry.

I remember being in the London office on several occasions when I would have various meetings and leave tasks for people. But they just sat on things and when I came back the following week all the momentum was lost. I found it impossible to keep motivating people by just popping into the office a few days a week.

I also felt I no longer commanded the same authority that I had before I moved to Monaco. Cliques were forming and staff seemed to line up behind the senior people. They didn't look to me for ideas and leadership: they looked to their bosses because they knew I would be off back to Monaco the next day.

This was illustrated one day in March 2008 when I was visiting my Sydney office. I was there for the week and as usual I was walking around the office chatting to staff. I casually interrupted a meeting between our head of the Asia-Pacific (APAC) region, who worked in our Sydney office, and our head of compliance. I just popped my head around the door and said, 'Everything alright?' The APAC head invited me into the office, and we chatted about some things – nothing too important. It was a beautiful office on the forty-fifth floor of Governor Phillip Tower with amazing views across Sydney harbour on a beautiful sunny day.

It was emotional to think where I had come from and where I was sitting. I then reminisced about when we worked in Bayley

Hall and when our APAC head worked in London and drove to work in a beaten-up old car. As I looked across Sydney harbour from our offices, I said, 'We have come a long way since those days.'

We all laughed, it was a joke, and I left the meeting a few minutes later and carried on my casual tour of the office. I like to think I am a man of the people and I walk around the London office every day saying 'Hi' to people. I get my own bowl of porridge in the mornings and speak to people in the kitchen.

The next day was Saturday and we had hired a couple of boats for some team bonding, sailing around Sydney harbour and then stopping off for lunch. We had invited people from the office to be on the boats with us and enjoy the day. It was a chance for people to meet outside of the office and to enjoy the sailing. I was the captain of one team and the APAC head was captain of the other team. It was going to be a lovely day.

Earlier the APAC head had arranged to pick me up at my hotel to take me to the boats. When he arrived, he said, 'Can we have a quick coffee?' He then said, 'Look, please do not undermine me in front of my staff. Yesterday, in front of compliance, I didn't like you discussing about my previous role with CMC and how I could only afford a cheap, old car.'

I exploded at him and let him have it with both barrels. I guess there was pent-up feeling from having lost control over CMC while living in Monaco. However, I wasn't going to take shit from my staff, and I let him have it, big time!

I said, 'Firstly, they are not your staff, they are my staff. Secondly, you are fucking working for me and not the other way round. Thirdly, if you do not like the way I speak to my staff in front of you then you can fucking well leave the company. I do not know who you think you are and if you ever speak to me like that again you will be out of the door before you have a chance to put on your jacket.'

I was furious with him: I felt like I was being put down and undermined. To this day, I do not know why I didn't point him to the exit on the spot. My blood was boiling but his response was to take it and then he did have the good grace to apologise and so I was happy to give him the benefit of the doubt, especially as he was doing a very good job.

We drove back to his house to pick up his wife who was joining us for the sailing. She was clearly worried as they had just bought their first house together in Sydney. I said, 'Don't worry, I didn't sack him, but it might not be like that next time.'

The day was uncomfortable but not for me, I enjoyed it even though it was raining, and I wasn't dressed for sailing. Unfortunately, I lost the race, but I gave every staff member on my boat a chance to take the wheel and steer the boat. It was, after all, a team bonding day.

The APAC head was called Captain Araldite by the professional crew we had employed to help us because he was the only one that seemed to steer his boat on his own. I think he thought it was a macho contest, him against me, but I saw it as a great day out and I wanted to enjoy it, it was not about one-upmanship for me.

The incident with the APAC head proved to be a turning point because, in 2009, Fiona and I returned from Monaco and started to live in London. The girls were at university in London and Edinburgh and I was ready to get a grip on CMC.

My starting point was our technology. I admired and respected all the developers that worked for CMC over the years. Terry Johnston had moved on to form his own new company after I bought the remaining shares in his company, Information-Internet, and made it CMC's IT department. There were a lot of Terry's original team still with the company, who had delivered fantastic technology over the years for CMC. However, this was old technology by 2009.

I remember one trip to Microsoft UK headquarters in Reading in the late 1990s, which I attended with Terry and a few of the team. Microsoft gave us the source code to their database technology Sequel Server, so we could configure it to work across our platform. The technology team were amazing and all of us non-techies looked up to them for what they could do with technology.

However, that same team were still working on the old platform and some tough decisions had to be made. In 2009, I came back from Monaco and decided to rebuild our technology with a new team and new software.

I knew change had to happen but there were two events that preceded all of this. One was an aborted flotation in 2006 and the other was selling a 10 per cent stake to Goldman Sachs in 2007.

Chapter 22

VOLATILITY CATCHES UP WITH ME AND THE COMPANY

2006 was meant to be the year that CMC Markets became a public company, listed on the London Stock Exchange. I always had mixed feelings about a public listing because we had been a private company for so long and I liked to control things. But I thought CMC would benefit from being public.

I figured that we would get more status, and it would give clients more comfort to know that they were dealing with a public company. Also, the EU's Markets in Financial Instruments Directive and major regulatory changes were coming in. This meant that all client money would have to be segregated, so we would need bigger banking facilities, and being public made that process easier.

I also saw being CEO of a publicly listed company as the completion of a journey that started as a fifteen-year-old school leaver. And the potential to earn £240 million from the initial public offering (IPO) was mildly appealing. At this time, Fiona and I owned 100 per cent of the share capital of CMC Markets and it was making approximately £40 million a year.

The company went through all the IPO due diligence and finance and audit processes, plus beauty parades to select a bank that could list us. All the banks we saw were polished. We could have chosen at least three, but we selected Deutsche Bank because we liked their style.

I remember their head presenter saying, 'Deutsche Bank is a flow monster and we understand your flow risk book.'

I responded by saying, 'CMC is a flow hamster.' That funny moment probably helped us choose them as our lead bank for the IPO, and we called the IPO process Project Hamster. We also chose Cazenove Bank as the secondary bank.

The bankers pitched the listing valuation at £750 million and, in early May 2006, my team and I set off on a two-week roadshow to sell the shares to new investors. We went to Frankfurt, London, New York, Boston and Edinburgh. It was a gruelling trip but nonetheless enjoyable. We used to maintain our energy and motivation between meetings by joking and playing the *A-Team* music.

IPOs are planned usually one year in advance, so we had to do all the preparation work long before we decided on a listing date. We predicted that May 2006 would be a good time to list the business. It would be before the summer slowdown and there would be momentum in the market as it was still early in the year.

There is not much science in listing a company. It is all about crunching the numbers, making sure the accounts are up to date and fully audited, putting together a business plan and showing historical data and performance so investors can gauge the future of the business. It was hard work and the whole process took us just under a year.

On Monday 15 May 2006, we were all set and ready to hit the road. 'So far, so good,' we thought, but our timing could not have been worse. In our first week on the road, the world's stock markets started to crash.

Between mid-May and mid-June, the FTSE 250 dropped by approximately 15 per cent. It was a bloodbath and it meant that investors had no appetite to invest as their portfolios were all nursing big losses. The whole financial world seemed to be in meltdown.

As we were on the road, we were a little detached from the turmoil. The feedback from our office was that we were making great profits, as volatility creates opportunity for us. We were on for a record month. But the bankers were managing our valuation expectations down as investor demand was slowing. Investors told us that they were looking to liquidate investments, not add to them.

By the Friday, it was not looking good and I had a conference call with Deutsche Bank and Cazenove Bank. The bankers told me that investor appetite was drying up and the valuation would be around £650 million, not £750 million. But they said I should carry on with the roadshows in case things picked up the following week. Their view was that the past week had been bad but hopefully markets would recover and there was no point in pulling out, especially as all the work had been done.

I was due to fly out to New York on Sunday 21 May and then on to Boston, but I didn't want to go. I said, 'Look, the company is having a record month, we are getting a record number of clients signing up and there is no way I will list the company at a lower price. I prefer to delay the IPO.' However, they convinced me to go to the States to keep my options open.

We had meetings on the Monday and Tuesday in New York and Boston and we flew back from Boston on Tuesday evening, arriving on the red-eye at five the next morning. The team and I showered and changed at the airport and we hit the road in our people carrier with the *A-Team* music playing in the background. However, we were soon to find out that even the A-Team has its bad days. Stock markets were still in the red and things had not changed. If anything, they were getting worse.

On Wednesday 24 May, we had various meetings, but I remember well the last meeting before we were due back at Deutsche Bank's offices in London Wall for the listing of the shares. It was around 2 p.m. with Andy Brough of Schroders. I didn't know Andy well, but he is a bit of a star in the City for calling the markets right and he has a stellar track record of investing. We left the previous meeting, with Tim Wise of Cazenove Bank, and just before we got to the lift, I asked Andy how the FTSE was doing. He said it was down 100 points – another red day for exchanges.

In the lift I said to Tim, 'OK, let's go to the pub and have a drink.'

Tim was concerned. He said, 'We don't have time, we have to be at Deutsche Bank's offices.'

I said, 'Forget it, I am not listing the company at a discount and I am cancelling the IPO.' I pulled the float one hour before we were due to list.

To this day, I am not sure whether we could have listed that day or not, and if we had, what the price would have been. I do not even know what the investor appetite was, nor whether we could have sold enough shares to list the business. But I do know that if we had listed that day it would have been on the back foot. As investors were suffering from negative stock markets, there was little if any enthusiasm to invest in a new IPO. Anyway, we had plenty of time to wait for the markets to recover.

I was looking forward to receiving the £240 million but, hey, it was just another deal in a lifetime of deals, even if this was the deal of a lifetime. To me, the money was important, but the company was more important. I was not going to sell shares in my company if investors were not going to pay the market rate, especially as CMC Markets was performing well and hitting record numbers.

It was not my fault the world's stock markets were crashing. My attitude was, I can try again later in the year if I want to.

I also took the philosophical view that if it was not meant to be, then it was probably the right thing anyway for the company and for myself.

Later that evening, we had a big meeting at the Deutsche Bank offices in London Wall and the bank confirmed that I probably did the right thing. There was decent investor interest but due to the crash in stock markets it would have been hard to achieve our expected valuation. They were clear that it was nothing to do with CMC but everything to do with the financial markets crashing and investors' lack of appetite for new investments.

It was hard to feel too disappointed. Deutsche Bank's offices are in Winchester House, where CMC had its second office, and as I sat there, I was looking across to the Western Union building in Great Winchester Street and remembering doing the night shift as a sixteen-year-old boy. I looked right into the offices where I used to work. It had a major calming effect on me and put things in total perspective. Here I was talking to bankers about not getting my £240 million when back then I was paid seven pounds, eight shillings per week and I had to clock in and clock out. I thought, wow, this is surreal, to think of the journey I have been on and where I am today.

It made me feel happy inside, not angry or upset, and I knew Mum would be looking down on me and smiling. If I had craned my neck around 180 degrees, I would have seen the offices we used to clean together in London Wall, where Mum would dust and I would hoover and empty the bins.

I was still a bit disappointed, but I brushed it off, went to work the next day and we recorded a record profits month for May 2006 as the stock markets continued to crash. My disappointment was not only because I was thinking about the company and its future but for another reason.

In early 2006, I was talking to David Dein, a director of Arsenal Football Club, and he mentioned that Granada Television was looking to sell its 10 per cent stake in the club. Television companies had bought into football clubs as a way of securing future television rights. Sky had bought into Manchester United, but it had to sell its stake because of the perceived conflict of interest. Granada had to do the same, so I had a chance to buy the 10 per cent stake. I had various meetings with Granada and had agreed a price of £40 million – we shook hands on the deal in their offices in Gray's Inn Road. The only problem was that I needed the IPO to finance the deal, but I told Granada this before we shook hands and they accepted it. When the IPO failed, my chance of buying into Arsenal FC was lost as well.

Although I could have afforded the purchase of the 10 per cent on its own, Mr Dein said that some other shareholders wanted to sell their shares and it was starting to get a bit out of control, so I let it all pass me by. A few months later, Stan Kroenke bought the 10 per cent stake and went on to buy and eventually control the club. I still regret not buying into the club because apparently it is valued at around £2 billion today – so a nice profit was to be made.

I wouldn't have sold to make a profit as Arsenal are my boyhood club and I still support them today. I would have held the stake and tried to buy more, in time. However, on balance, it was probably the right decision. Again, it was another deal in a lifetime of deals that passed me by. But hey, that's life.

I always took the view that if I did what was right for the company, it would in the end turn out to be right for me. Who knows if pulling the IPO was the right decision? But it was my money anyway. I owned 100 per cent of the business. We had no debt and we were making good money. It was a no-brainer for me. I sent the staff an email pointing out that we were in illustrious company as Goldman Sachs had also pulled their first IPO. I said it was not a change in company policy, it was due to market conditions. We were not the first and we would not be the last.

I didn't see this aborted IPO as a failure. I thought, 'Oh well, we carry on, wait for the markets to recover and we can have another look at it.' At heart, I am a trader and I saw this as just another trade – you win some and you lose some.

Later that year, Deutsche Bank said if I wanted to have another go at listing the company I could, but I passed on the opportunity as it was exhausting the first time and I felt we all needed more time to recover from the process. I also felt that the financial markets needed to be more stable, which they certainly were not at that time.

I had also lost my appetite a bit for being public as the markets at times were so volatile and unpredictable. It is an irony because CMC makes more money when the markets are volatile and unpredictable. On this occasion, the volatility worked against me and you could say it caught up with me.

Cancelling the IPO created some internal issues that needed to be resolved. As part of the IPO process, I had gifted staff lots of free shares which incurred a tax liability for them individually. Loyal long-term staff were given sufficient shares to sell at the IPO to pay the benefit-in-kind tax. Then they would be left with enough shares to keep as an investment in CMC. This was a reward for their hard work and is typical when companies IPO, to tie in key staff to the business.

The problem for our staff was that the IPO didn't happen. But they still had the tax liability as they still owned the shares, only now they were holding private shares, not public company shares as expected.

I had gifted the shares because I was following advice I received at the time. It would have been good advice if staff had been able to sell their shares on the open markets after IPO, but now they were left with a big tax liability and they had no one to buy their shares in a private company, so they needed help.

I had to resolve the issue as it would cause lots of problems for people without the money to pay their tax bill through no fault of their own. So I bought back the shares from staff, the same shares I had gifted them a few months before the potential IPO. It did make me wonder: here I was giving shares away for free and then buying them back a few months later just to pay the taxman. Such are the intricacies of listing a private company on the stock exchange.

I paid around £17 million for the shares in total and staff used the proceeds to pay their tax bills. I felt this was the right thing to do, but it didn't always sit comfortably with me. I felt that, since I started CMC Markets, I had taken on risk every day to make the company a strong and profitable business. There were many occasions when, as a market maker, we were running losing positions and losing money on open positions or losing trades. It was constant pressure as the business expanded, overheads were increasing every month and profit targets kept rising.

Market making is a volatile business and the plan for any market-making company is to come out ahead overall. But there are lots of losses in between before you achieve your net overall profit. There are one or more losing trades at some point every day and it can get scary at times. This is grown-up stuff and although the staff added a lot to the business, it was not their company on the line every day.

The staff turned up every day, drew their salaries and worked hard. They expected rewards in return, but the only risk for them was losing their jobs and most of them could get new jobs anyway. Every day, the risk for me was keeping the company solvent and paying the overheads. Their tax liability became my liability if I wanted to keep them and deal with an issue that was created by my own generosity and kindness.

I wanted to reward them for their hard endeavours but here I was bailing them out and, who knows, most of them could have resigned once I had taken care of their tax liability and kept their residual shares in CMC. I felt frustration because I was taking all the risk in the company. But I guess that is what happens when you own 100 per cent of the business and there are issues to be dealt with.

I have become wealthy over the years, but I have had to work for it and deal with all the pressures. When people tell me how lucky I am to live in a nice house and drive a nice car, my immediate response is, 'It's not luck.'

However, all turned out well in the end because in 2007, I sold 10 per cent of the business to Goldman Sachs, and staff were able to cash in their remainder shares at a profit. I was also able to recoup my losses on the share buyback scheme.

Chapter 23

GOLDMAN SACHS ARE
ON THE LINE

The rest of 2006 was uneventful as CMC Markets kept opening more offices and looking at opportunities. In 2007, I
started looking at buying a stockbroker in Australia. At that time,
regulators the Australian Securities and Investments Commission
were oriented towards trading on exchange and they were supportive of local exchanges. They encouraged over-the-counter trading
but were new to how to regulate it and apply capital constraints
on companies. They were and are a good regulator, they are pro-
business and supportive. But I felt we needed a broader offering
in Australia, more for perception than commercial reasons and, in
early 2007, we got the chance to buy Andrew West Stockbroking
in Sydney.

While these negotiations were going on around July 2007, I got
a call from Mike Sherwood, joint CEO of Goldman Sachs bank. I
didn't know Mike at the time so I checked him out and I could see
he was one of the most powerful people in the City. Mike invited
me for a breakfast meeting at Goldman's offices in Fleet Street,
which was very nice, and we discussed CMC as a business.

Mike explained that Goldman Sachs saw retail as a growing
sector as more and more firms offered online trading, and that retail

flows were beginning to impact exchanges and underlying markets. Goldman Sachs didn't want to develop retail technology as he said it was not their thing, they were more wholesale than retail. But he said the bank was interested in taking a stake in CMC Markets to have a strategic position in the retail space.

The bank had pitched to us for the IPO process and didn't get the job, but they were an impressive bunch and we could have easily appointed them for our IPO in 2006.

Mike liked our technology. He thought we were cutting-edge. He noted that we had tried to list the previous year and asked, if I was prepared to sell shares to the public market, would I be prepared to sell a stake to Goldman Sachs?

At first, I was flattered and honoured that such a big organisation even knew I existed let alone wanted to buy a stake in my company. But this was a powerful organisation run by powerful people, so I had to watch myself.

Mike explained that the bank would like a meaningful stake of 30 per cent and a seat on the board. This worried me slightly because I had always controlled the board and I had always owned 100 per cent of the business.

In the end, we compromised. I said I would sell them a 10 per cent stake to begin with and later if they wanted more, I would consider it. The condition was they would help me develop CMC Markets around the world and help me with acquisitions.

I enjoyed the negotiations with Mike and his team. Jan Boomaars, a Dutch Goldman banker, was also helpful and supportive of the deal. I remember one time during our negotiations when I was throwing numbers around with Mike and Jan, Mike just smiled and looked away. I am not sure why he smiled but I think he recognised that I was a self-made man, a trader at heart.

Probably he had seen it all before but I think he liked me. I liked him. He is a man of integrity and grit.

Once we closed the deal, Mike invited all my senior team to his spectacular villa in the south of France for dinner. It was a kind gesture and a message to my team that we were part of the Goldman family now.

The sale document restricts what I can say about the valuation of CMC Markets, but I can say that overnight I became a sterling billionaire based on the value of the 90 per cent of the company that I still owned and the shares that I had sold. Since I had cancelled the IPO a year earlier CMC were making record profits and the valuation was justified and fair.

It also vindicated my decision to cancel the IPO when the valuation was lower because of a falling stock market. Also, this was in the run-up to the 2008 financial crisis when valuations were at their highest. Volatility may have caught up with me in 2006 but it was in my favour in 2007. 'Fortune favours the brave' springs to mind.

This was also a good deal for Goldman. We were growing at 40 per cent a year and we were constantly developing our technology to the retail sector. We also gave them a strategic foothold in the retail client trading space. It was almost like an insurance policy for Goldman should retail really take off. Also, if we were to IPO again, they could handle the transaction and help us with timing and getting through the process.

Their stake in CMC Markets at the time was just what they were looking for and it was a fair market valuation. They asked me twice more after their initial purchase to sell them more shares, but I declined because I wanted to wait and see if we could list again. My plan was to sell them some more shares ahead of any IPO, so they were incentivised to get the listing completed. I didn't want a repeat of the last IPO effort, and this was a powerful bank and a great ally.

I would have sold more shares to them pre-IPO, but 2008 was an even worse year for the world's global markets. We were all about to find out that another crash was on the way which made 2006 look like a tea party.

Chapter 24

GLOBAL CRISIS AND THE NEXT BIG CRASH

While I was living in Monaco, between 2001 and 2009, there were two major events that created a lot of volatility and uncertainty. One was not only difficult from a work perspective but also shocking and upsetting from a personal point of view.

I was over from Monaco visiting our offices in Hertford when the first event unfolded – the World Trade Center terrorist attack in New York on 11 September 2001 (9/11). During the 9/11 event, the New York Stock Exchange (NYSE) declared a force majeure – an unforeseeable circumstance that prevents someone from fulfilling a contract legally. In the case of 9/11, the NYSE suspended trading of all US shares on the exchange.

This meant that our clients could not trade out of their existing US share positions. They just had to wait for the NYSE to reopen, which it did four days later. While waiting for the exchange to open, clients were trying to short shares (to hedge their positions) in similar sectors on other exchanges as it was obvious that, when the NYSE did reopen, stocks would be lower across the board. If a client was long a US telecom stock for example, during the force majeure period they could try to short a European telecom stock in the hope that it would mitigate some of their losses when the NYSE reopened, a so-called sector hedge.

Over the first few days following 9/11, there was so much uncertainty around whether the US would go to war and invade other countries that the financial markets were spooked into an instant bear market. Clients were frantic as they were sitting on potentially big losses on their open share positions. They switched into gold and looked to mitigate their losses through sector shorts and index shorting. Clients tend to buy gold when there is a crisis and uncertainty. They see it as a (safe) haven product.

The NYSE reopened 12 per cent lower – what we call a gap open. Then all hell broke loose as clients tried desperately to close out their existing US share positions.

However, for us there were other considerations apart from market volatility. We would generally only ask a client for a small amount of upfront cash deposit (margin) to cover their trading, then lend them the balance of, say, 95 per cent of a total position exposure. This meant that we generally only had a 5 per cent deposit against a major market movement.

Let's say a client deposited with us 5 per cent to trade a NYSE share and the opening share price was 12 per cent lower following the ending of the force majeure period. You don't need a calculator to know that the client would be overdrawn and owing us money, because the value of the share had dropped 12 per cent and we only had 5 per cent cash deposit from them.

In addition, we were sitting on sizeable NYSE hedge share positions – hedged against our client positions – with our prime brokers. These hedges meant that we owed money to the exchange for any unrealised losses due to the price gap. The losses may be the clients' – we do not trade the markets for our own positions – but we are liable for our own hedge losses.

Force majeure is covered in our account opening documents, which make the client legally liable. But we usually come to a settlement with our clients, who pay all or some of their overdraft or occasionally none. In this scenario we can sue the client for their losses, but we very rarely do this.

However, we must always pay off our own (hedge) losses with exchanges and prime brokers – we cannot negotiate with them. So, when clients generate bad debt, we must pay it off first. Then we must write off anything we do not receive from clients against trading profits and it becomes a trading loss even though it is bad debt. Bad debts effectively all end up in our risk book as losses.

Clients understand the risks involved with trading, especially on margin. They know there can be a big market movement at any time, and they could end up owing us money. But they, like us, take the risk of gap markets because they do not happen often.

Not all clients lose during a force majeure period; some can make lots of money from market volatility and uncertainty. Those who are short share index or long gold usually make money as they are on the right side of a big movement in the financial markets.

During the terrible events of 9/11, there were rumours that some of the terrorists had, through third parties, taken short positions on the world's stock markets ahead of the attacks in anticipation of the markets dropping rapidly. This was presumably to finance their future terrorist activities. This was never proven or substantiated but stranger things have happened.

Commercially we got through the 9/11 terrorist attacks without too much client bad debt. The office for that week and a long time after was subdued. Our feelings and reactions were the same as everyone else's, especially as the stories of bravery and tragedy unfolded. It truly was a surreal time to be working in the financial markets.

In 2008, the global economic crisis (GEC) was another event that would cause extreme volatility in the markets and test our market-making capability. The events of 2008 are less clear in my memory than 9/11 because the latter was a shocking instant event, whereas the GEC built up with lots of worries over time.

During 2007, there were concerns about US sub-prime mortgages. But things came to a head on 15 September 2008, when Lehman Brothers, a bank that traced its roots to a company formed in 1847, filed for the biggest bankruptcy in US history. This caused the Dow Jones index to crash by nearly 5 per cent in a day – in total, stock markets would fall more than 30 per cent that year. In October 2008, the British government took a 58 per cent stake in RBS and there were further bailouts and mergers, including Lloyds Bank with Halifax Bank of Scotland (HBOS).

This was another seismic financial event and volatile period for the company, but we coped well. We were generally selling shares to our clients and there was so much volatility that it proved a lucrative period for the firm.

However, my overriding feeling at the time was anger towards the Labour government and Prime Minister Gordon Brown. Labour politicians were lining up to criticise the City and bankers for the mess they had got the country into. But previously these same politicians had been touring the City telling us to go for it and generate more taxes for the government. It was called light-touch regulation and the Labour ministers were the architects of this and now they were blaming the City for the mess, when it was they themselves that had encouraged the City to push the limits of regulations.

It was crazy that the British government allowed a bank like RBS to leverage its balance sheet over thirty times to buy an overseas bank. Most hedge funds leverage around five times, but here was a British bank rolling the dice on an acquisition – yet the government makes the rules for these financial institutions, not the bankers. Thankfully, things have since changed and this could not happen again. In theory!

There had been a policy of light-touch regulation from when Tony Blair was Prime Minister and Gordon Brown his Chancellor, as there seemed to be a threat from Frankfurt and Paris to London as the financial capital of Europe if not the world. Blair and Brown wanted the best of both worlds and when the GEC hit, they were looking to blame anybody but themselves. The bankers seemed to be the easy target and fitted their political agenda – the rich City bankers (who finance the Conservative Party) lining their own pockets at the expense of working people.

Bankers were to blame for some of the problems, but ultimately it is up to the government of the day to set the rules and make sure they are implemented. The Labour government at the time could easily have set rules to restrict the leverage of bank balance sheets, as is done today. But at the time this was not government policy – it was almost the opposite.

Then when the shit hit the fan, the Labour government were bailing out banks and blaming everybody else for the mess. This was the same government that sold off half of our gold reserves between 1999 and 2002 and told the world they were going to do it beforehand, costing the British taxpayer around £5 billion – the price of a few hospitals.

It seemed the lunatics were in charge of the asylum because a few years later, when the Labour government lost the 2010 general election, Liam Byrne, who had been Chief Secretary to the Treasury under Gordon Brown, left a note to his successor saying, 'I am afraid there is no money, good luck.' Labour's failure to regulate the banks and the City in the way they are regulated today ultimately cost them that election. The words 'piss up' and 'brewery' spring to mind.

Chapter 25

THE PRODIGAL
BOSS RETURNS

Towards the end of 2008, our time in Monaco was coming to a close and in 2009 we moved back to the UK. We wanted to be closer to our girls, who had gone to British universities, and I needed to be more closely involved in the business again.

As always, if I was in Monaco for tax planning then I was crap at it. Because when I got back to the UK, I faced an additional tax bill for approximately £2.5 million for some interest on money that I had invested in CMC Markets as a subordinated loan while living in Monaco. I had never received the interest on the loan because I had had to convert the loan and accrued interest into CMC shares as an injection of capital to the company. But technically, I had received the interest, even though it was immediately converted into shares. From a tax perspective, even though the money was not paid to my bank account I was deemed to have received it. So, I had to pay approximately £2.5 million cash from my own pocket to HMRC on income that I had never had. Tax exile was not a status I could call myself.

On our return to the UK, instead of moving back to our beautiful house in Hertfordshire, we rented an apartment in Mayfair and we have lived in Mayfair ever since, eventually buying the house described in the first chapter of this book. We love Mayfair. I believe around 25 per cent of the country's Michelin-star restaurants are within a ten-minute walk from where we live.

By then, Jim Pettigrew (the previous group finance director of the City brokerage firm ICAP) had become CEO of CMC Markets. I wanted someone else to run day-to-day operations so I could concentrate on the wider strategy. I became chairman, with Jim Pettigrew and then Doug Richards as CEOs. I bought myself a beautiful Rolls-Royce with a personal number plate. I have owned personal number plates for nearly forty years and paid a pittance for them. I am sure they are worth a fortune now, but I just put them on my cars and enjoy them.

I also employed a full-time driver for the first time. I felt that not living in Monaco was a step backwards from a lifestyle point of view. Also, I felt getting the Piccadilly line then the Central line to the City would have been too much of a culture shock on my first day back from sunny Monaco.

Once I was back in the UK, I went into the office daily, and still do. I needed to see what I had to do to improve the business. As explained in previous chapters, CMC was under-performing and lacked direction. The starting point for revitalising the company was technology.

At that time, we had a talented software engineer called Kerem Ozelli. I had met Kerem in Berlin when he was working for a German bank and we both attended the launch of a book by George Soros, which CMC Markets was sponsoring. It was near the end of the evening and I was tired, but Kerem rocked up to me and impressed me immediately. He knew a lot about online financial trading and told me where our platform was falling behind.

He immediately got my attention and a few months later he was working for me.

Once I was back in London and with the company full-time, Kerem and I would discuss for hours what we needed to do. Kerem had lots of ideas and CMC had the resources to get things done.

By 2010, I had decided that we needed to start again with technology. The Market Maker platform was over fourteen years old and no longer able to operate effectively across mobile devices and streaming web pages. Kerem thought that computers would become less relevant than mobile devices as people would use their phones more for accessing the internet. Facebook and Twitter were just getting going. Also, in April 2009, Apple launched the iPad and Kerem flew to New York to buy one of the first iPad releases so we could play around with it and try to get software to work on it.

Kerem and I wanted to build a new platform based on mobile devices. We discussed how we could build and launch a new trading platform, which was not easy given that clients were still trading on Market Maker. We also employed a hundred developers that were committed to keeping the old platform working. I had to find a way to circumvent our already stretched IT department to get the new platform built without disrupting the existing business.

I thought back to the old Bayley Hall days in Hertford when we had configured the platform to think that a share deal was a forex deal. However, this was a completely new build of a new platform that needed to work across a much faster internet and across mobile devices, and needed to service a more mature and demanding sophisticated client base. Clients were getting used to trading via the internet.

The world had changed as exchanges were going electronic and clients were using mobile devices more and more. There was no way we could fudge our new platform. It needed to be a complete new build.

Fortunately, as mentioned earlier, I had previously bought a small technology company in Austria called Red Monitor. It was developing some options and binary products that we were hoping to add to our product offering. We came up with a plan, to get Red Monitor to concentrate on building our new trading platform, independently of our existing developers. We had to abandon the options projects it was working on so it could develop our new platform without disrupting the UK development team.

Kerem did a great job in organising everybody and getting the right teams together. He put together another team based in Germany that he had worked with before and we got going on the new platform.

Building a new platform in 2010 was in some ways easier than when we built Market Maker in 1996, mainly because the more modern software applications were much more advanced. Oracle, for example, were building fantastic new databases so building a new platform was about bolting things together rather than breaking down other companies' software to get it to do what we did with Microsoft's Sequel server. But we still needed lots of hard work and lots of smart people.

We called the new platform Next Generation or Next Gen for short. We essentially built it for mobiles, not desktop computers, and we built it outside of our existing development infrastructure. This was lateral thinking at its best – maybe not the cheapest method, but definitely a good way to get things delivered. We would recover the costs in due course as we used Next Gen as the foundation to expand the business and replace the old platform.

The various platforms we have built over the years put CMC Markets on the map and turned us from a UK-centric business into a global player. Many people were responsible for delivering our platforms over many years. However, all developers need something to build, so they can be creative, and some of the ones I have worked with are unbelievably intelligent and creative.

But I was the catalyst for creating online trading. I saw its potential and I believed in it all the way. When I started developing platforms, there were none to compare ours to. I had a blank canvas and a vision and belief and the excitement to try something new. And once you get into technology there's always something new to develop.

Chapter 26

NEXT GEN AND
A NEW ROLE

Once Next Gen was delivered in 2010, I wanted to keep improving the platform as I was determined not to get left behind again after having been in a position of dominance.

Kerem left the company. He felt he could do some amazing things with technology and wanted to set up on his own. His vision was to get millions of clients to download a trading app – his expression was that he wanted 'to create the Farmville of trading', referring to the agriculture simulation social media game.

I didn't mind the idea of attracting a million clients, but I worried that it meant that clients would be onboarded like they were downloading a computer game. It would have effectively made us a type of gaming company. I set CMC Markets up as a financial services company, not a gaming company, and it was not my vision.

After Kerem left, he set up his own company and launched an app called Flick a Trade. It did what it said – you flicked, and you traded. Kerem even launched products that could be traded over the weekend when the markets were closed. He created fantasy commodities to invest in such as kryptonite and explodium. I am not sure what happened to Flick a Trade – Kerem sold the business. But I had another vision completely and I was focusing on that.

Over the next two years, from 2010 onwards, I kept developing Next Gen and I employed a creative team to concentrate solely on front-end technology and client requirements. I made them sit outside my office so I could keep watching what they were doing, and I could get instant demonstrations as I passed their area regularly.

Their sole purpose was to keep innovating the front-end technology by adding features such as charts, pattern recognition, client sentiment, module linking and price-depth ladders, to name but a few. There was a never-ending supply of ideas from the team as they kept researching technology and monitoring innovations from around the world.

In 2012, the CEO was Doug Richards and Goldman Sachs still had around 10 per cent of the company. There was a small dilution for them when I converted my £30 million subordinated loan into shares (which caused the tax payment mentioned in the previous chapter) but effectively Goldman still held 10 per cent of the shares.

Doug had been promoted from CFO to COO to CEO, but he was coming in every day to work alongside the founder of the company, who still owned 90 per cent of the business. This could not have been easy, especially as we were still a private company. Owning 90 per cent meant that I could control the board and if I wanted to, I could completely run the business the way I wanted. This could not have been easy for anybody in Doug's position.

I was liberated from overseeing the development of our Next Gen platform as it was up and running and we were migrating clients over to it from the old platform. I had achieved what I thought the company needed, which was a new trading platform, and now I was looking for my next job.

That job was CEO.

I had had enough of being chairman and watching other people run my company. This started when I was in Monaco but now I was in London it was even harder to watch other people making decisions about the business that I felt I should have been making, especially as I didn't always agree with some of the decisions.

However, this change was not just about what I wanted. The company was struggling financially. The lack of investment in technology over the years was catching up with us and we had been losing clients because of it. Next Gen was launched but it was taking time to get clients on board to use it and to migrate over from the old platform.

Most businesses are about keeping clients happy and although our clients liked our new Next Gen platform, there were a number of reasons why they were slow to migrate over. They wanted to keep their chart configurations; and to move over when they were out of existing trades. Plus, there were some aspects of the old platform that they preferred to the new one and clients do not always like change.

Next Gen was necessary from a business perspective, to stop clients leaving us and going elsewhere as the old technology struggled to keep pace with the modern world. But we had a solid, loyal client base that liked us for being pioneers. For some, we were the first company they had ever traded with online. The general client view was, 'Market Maker works and if we move over, we have to learn something new.'

To deal with this, Doug and the team implemented a client migration strategy, giving clients deadlines to move over to the new platform. Clients would be called and told that the old platform was closing and unless they moved their business over to the new platform their account would be closed.

It is easy now to look back at this period and say that was the wrong decision. The company was struggling financially, and something had to be done quickly to cut costs. But I did not like it and I did not agree with it. That is why I needed to get back in charge and take control of the business. It felt just like 1997, when I had a mass changing of staff and brought in young new people. I felt that I had to take control of the company and make big changes.

I also felt that control should start with me and work its way down to the team. So I sold the Rolls-Royce and decided to drive myself to work every morning, which meant I no longer needed my own driver. Change was needed and it had to start at the top.

On 3 January 2013, I drove to work, parked my car in the company's parking space and walked into the office as the CEO. Doug had left between Christmas and the New Year. It is never easy when a valued colleague leaves the company, especially as I liked Doug. He had bags of energy and used to run marathons, but it was time for me to take control of the business and get the company back where it belonged. Doug's departure reflected what I wanted to do and my vision for the company, not his performance.

The first thing I did on 3 January was call a meeting in my office with the executive team (Exco) and explain my thinking. There were about ten of them with a couple dialled in on conference calls from Singapore and Sydney. The meeting didn't go too well because Doug had appointed most of Exco and they were loyal to him. I was also an unknown entity in the sense that when I was chairman, they were not reporting to me. Now the whole of Exco reported to me.

I remember the meeting clearly because one or two of the team asked questions that gave the impression they did not agree with me being CEO. It was nothing rude or aggressive. It was more out of loyalty to Doug than a lack of belief in my ability. However, I thought this showed a lack of respect for what I had achieved and how successful I had been over a long period.

My concern was that if I did not have a united team, it would be much harder to implement change and move the business forward. So, we chatted about it and I tried to give some guidance, but I felt I was not making inroads. I felt that some of Exco were Doug's merry men and they felt too much loyalty to him.

I said, 'Your loyalty is to your family.' At the end of the meeting, I said, 'Look, this change has happened whether you like it not. If you have any doubts about the change then go home tonight and ask yourself: how many people do you know that have turned £10,000 into a £1 billion company?

'When you work out the answer to that question, that is the person you should be backing. If you cannot work out the answer to the question, then you might as well leave.'

The head of HR was the last person to leave the room. When she was on her own I said to her, 'Now I will show you what being a CEO is all about.' I'm not sure she believed me, but within a year she was my number one fan.

Chapter 27

IT'S GOOD TO BE BACK IN
THE DRIVING SEAT

I had to get a move on because when I started as CEO in January 2013, the company had made a loss of approximately £17 million for the nine-month period to 31 December 2012 (our financial year ends 31 March). If we had continued that trajectory, the company would have had severe financial difficulties. We had around £40 million in the bank but with overheads running at £10 million a month it was time to act and get CMC Markets back on the road to profits.

Morale was low as we were losing money, there was no bonus pot and we were losing clients due to our forced platform migration strategy. However, I saw lots of quick, easy wins to get back on track. I started with the assumption that my team were good enough, but they needed some guidance and leadership.

The first thing I did was contact all our offices to stop them from forcing clients to migrate onto the new platform. I told them that the old platform would remain operational indefinitely and if clients wanted to stay on it that was fine.

I called it Project Hug-a-Client – because I wanted to focus the minds of the team and make sure they were delivering a specific outcome. I told them, 'We spend millions every year onboarding clients and with forced migration all we are doing is pissing them off. We have to treat clients better and the starting point is to give them the choice of what platform they want to use.'

A new message went out to clients: 'We have a new platform built for you. It is great and works much better than the old one. But take your time and when you are ready you can switch over. Just give us a call when you are ready or click on the link and we will transfer your old positions to the new platform.

'One caveat is that we will not be upgrading the old platform, but it is yours to use for as long as you want.'

I wanted to empower clients to make their own decisions, giving them the feeling that we were working for them, not the other way around.

Also, as part of Hug-a-Client, I employed sales traders to speak to clients. I gave large, important clients their own account managers and I upgraded our client support service team. I combined two departments – business intelligence and marketing – so we could understand what clients were looking for and why they didn't always get through the account-opening process.

We also invited clients to feed back to us what they wanted on the new platform and what they thought was good or bad about it. We always responded to them and often we made changes that they had recommended. We always made a point of telling them that we had listened to them and thanked them for their support.

As part of Hug-a-Client, I promised all clients a cash rebate on their trading spreads if they reached a certain turnover level. My logic was that the more business a client does the more valuable they are to the company. Why should it be one-size-fits-all for small and big clients? In some cases the rebates amounted to thousands of pounds in cash each month.

Sometimes, clients would call us before the month end asking if they could have their cash rebate early as they wanted to trade on it. My response was, 'Yes, it is your money, you can have it when you want.'

Sales traders would call larger clients at the end of each month to tell them they would be receiving a nice cash rebate from CMC as a thank you for their business. One large client told me once that he bought his honeymoon flights to the US from his cash rebates. It seemed that Hug-a-Client was extending to Hug-a-Wife.

Hug-a-Client proved a great success for clients and for staff, because it turned the negative job of forced migration into a positive. It started to shift morale among staff and clients. I told staff, 'We are here to make money. It is hard to make money if we don't have clients. It doesn't matter what platform they use so long as they trade.'

The reversal of forced migration was a big relief to most of the offices because it had been tying up lots of resources, and the salespeople barely had time to process new client accounts. Suddenly, they could do their job and sell. This liberated each office to go out and find new clients and I built in bonus schemes and incentives for each office to push on with client recruitment.

Dealing and risk management were other glaring areas for me to look at. Almost immediately, I sat down with our head of trading, David Fineberg. David is intelligent and always open to challenge because he always wants what is best for the company. He will challenge you back hard if he does not agree with what you are saying, I like that in my team. Also, David doesn't challenge unless he has the facts in front of him, so if you ask him something, he does his homework before he answers.

David and I sat down with the traders and we talked about how to manage the company's risk. It was a great meeting because the traders know I understand risk management and we could challenge each other. We didn't make radical changes, but just as I empowered clients to decide when to migrate platforms, I liberated the traders to express their views and tell me how we could make more money and improve the company's financial performance.

I just sat back and listened to their ideas. I also said what I thought we should do, but most of the ideas came from them. Most of the traders had been with me for over ten years and some for nearly twenty – I had had a great influence on them over the years.

By the end of the meeting, I had effectively empowered them to get on with their jobs. They were good traders, but before they had been working within tight controls imposed on them by the previous management. They had been hedging when they didn't need to. They had been backing off trades and positions to our prime brokers when they felt they should be managing the risk alongside other asset classes – for example, running an index position against a share position – known as portfolio hedging.

The previous management team did not understand risk management as they were primarily from an accounting background, so they were always risk averse or nervous when markets were volatile. My view is the opposite – let's take on risk. We quantify it first and analyse the downside. If we can tolerate the downside, we run the upside to the maximum levels. Run your profits and hedge your losses!

After this meeting, the dealers were able to run more exposures, still within pre-defined limits but those limits had been increased with the help of David and the dealers. Also, I said that the company had a maximum risk appetite across all asset classes but that individual asset class exposures could be fluid. We did not have to apply the company's risk limits in silos. Dealers were free to increase exposures in individual asset classes provided the company did not breach its maximum exposure.

For example, if we applied individual limits for shares, index, forex and commodities, then the total company risk limit could be applied across just one asset class and not spread evenly across each asset class. If index markets were going up and we were net long the index book then total exposure could all be on the index markets, especially if clients were trading them more than, say, the forex markets. Dealers could take exposure limits from the forex book if forex was quiet or not performing.

The caveat was that they had to work as a team and run increased exposures across a winning book, not a losing book. And they should not let exposures increase to get out of losing positions. In other words, run your profits, cut your losses.

I also said that if, during the day, they had hedged up client net exposures with our prime brokers in, say, the Dax index and then the clients reduced their Dax positions throughout the day, we could run the prime broker Dax hedges even if the clients had no net exposure with us.

'If there is money to be made from running hedges, we should do that. It doesn't matter where the risk exposure comes from, either clients or hedges. If it is winning, run the positions with "take profit" and "stop loss" limits around the exposure.

'We are here to manage risk and make money, either from client flows or our own hedges. It is up to us when we reduce our hedges, we don't have to do it just because our clients have closed their net positions.'

This practice is different to trading for the company's own account. When you trade for your own account, you decide when to buy and sell and run your positions and then you decide when to take a profit or a loss.

We only put on hedges to cover existing client positions. I proposed that, when it was time to take off the client hedges because clients were reducing their positions and we were over-hedged, then if the hedges were making money because the market was moving in the right direction, we could delay taking off the hedges as we might make some extra money.

At the same time as changing the risk management strategy, we created a risk management team. This was run by some super-bright guys who would manage our daily value at risk (VAR) book against market movements. This underpinned our expanded risk management model and ensured that dealers' VAR risk was monitored and controlled. The risk team were also there to support the dealers' decisions and challenge their thinking. Dealers were given a lot more autonomy, but they also had to be held accountable and the risk management team was created to do this.

One other important decision I made, though it was David's idea, was to get the quantitative analysts (quants) to report directly to our chief trader (him) and not to the head of IT. We had employed quants to manage pricing and execution and analyse flows but David wanted to expand the team and bring in more quants to analyse risk. It was a great idea and one that would reap rewards as the changes progressed.

After this meeting, the dealers knew that I understood their job and that I would not get upset if they lost money running risk. However, they knew I would get upset if they did not run risk and it cost us money through missed opportunities.

This is the mindset of a CEO that has a risk management background. I get upset not at losing money but at not maximising profits. I even get upset if we make money, but we have not maximised what we could have made.

Understanding how to manage risk is the reason I set up CMC Markets and why we have been successful over a long period of time.

Chapter 28

FOCUSING ON QUALITY
NOT QUANTITY

By mid-2013, business was picking up with profits improving again and people were getting used to me as their CEO. Staff had more structure to their daily working lives as there was now a flat-line management system. This meant they had a voice through their boss, who had a seat on Exco. More importantly, Hug-a-Client had given people a focus and guidance on what was expected of them and what the company was trying to achieve.

Combining marketing and business intelligence meant the overseas offices had a bit of science around where they should spend their marketing money. Business intelligence would feed back to marketing the optimal areas to invest in. It was joined-up thinking.

In addition, decisions around client commercial terms were being centralised and ultimately made by David. Previously, local offices had had some autonomy around negotiating commercial terms with mainly larger clients, but I took it out of their hands and gave it to David – only he could cut deals with larger clients. We did this because it was up to the dealing desk to decide on spreads and financing terms as ultimately, they had to manage the client trade flows.

The changes were about creating consistency and focus through the whole company and sharing in the journey with all the teams who could contribute to all aspects of the business either directly or indirectly through Exco.

Centralising commercial terms was a good example of why the company needed an ex-trader as its CEO. As an ex-trader, I understood that you cannot have salespeople or office heads negotiating trading terms. Often these staff are conflicted as they have key metrics to meet like opening a certain number of accounts. This can cloud their judgement and lead them to offer the potential new client favourable terms just to get them to sign up.

Also, because David had the quants working directly for him under the new changes, he could quantify the value of each client and their contribution to the business and which clients were valuable to the dealing desk. David created a much broader understanding of the value of clients, rather than local people trying to judge what was good for the company without having all the facts. Centralising commercial terms also left office heads and others to concentrate on servicing clients and pushing the business forward.

Valuing overseas offices on their contribution to the group's profits instead of accounts opened improved team morale, especially when I created a league table showing which offices were more valuable. This gave smaller offices a boost as they could see that if they focused their marketing spend on quality of clients over quantity of accounts opened, they would be more valuable to the group, even if they opened fewer accounts than some of the bigger offices.

In the back of my mind, I was also trying to rebuild the company's brand, as it had been damaged by the forced migration process. We lost lots of clients during this process, but if I could get the teams to focus on quality through service, then we could rebuild our brand. We were already doing this through platform technology, but 'quality over quantity' was also part of the process.

Furthermore, I wanted to transform the company from being sales-oriented to being service-oriented. I have always found acquiring clients with incentives to be a short-term measure. It doesn't breed loyalty among clients because the moment a better offer comes along, they leave you or they use it to renegotiate terms with you.

Another thing that helped motivate staff in 2013 was buying everybody in the company a brand new, more powerful computer. I am not sure how many we bought – probably about 500 globally – and the cost was around £1 million but it was one of the best things I did to motivate staff. They saw it as a personal gesture to individuals from the CEO and sending the message that I valued their contribution. It also made staff feel like I had a personal understanding of their needs, and they felt valued. It was a quick win to show staff that the company was doing better, and they were part of my plans.

The company was moving forwards now because there was direction and consistency across all offices globally. The teams were embracing Hug-a-Client and business intelligence and marketing were integrating more and sharing client feedback so they could be more targeted in their approach. More importantly, dealers were generating more income and managing risk more efficiently.

At the same time as making the internal changes, I had been following our competitors closely. It struck me that two of them had overtaken us, but they had not created a niche for themselves. They were building brand and doing well but with a one-size-fits-all mentality and approach.

I often asked Exco, where do you think we fit into our industry? What's our unique selling point? How are we different to our competitors? We had the best platform; my restructuring of the management and overseas offices was moving the company forward and we were making more money. But I felt we could do more – we needed a clear business plan and focus.

When I took over as CEO in 2013, the company was being run in silos. Overseas offices were kept apart from each other without sharing information. Sometimes, following lengthy meetings, staff were given tasks and when the work was completed, they were given more things to do just to keep them occupied, without any real purpose or plan.

I started to change this. I created an intranet site, so offices and staff shared information. On the site, we also posted my 'town hall' presentations (to all staff) so people could view them if they were out of the office when I gave the talks. I also made sure that Exco minutes were available to key staff and all Exco members, and I invited the head of HR onto Exco. In the past minutes were not always widely distributed to Exco members. It was done on a need-to-know basis.

We were at the stage now where we needed a plan that would unite the company around our goals, but more importantly our differentiators and where we fitted into the industry. It was about creating our own identity, not just following the competition. This is what I had done back in 1996 when I launched internet trading, in 2000 when I launched deal4free.com for CFD trading, and in

2001 when I launched 'compare the spread' and the rolling cash spread bet for the spread betting business.

I was not used to following others, I was used to leading from the front, and this was on my mind in 2013 and 2014. Once again I had a master plan.

Chapter 29

I DON'T LIKE SUSHI,
BUT I DO LIKE TUNA

The CFD and spread bet industry generally generates about 80 per cent of its income from 20 per cent of its client base. This 20 per cent of clients are generating more commission, spread income and financing, mainly because they trade in larger amounts. Some larger clients can generate tens of thousands of pounds in monthly commission on their share trading alone. It therefore seemed logical to me that if we wanted to increase our profits, we had to concentrate on growing that 20 per cent – the larger clients.

Our competitors had done well at marketing to anybody and everybody through spam marketing. A good example is appearing on the front of a Premier League football shirt, or around the stadium during a televised sports event. Millions of viewers watch the game around the world and most of them have no interest in online trading. However, competitors hope that there are sufficient people watching to generate enough new accounts to justify the expenditure. By spam marketing, competitors were hoovering up as many clients as possible with little focus on targeted marketing for higher-value clients.

This scattergun approach to onboarding clients works but it was being well serviced by competitors who had bigger marketing budgets and were sales-oriented with lots of commission-based salespeople. Their focus was mainly on quantity, not quality. My strategy was to grow the valuable part of the sector, which I thought was our niche because of our platform and technology. I felt that this was where we could fit into the sector.

We geared all our offices to bringing on quality clients and our Next Gen platform appealed to the more professional client because it was crammed with trading tools and features. It's not the Fisher Price of online trading.

This was a simple enough strategy, but nobody in the company had thought about it in detail or had a plan to attract and retain the higher-value clients. I described it as like fishing for tuna, as they are the most valuable fish in the sea, mainly because they are in big demand from the sushi restaurants. I also said that we must be more targeted in the way we attract valuable clients. We need to target the right clients instead of just throwing our net over the side of the boat and scooping up whatever we can find. I named our new targeted approach Project Tuna.

Project Tuna was about making sure we attracted high-value clients that didn't burn out and lose all their money in days and weeks. We were looking for clients that traded, put in stop losses, then took their profits and traded in larger sizes. Professional, long-term clients that generated consistent high levels of trading income and were investors, not gamblers.

The longer you retain a client, the longer the income keeps coming into the business. This is the type of client that every company wants but they are not always geared up for them or targeting them. You cannot hope to attract valuable clients consistently with a scattergun approach to marketing. It must be highly targeted and backed up with good service and a good platform.

Tuna clients are valuable but also demanding. They understand the markets and the risks involved and they expect a high level of service. They need individual attention and they want a service built on trust and transparency. They are also looking for a feature-rich trading platform full of charts, news, expert pricing and research tools – effectively a Bloomberg- or Reuters-type terminal.

I introduced Project Tuna to Exco in September 2013, before I was due to go to Australia in October. The team understood it immediately, but the key question was, how would we attract the tuna clients? We had already picked up our fair share of high-value clients, but this was a major strategy change and it needed a new approach based on service and technology.

We already had a good platform but, from the end of 2013, we started to create a fantastic Next Gen platform crammed full of features that no other company could compete with. We had a technology advantage and now we had to capitalise on it. We wanted to help our clients as much as possible and to elevate the platform to be the best in class.

At the time, we were upgrading our real-time charting packages and adding features like real-time news from Reuters. We also added other features like automated pattern recognition software that highlighted price movements within our charting packages. We added a client sentiment pie chart showing what our winning clients were trading. We also segmented the pie charts to show other products that winning clients were trading. If they were long the Dax and making money, we showed if they were trading products like gold. Not by client name but by product so winning client details remained anonymous.

This and many other such features worked fine, but we needed more, so we introduced automated execution of client trades. This meant that clients effectively traded with a computer not a person. Clients would click on the latest price and trade and the whole process was handled in milliseconds by computers.

Because the process of executing a client's trade was automated, we wanted to give clients transparency. So as part of our pricing we offered a touch price, which was the current market price alongside the amount the client could buy or sell at that price. We also added price-depth ladders, which showed the prices and volumes below the displayed touch price. So, if a client wanted to trade 5,000 shares but there were only 3,000 on offer at the touch price, the client could see where the balance of their 5,000-share order could be traded. This was all done electronically, and the trade execution was fully automatic.

We added a further set of features that gave clients control over their trade execution – this appealed greatly to tuna clients. We called it 'boundaries' and they allowed a client to set a slippage tolerance on their trade order execution. For example, if the market price moved in the milliseconds it took for the trade to be executed on our platform, the platform would automatically reject the trade if the client had set a boundary tolerance of zero. This meant the client did not execute a trade when the price was not what they saw.

Price slippage is not always against the client – it could move in their favour. We are talking about milliseconds of trading across a public network, the internet. But the point was to empower and build trust with the client by showing that their trade execution was within their control and they could reject trades if they didn't get the price they had seen on the screen.

Price slippage happens on all exchanges and platforms simply because financial markets can move quickly during volatile times.

If clients are prepared to accept some price slippage due to market volatility, they can widen the boundary levels and trade within their own slippage boundaries. The whole process is automatic without any (CMC) trader intervention and the control is with the client as they can set their own boundaries. Boundaries are high-level price and transparent execution tools, but necessary to attract the best tuna clients. It is one-click trading at its best and is great for client trust.

Chapter 30

JUDGE ME ON
THE NUMBERS

When I took over as CEO in the first week of January 2013, a journalist asked me why I was so confident that I could do a better job than the last CEO. My response was, 'Well, no need for me to talk now, just judge me on my numbers over the next few years.'

The numbers spoke for themselves. Before I took over as CEO, we had lost £17 million for the previous nine months. In the first three months after I became CEO, we had our best profits quarter for the year and our loss year to date was almost wiped out, being reduced from £17 million to £3 million. This equated to a profit for the quarter of £14 million as opposed to the £5.6 million loss per quarter in the previous nine months.

In my first full five years as CEO I produced a total profit before tax (PBT) of £246 million, an average of approximately £50 million per year or approximately £12.5 million per quarter. If you add the last quarter of 2013 when I took over as CEO, that is approximately £264 million profit before tax. The total dividends paid since I became CEO to the end of March 2018 were £110 million.

Alongside the improved financial performance, in December

2016, we signed the largest partner's technology deal in our history when we agreed to take over ANZ Bank Australia's stockbroking business through a white label agreement (more on this in the next chapter). Earlier that year, on 6 February, within three years of taking over as CEO, I listed the company on the London Stock Exchange 2016 for a market capital of £700 million and with the company making profits of approximately £60 million a year.

I had no advantages on taking over in 2013 over any of the previous management. The new trading platform had been available throughout the whole of 2012 when I wasn't CEO and we already owned the stockbroking business that did the ANZ white label transaction. The changes I made were about cutting out unnecessary meetings and reports and trusting people and empowering them to do their jobs. By backing them and supporting them, we could get more productivity from each individual. I gave staff leadership and mentoring through various projects including Project Tuna and Hug-a-Client.

I also empowered clients and built their trust by giving them new upgraded technology, boundaries, automated execution and price depth ladders, and by letting them choose when they migrated onto the new platform.

The company now had direction and that meant staff did too. It wasn't rocket science. We were here to acquire clients, offer a service and make money. I told everybody to do their day jobs. For example, dealers were tasked with managing client risk flows and not with attending endless meetings and building flow reports for the board.

I always remember back to the mid-2000s, when there were some issues with trading that needed sorting out and I did then what I do today. I asked the dealers what they thought I should do. They have all the answers, you just ask them, get their feedback, and work out what needs to be done.

Someone once asked me if I am a control freak and my answer was no, I am the opposite of that. I keep pushing responsibility back onto people. I ask them what should be done, discuss it with them and then tell them to get on with it.

In the past under the previous management there were just too many meetings. I always thought that if you are having a meeting, you are not doing your job. Meetings are important but they are there to support you doing your job. If they take up so much time, something is wrong.

On one occasion when I was still chairman I was passing David Fineberg's trading desk. It was a Monday morning around 10 a.m. and I asked David to pop into my office for a catch up.

His response was, 'Sure, I have a few things to do for the CEO and then I will come in.' He turned up the next day at 3 p.m.!

I said, 'What happened to yesterday's meeting?'

He replied that he had been tied up in meetings with the CEO and then he had to write some reports.

I said, 'Dave, you are head of trading. You should be managing risk, not pushing a pen all day.'

This was late 2012 and I took over as CEO in January 2013.

About a year after I had taken over as CEO, I was sitting with some of the traders watching the markets on their screens and having a coffee. One of my senior traders summed it up. He said, 'Peter, I have worked for you for over eighteen years. I have seen you build this business from scratch and we are all behind you. We will deliver good results for you, but you must promise us that you won't bring in another CEO. Please stay as CEO – you are the only one that understands this business.'

I promised him that I would not bring in another CEO so long as I was the majority shareholder. But it showed the respect and support that I had within the business. The team had had enough of other people trying to run the business and not doing a good job.

I have kept my promise even after we listed the company on the LSE.

Chapter 31

ASIA PACIFIC ON
THE RADAR

In October 2013, with a solid start under my belt, and the company getting back on track to making money, I made my first overseas trip to our Sydney office where a new man was in charge.

Matt Lewis, who was born in Sydney, was running our Singapore office, but I wanted him back in Sydney. I had bought an Australian stockbroker (Andrew West Stockbroking) in 2007 and our CFD business was bigger in Australia than it was in Singapore.

Matt had been our head dealer in Sydney but took off to Singapore to set up our dealing room there. The plan had been to make Singapore our APAC hub for all business, but it was not my plan and as the new CEO I wanted to change things. To me it did not make sense to have a big stockbroking business in one location and a CFD dealing room in another. There were synergies between the two businesses and while they were in different countries it was hard to monetise those synergies.

It was obvious to me that the APAC dealing room should be run out of Sydney, not Singapore. The Australian business was bigger and, to service our Auckland office, the Singapore dealers had to start at 4 a.m. because of the time difference. This seemed ridiculous, so I asked Matt to move back to Sydney to be the head of our whole APAC business from there. My plan was to run the APAC region business out of Sydney and create synergies between the stockbroking and CFD businesses.

Matt was only thirty-five at the time but he had been with the company ten years. I felt we needed change and Matt was an experienced dealer. I also felt that dealers needed to run the company. As the new CEO I wanted more like-minded people in my top team.

We are a market-making company, so it made sense to put an ex-dealer in charge of our most important office outside Europe. It also made sense to put a local in charge of a local office. It galvanised the Sydney team to get behind a Sydney-born office head.

Matt was a bit put out at first because he had only been in Singapore for a year. But he could see that his long-term future was back running CMC's Sydney office. It was also a major promotion for him, and he is still running the APAC region out of Sydney for us today and is now a main board director.

The purpose of my first overseas trip was to explain the changes to the team personally and support Matt in his new role. I wanted the office to understand why I changed things and why I put my faith in Matt to replace the existing person (who did not have dealing experience).

I stopped off in Singapore on the way to explain things to the team there and to let them know that Singapore had a big future and that I was committed to expanding our office there. I also asked Chris Smith, the head of our New Zealand office, to come to Sydney to hear my strategy first-hand.

In Singapore I explained that I was moving Matt for strategic reasons, but we would invest in Singapore and keep expanding it. It was important that I explained all this personally as there had been a lot of changes in the company and I needed to show my face to demonstrate my commitment.

Having lived in Monaco for eight years, staff naturally assumed that I was semi-retired and what I was doing now was a short-term fix before I went back to Monaco again. I wanted them to hear from me that I was committing myself long-term to the business.

In October 2013, I arrived in Sydney to show support for Matt and the team. I gave a town hall presentation in the office and said that Matt was part of a new flat-line management structure that I implemented almost on day one. I explained that Matt would be reporting to me and he would sit on the Exco board. I said Matt had a voice at the top table, his voice would be heard, and he had me on speed dial. I said Sydney was the second-largest office in the group, that it was important to the future of the company, and that was why it was my first overseas trip as CEO.

Also, on this trip, I sat down with Matt and the stockbroking team. I asked them how much stockbroking was making annually and they said around two million Australian dollars (AU$), which is just over £1 million.

The first thing I said was that the stockbroking business was no longer for sale. This was a complete reversal in attitude and strategy, because in late 2012, the board had put it up for sale to cut costs and reduce overheads. The staff were low in morale as they didn't know their future. The stockbroking business had been slowly declining under the previous management regime. There was no love for it. I knew that it could contribute to the business, it just needed investment and belief to extract its true value.

Then I said, 'Right, for the next three years, all profits from stockbroking will be ploughed back into the stockbroking business, investing in new people, technology and marketing.' I also invited the head of Sydney IT to our London office to learn about Next Gen technology so he could upgrade our existing stockbroking platform.

Stockbroking was a great business, it just needed some attention, focus and belief. Even though it was not exactly shooting the lights out with profits, it was net positive. But more importantly, it was a major brand enhancement and gave us a different perception in Australia as a financial services company.

It was a wise decision, because three years later, in 2016, we agreed a white label deal to take over ANZ Bank Australia's stockbroking business. This made us the number two retail stockbroker in Australia, propelling us from number forty-three in 2013. As part of this transaction, we acquired one million ANZ stockbroking clients and over AU$60 billion (£27 billion) in client share assets. We also acquired 103 intermediaries who were clients of ANZ Bank's stockbroking. In stockbroking alone in Australia we have around 150 people working for us. Our stockbroking business today makes over AU$50 million a year and rising.

In my town hall talk in Sydney, I explained as much about the company as I could. I wanted to tell the staff how excited I was about the future. I told them about Project Tuna and our renewed investment in the stockbroking business. I told them Michael, their head of IT, would be coming to London to learn about our new technology; and I talked about my commitment to the business.

I thought it was one of my most inspiring speeches and I felt good about it, so I opened the floor to questions. I said to the staff, 'You can ask me any question you like, and I am happy to answer it.'

The first question was 'What watch are you wearing?', which I thought showed how relaxed and happy the staff were. I told the guy it was an IWC Tourbillon, serial number 2, and I said, 'Mind your own business about the cost.' We all laughed, and it was clear that the team were happy and so was I. Australians love successful people. The Sydney team saw me as a successful person, and they were pleased to see me energised and committed to the business. All of a sudden, they had direction and they were ready to dig in and make a success of the business.

I left the Sydney office with morale improving, with a clear business plan and structure. They knew I loved the stockbroking business and that I was in town to invest not withdraw money.

The team laughed at Hug-a-Client and Project Tuna. I said I would come up with a few names like Project Billabong and Didgeridoo but that would be on my next trip. It felt good to be CEO again.

Chapter 32

CULTURE CLUB MY ARSE

When I was preparing the company for listing on the London Stock Exchange, I was meeting potential investors on the pre-float roadshows in 2015. Lots of the questions around my role were about how I ran the business. I got the impression that investors thought I was a control freak and that I wanted to control every aspect of the business.

This was a reasonable assumption because I still owned 90 per cent of the business and we were extremely profitable. But investors learnt quickly that this is the complete opposite to how I run the business. As I have said before, I constantly push responsibility back to staff. They do not need a running commentary on what they are supposed to be doing because I am always telling them to get on with their jobs.

This goes back to 1994 when I needed to employ super-smart developers to build my first internet trading platform. I quickly realised that, if I wanted the business to expand, I had to depend on others to deliver, especially in areas that I knew little or nothing about, and technology was one of those areas.

With the advent of the internet and laptop computers, more and more young people were working for financial institutions and they brought a different attitude to the workplace. In 1994, when we started developing our first platform, often the developers would get in around lunchtime and work until two in the morning. They preferred to work on their own terms and often when we arrived in the morning there were empty pizza boxes in the office. They were untidy buggers. But they were a smart bunch of guys, young and excited about technology and the challenges involved, and they were left alone to create and develop our first platform. But with a lot of input from me.

Another example of my management style was this – one day in 2017 there was a knock on my office door and our new head of marketing walked in. He laid out in front of me a twenty-page report that had taken him weeks to prepare. He presented it proudly, declaring, 'This is what needs to be done in the marketing department and how to do it.'

My response was, 'What do you expect me to do with the report?'

He replied, 'Well, read it and let me know what you think.'

I replied immediately, 'I am not reading it. That's your job. I brought you into the company to sort things out and I don't need reports, I need the job done.'

When I took over as CEO, this was the tone I wanted to set for Exco. My style was to give staff more responsibility, liberate them from meetings and reports, and tell them that I trusted them to do a good job.

I didn't know if they were entirely capable of doing the job. But I wanted to give all the senior people a chance because, even if they were not capable, at least they would try harder and it gave me breathing space to decide who I should keep and who I should replace.

However, it was also important to set the tone and my style of management for the rest of the company. During a town hall speech to staff in mid-2013, which was recorded and transmitted on our intranet site, one of the team in Singapore asked me, 'What can I do personally to make the company better?'

My response was immediate: 'Just do your job. If everybody applies themselves and does their job it will be a much better company and our best years are ahead of us.'

Funnily enough, this was the town hall that got reported in the press, because I banned free fresh fruit, jeans and flip-flops. The press reported it out of context as me cutting costs, but what I was saying was that if I was coming back as CEO and having to work hard then I expected everybody else to work hard and not turn up as if they had just rolled out of bed. I said, 'Working for CMC is about having the right attitude. If you stroll into the office not having washed and shaved or put on some decent clothes, then your attitude must be wrong.

'If you work at CMC Markets you are here to make good money for the company and for yourself. I want to pay everybody a big bonus, but you must earn it. If you want a lifestyle job, you should go and work for one of the big technology companies like Google or Facebook.'

I laid down a marker to staff of what was expected of them, so they knew that change was coming. Under the previous management, there was a so-called culture club – an attempt by the head of HR to create a homely working environment whereby coming to work should be enjoyable and not too stressful. But I thought this was dumbing down the working environment and not pushing people to work hard or at least do a fair day's work for a fair day's pay.

This may be alright for millennials, but I was from the old school. I was office cleaning with my mum at sixteen after a fourteen-hour night shift at Western Union. So fresh cream teas watching the Olympics was not my style of running a company. My style is, 'You are here to work. I am getting in every day before 8 a.m. and leaving ten hours later. If I can work hard so can you.'

More importantly, this lifestyle working environment was affecting the company's performance. So, I banned working from home. Technically, back in 2013, I am not sure that was legal at the time, but I did it anyway. It was funny that most people wanted to work from home on a Friday or a Monday and HR seemed to be saying, 'Sure, no problem, pop in when you are passing next time.'

When I banned working from home, somebody asked me, 'What if the plumber is calling and I need to be at home?'

I said, 'Well, take a day's holiday and don't deal with the plumber in my time, it has to be done in your time. If you're speaking to the plumber, you cannot be working.' It was probably a bit harsh and unfair, but you need the right attitude when you come to work and if I had it, so should the team.

Much of this town hall talk was about setting the tone and trying to change the culture of the company. It was also about releasing my own frustrations at seeing a market-leading company that I had built with my own hands going slowly backwards. These were the frustrations I felt when I had other people running the company and making lots of mistakes. It was about not having my voice heard and I had had enough. I was releasing all this pent-up frustration and driving the business on to greater things. I wanted everybody to know that I was back big time and that I was taking back control.

Welcome to the Muppet Show

At my staff town hall speech in early 2013, I mentioned something that had happened to me outside of work. It was a sting operation by the *Sunday Times* when I was treasurer of the Conservative

Party in 2012. Practically everybody in the company had seen my face splashed across the front pages of nearly every newspaper and on their television screens. I felt that the issue could not be ignored.

I wanted staff to know that I was going to concentrate fully on business. I said that I would only work for CMC Markets and my charity, the Peter Cruddas Foundation. I would not get involved with politics.

However, I also said there was a pending court case against the *Sunday Times* which I had to deal with, but it would not take too long, and it would not be too much of a distraction. I said I was confident I would win my case against the *Sunday Times* and their libellous allegations and once I had sorted out the *Sunday Times*, I would sort out David Cameron, the Prime Minister.

People laughed when I said this, but I told the staff that I was not joking, I was serious. They laughed because I said that I was going after Waldorf and Statler, two characters from *The Muppet Show*. I had to explain that I was referring to David Cameron and Conservative Party chairman Andrew Feldman, after they forced me to resign as treasurer following the *Sunday Times* sting. Like Waldorf and Statler, they were two unaware observers watching from the wings oblivious to the real goings-on and what had happened in the sting by the newspaper.

This was because they had cut all ties with me and just moved on. They did not know my side of the story. The names stuck because, whenever the court case was discussed, we always referred to Cameron as Waldorf and Feldman as Statler. By the end of 2013 they were proven to be a right couple of muppets. More about that later.

I finished the speech by saying, 'I will sort this company out and when I have done that, I will sort out the muppets. You must decide whether you want to be part of this company's future growth and ambitions, with me at the helm.' I said that I was going to make this company great whether the staff were with me or without me. If I was going to take on the role of CEO then I was going to do it properly. It would mean hard work and a change in attitude. No more culture club and cream teas.

I explained I wanted staff to dress smartly and be ready for work every day. If that's not for you, then good luck, have a great life. But if you are on board, CMC's best days are ahead.

Chapter 33

A NEW CHAPTER BEGINS

By 2015, the company's profits were continuing to grow. When you have a profitable business built on great technology, the bankers are never far away, sniffing out opportunities to make some money.

Many of my team had been loyal and hard-working and I wanted to reward them through a share option scheme. I still had bags of energy and I was enjoying working, so I thought a public listing was the right step for the company and for me. It had also been approximately ten years since we last tried to take the company public.

In early 2015, the decision was made to go public and list our shares on the London Stock Exchange. We selected Goldman Sachs and Morgan Stanley as the lead banks, with Royal Bank of Canada as specialists on the FTSE 250 listings.

My instructions to the bankers were that I wanted to sell the minimum amount at the initial public offering (IPO) and, to prove my confidence in the business, I was happy to sign a long-term lock-in on selling the remainder of my shares. I also agreed to stay on indefinitely as the company's CEO.

I signed one of the longest share lock-ins in LSE history, with three years for 50 per cent of my remaining shares and two years for the other 50 per cent. This meant that the earliest I could sell any more shares would be two years after the IPO.

After the IPO, my family and I would still own around 63 per cent of the company as we would sell around 27 per cent of our shareholding. Goldman Sachs still owned approximately 10 per cent. It is quite unusual for an individual to have control of a public listed company. But as I owned (with my family) 90 per cent of the company we could be listed and I could still control the company. It was the best of both worlds as far as I was concerned. Especially as I expected to work for another ten years once we became public.

The due diligence and investor meetings were another gruelling time as we embarked on early-look, pre-IPO meetings around the world. But following the early-look meetings, we were encouraged to move to the next stage and eventually we listed on the London Stock Exchange on 5 February 2016. This time there was little market volatility to prevent our listing.

As I pushed the button at the launch ceremony, I felt proud to list the shares surrounded by my family and many of my colleagues. It was amazing to see our share price (CMCX) up in lights and I gave a small speech to everybody gathered there that had been part of the CMC journey. I felt emotional as Fiona had handed me a lovely card before the ceremony, telling me how proud she was, which contained this handwritten rhyme:

> With £10,000 and a basement room
> Nobody guessed how the business would boom
> You've relished the highs and battled the lows
> Where your energy comes from, God only knows!
> But for 26 years, you've led all the way
> To gain the success and respect achieved here today
> So, raise your glass and shout 'chin-chin'
> Congratulations! Good luck! Let the new chapter begin!

For me it was an epic day, and the only thing missing was not having my mum there. I knew Mum would have been immensely proud to see me up there giving my speech at the London Stock Exchange, especially as she used to clean the LSE offices forty-five years earlier and I used to help her empty the bins. I didn't mention this in my speech, but I remembered it well. I know Mum and I would have smiled at each other because we would have both known that listing a company on the LSE beats cleaning their offices. I kept this to myself because I felt that this was a joyous day, the team were happy, and I didn't want to be too emotional. I didn't trust myself as I knew I would have broken down in tears and embarrassed myself.

In the 1960s, the LSE was just off Old Broad Street and near to the offices above Boots the chemist which we cleaned in Bishopsgate. Now the new offices were by St Paul's, but it was still the London Stock Exchange and instead of helping my mum clean them I was there to list my business. Wow, what a journey.

I have to say they were nice, clean offices. It was good to see standards had not dropped since Mum and I used to clean them.

Once the shares were listed, at £2.40 with a market capitalisation of £700 million, they quickly moved up to a trading high of £2.93 in July 2016, valuing the company at approximately £850 million. It was all going well, even though I felt the value of the company should have been in excess of £1 billion. The bankers told me that, having been a private company for over twenty-seven years, we had to prove that we could operate effectively as a public company. Then, they assured me, our shares would get a higher rating.

Everything was on track until 6 December 2016 when City regulator the Financial Conduct Authority (FCA) decided to review retail client leverage on certain derivatives including CFDs and spread betting. Their logic was to improve client outcome and help protect retail clients from excess losses. They started a review process that lasted for nearly two years. This was all noble and although I agreed that the regulators should review retail client margins, it was not good for our share price, which immediately dropped 40 per cent and would eventually settle at around £1, valuing the company at approximately £300 million.

So, in the eight months of being listed our shares hit an all-time high of £2.93 and an all-time low of 90 pence. The low share price reflected how investors thought regulation changes would affect our future earnings regardless of how we were performing at the time. Also, until the regulators published the proposed changes it created an overhang on our share price due to the future uncertainty of the industry.

Somebody asked me if I liked seeing the company's valuation reduce overnight by around £300 million and my response was that I lost 60 per cent of something that I never had. A large chunk of my wealth was tied up in CMC shares and, like a property, valuations can go up and down. I still owned the shares, so I didn't feel any different. I was more annoyed for our shareholders, who were very supportive.

The FCA wanted to improve client trading outcomes, which we all agreed with. But the industry generally felt that we were being penalised for a few firms that were not onboarding clients appropriately and were exploiting inexperienced clients through over-leverage. Most of these rogue firms were not even operating out of the UK but from less regulated overseas jurisdictions. But they could market to UK clients because of the passporting rights allowed by European regulations. Since I launched online trading in Europe in October 1996, the retail trading space had exploded with retail clients wanting access to shares like Facebook, Google, Apple and products like gold, oil and cryptocurrencies.

More galling was that our clients were generally happy with existing leverage levels and they didn't want to be told how much leverage they could use. It was their choice and they were annoyed to be told their trading would be restricted. One client said, 'It's a bit like the government saying, "We are not going to ban smoking, but you can only smoke ten cigarettes a day."'

The regulator's changes took nearly two years to implement, because of a lengthy and thorough consultation process. Eventually the FCA implemented leverage restrictions on retail clients, along with other onboarding changes, on 1 August 2018.

Following the new margin restrictions, many retail clients started to open accounts offshore in low-regulated jurisdictions to find higher leverage. Regulatory arbitrage was always a concern of ours because there were no restrictions on clients opening accounts with overseas companies. This effectively made it an uneven playing field for companies like ours that complied with the new rules.

However, the regulators usually get it right and, as a firm, we must adapt to the changes. Usually, regulations make the strong firms stronger and the weak firms weaker, so we were in a good place. Effectively it would just be a matter of time before the share price improved as new rules and regulations took effect and the stronger firms picked up the lion's share of the business.

We were confident this would be the case because in December 2016, just after the regulator's announcement about proposed changes, I got a call from Matt Lewis from Sydney. He said, 'I have a nice Christmas present for you.' He told me we had won the technology mandate to white-label the whole of ANZ Bank's Australian stockbroking business. With around 1 million clients and AU$60 billion in client share assets, we could expect profits in excess of AU$10 million (£5.5 million) from this transaction alone. I didn't know whether to laugh or cry because our shares on the LSE were dropping, and yet profits were the same as before the announcement and we had just signed this big ANZ deal.

It took me back to 2006 when I cancelled our listing on the LSE due to market volatility, against a backdrop of record profits in the company. This is one of the dichotomies of being a public company. The business can be doing well but if the sector is under pressure then that affects the value of the shares. Events outside of our control affect the value of the company. All we can do as a business is keep making money to drive the value of the business. If outside events affect our share price, there is nothing we can do.

Since we became a public company, we have delivered record profits; we signed the biggest partner deal in our history with ANZ stockbroking; and, before our London listing, we spent £100 million on our technology and trading platform, which was all paid for before the listing. We went into the IPO with no debt and no borrowings.

Also, we were sitting on the largest cash pile in the company's history – approximately £200 million. The company may have been performing well, but the sector was under-performing because of the changes in regulation, and our shares were being de-rated because of the uncertain outlook. I was frustrated, because I thought, what was the point in being a public company if the valuation of the company was barely its cash value?

I was finding being a public company difficult because our valuation was dropping due to events outside our control. Also, despite having some good long-term investors, there were plenty of people who were just punting the shares and jumping on any movement up or down. This is normal but I was the one with a long-term lock-in on my shares and staying loyal to the company while others just took a punt.

One issue we have as a public company is the lack of liquidity in our stock because I still own around 63 per cent of the shares with my family. The problem with this is a small purchase or sale can exaggerate the share price movement and cause a big change in price. Also, some potential investors are restricted in buying shares in a company that has less than 40 per cent free float. Which doesn't help because a lot of the bigger funds that automatically buy into FTSE 250 companies are restricted in buying our shares because of the small percentage of free float, the portion of shares not owned by me.

However, I wanted to be the controlling shareholder and keep on working and developing the company. Therefore, I have no room to complain because I listed the company on my terms, which is fair enough. Before listing, having a controlling shareholding was deemed to be a good thing because it showed commitment from me. Post IPO it became a liquidity issue. *C'est la vie*, as they say in Monaco.

But now, I am glad we are a public company. I like the new regulations, which in the long term are right for the industry and right for CMC. They also fit very nicely into Project Tuna.

Back in 2013 when I became CEO, I changed the strategy of the company to focus on experienced higher-valued clients, our Project Tuna underpinned by Hug-a-Client. The new regulations that are targeting lower-valued inexperienced clients are a good thing for the industry and a complete vindication of our business model. The regulator wants to ensure that inexperienced clients understand the risks of trading on leverage. We agree with them, especially as this has not been our target market since 2013 and is not today.

Business is about challenge and change and you must keep adapting. Often, we have been ahead of the curve with technology, but Project Tuna put us ahead of the curve of regulations. Five years ahead to be precise.

Chapter 34

DIPPING MY TOE INTO
POLITICAL WATERS

I got into politics when, in 2009, I donated £200,000 to the Conservative Party when David Cameron was its leader. I had never made political donations before, but I was so fed up with Blair and Brown and their mismanagement of the British economy and the Iraq War that I thought I would donate to the Conservative Party. I felt the country needed change and I was able to do my bit.

I was always a Conservative and I had voted for them in every general election since I was old enough to vote. My mum had also always been a Conservative and had strong political views. She was a typical centre-right Conservative but sometimes hovered between centre and far-right. She was always a big Churchill fan because of her experience during the Second World War. My dad was from a coal mining community in South Shields and was a typical Labour supporter. He was also a big Churchill fan for the same reasons as my mum, but he always voted Labour.

In 2009, I was a British resident, having returned from Monaco, so I was able to make political donations. My donation went towards the 2010 general election campaign. David Cameron became head of a coalition government with the Liberal Democrats. This partial election win was the beginning of my own political journey that would lead to a lot of grief.

I cannot say I wasn't warned.

A prominent businessman and well-known figure told me over dinner one night, in no uncertain terms, that I would be mad to get involved in politics. He had some choice words to describe some politicians.

Fiona gave me a similarly good piece of advice. She said, 'It will end in tears. Do not get into politics, just concentrate on business.' Unfortunately, I ignored her too even though I knew I was playing with fire and I went into it with my eyes open.

At first it started off well. After the 2010 election, I was firmly on the radar of Conservative Campaign Headquarters (CCHQ). I was one of their key bigger donors and they knew that if they needed short-term help, they could rely on me.

Lord (Andrew) Feldman, David Cameron's Oxford University friend, and co-chairman of the Conservative Party, asked me to be part of his close circle of top donors.

I said, 'Yes, sure, call me any time.'

It didn't take long, and Lord Feldman called me in February 2011.

Andrew Feldman was head honcho at CCHQ, and people were wary of him because of his close friendship with Cameron. According to Wikipedia, Feldman was apparently Cameron's longest political friend as they went to Oxford together. He had raised the funds for Cameron's Conservative Party leadership campaign in 2005.

Cameron and Feldman were close. Often, I would see donors at events slip a cheque in Feldman's top pocket. He would pat his pocket and say, 'Thanks very much, I will make sure David knows about your donation personally.' Andrew was excellent at raising money for the Conservative Party because of his close friendship with the PM, and he knew how to work a room. Donors bypassed other treasurers as they felt a cheque given to Andrew would mean that he would put in a good word for them at No. 10 and help push them up the pecking order. Whether this was true or not I do not know, but it certainly helped to raise money for the party, and it made Andrew important to the party as he was by far its biggest fundraiser.

Andrew had supported David Cameron all through his political journey to become leader. He was Cameron's right-hand man at CCHQ, and he had his own pass to No. 10 Downing Street. It was all very cosy.

Andrew talked frequently at donor dinner parties about how he and David would meet for dinner at the PM's Oxfordshire home, open a bottle of wine and smoke a cigar. Andrew would also auction off a doubles tennis match against him and the PM to the highest bidder at Conservative Party fundraising events.

It was the David and Andrew show at CCHQ and it worked because Andrew sorted out the party's finances, wiping out previous debt and putting the party on a solid financial footing. Everything was above board, and the friendship connection was leveraged to the maximum.

In early February 2011, I was sitting in my office when I got a call from Andrew. He said he wanted to see me urgently and asked when I was free to meet. I said, 'Give me an hour, and I will pop over to Millbank.'

Andrew explained that the government was going to launch a referendum on the alternative voting system (AV), which was part of the Lib Dems' terms to form a coalition with the Conservatives. Andrew said it was important to the party and to the Prime

Minister that the 'no to alternative voting' (No2AV) campaign won the referendum. The Lib Dems were backing Yes2AV.

I thought it was strange that Andrew used the term 'Prime Minister' when he wasn't asking me for money, and I inferred that this was important. It was more about politics than money. Andrew said the party could not afford to lose this referendum, especially as it did not have a majority in the House of Commons following the 2010 general election. If it did lose, it could lead to future hung parliaments.

The purpose of the chat was to offer me the job as treasurer of the No2AV campaign. But there were some terms. He said I would need to inject £500,000 into the campaign immediately. I would also need to put in sufficient time to really help the campaign.

Before I accepted his offer, I pointed out that it was February and the referendum was on 5 May 2011, so we only had a few months to sort things out. He wasn't giving me much time to win this referendum.

Andrew said that there was already a team in place headed by Lord (Rodney) Leach and Matthew Elliott. But the campaign needed funds and direction and the Prime Minister and Andrew thought I was the right man for the job. He said that if I accepted the job it would put me in very good light with the Prime Minister, who would be grateful, especially if we won.

Andrew also said that if No2AV won, the Conservative Party's treasurer's job was mine if I wanted it. Andrew said this as if he was doing me a favour when I knew that being the Conservative Party treasurer normally costs the treasurer around £750,000 per annum in donations. I said, 'One thing at a time, let's win No2AV first.'

I accepted his terms and said that I would get on with it

immediately, arrange to meet Matthew and Rodney, and send the cash within one week so we could ramp up the campaign.

Andrew explained that the No campaign had to be completely independent of the Prime Minister as all parties agreed that this had to be an independent referendum. However, No. 10 would be in touch to thank me for supporting the No campaign.

A week later, I was summoned to Downing Street for tea with the Prime Minister. It was 4 March 2011, the day the PM's daughter Florence was being christened. So he couldn't hang around, he had to go to Oxford to attend the christening.

I had been to No. 10 before but usually it was to attend charitable or social functions. This time, I turned left and went into the PM's office and there he was sitting at his desk waiting for me. He must have seen me looking around and asked me what I thought.

I said, 'Well, it's a bit small for the leader of our country,' and so he got up and opened the double doors behind his desk to reveal the famous big oval Cabinet table. I said, 'Ah, that's better. Much more fitting for the PM.'

We had a cup of tea and I proceeded to spill milk all over his nice coffee table, which I quickly mopped up with my handkerchief.

The conversation was bizarre as he sounded removed from the topic. He said something along the lines of 'Oh, I understand that you will be taking on the treasurer's role for No2AV. I hope you do well, and it is a good cause. But No2AV really needs to win.'

It was as if it had nothing to do with him. We all knew in the room that the party and he wanted the No campaign to win. But he had to distance himself from the process as he was in coalition with the side that wanted the Yes campaign to win. They needed to remain on friendly terms, being in government together.

I couldn't see the point of the meeting at Downing Street if he wasn't directly supportive, but I guess he had to be careful, which he certainly was. We only had about twenty minutes, then I was on my way and thanked the PM for the nice chat and cup of tea. It was all very British and a nice gesture, even if it was a bit of a waste of time.

A few days later, I met Matthew Elliott and Lord Leach and we discussed how to approach the campaign. I told Matthew it was time to ramp up the campaign as we didn't have much time to win the referendum and I would be sending £500,000 in the next few days.

Matthew and I got on well. He was grateful for the injection of energy from me as well as the cash. Rodney was the intellectual and he always spoke well and was supportive of me coming on board. We also liked each other.

After this initial meeting, Matthew and I met again, and we agreed it was time to get our hands dirty. I said we needed to be more aggressive and Matthew agreed, and he was up for the fight. We also had other team members that I met at our regular Wednesday morning update meetings in Tufton Street. Among them was Sarah Southern, whose path I would cross again after the AV campaign, but more about that later.

Matthew and I got on well and we are both Conservatives. However, we had a cross-party campaign group and at our headquarters in Westminster Tower on the south side of the Thames, adjacent to Lambeth Bridge, there were plenty of Labour Party people also working for the campaign.

I asked Matthew why Labour were supporting us and he said, 'Well, Labour and Conservatives have been in power between them for the last hundred years or so and they don't want anything to change because, with a new voting system, they might not get voted in.' I thought, 'Nothing like the thought of losing an election to galvanise the left and right of the political divide.'

I said to Matthew, 'We need to win this thing and we have to put politics to one side and just go for it.' Matthew was concerned that our aggressive stance would upset CCHQ because the Conservatives were in a coalition government and his mandate, up until I joined, was to push to win but not upset our coalition partners. He said he had to be politically sensitive. I agreed with this to a point, but I argued that if the Yes campaign won, we would have proportional representation governments for ever. That would mean that the Conservatives might never win another outright election again, or at least for the foreseeable future.

I told him this was serious. I told him not to worry about CCHQ, as I would deal with them. I said, 'If you get any calls just refer them to me.'

So, Matthew, the team and I decided to fight hard to win the campaign. When I joined in February 2011, the Yes and No campaigns were level in the polls. By the time of the referendum on 5 May, the No campaign won approximately 68 per cent of the vote. But to win such a big majority, we upset lots of people, not least the Liberal Democrats, who were complaining about our tactics.

I heard several stories that found their way back to me, along the lines that the Conservatives were fighting dirty and it would upset future relations between the two parties in power. This was probably true as I heard afterwards that the Liberal Democrats withdrew their support for boundary changes that would have benefitted the Conservatives, as they were so upset with the No2AV campaign tactics.

The Lib Dems did have a point because our campaign was hard-hitting. We were saying things like 'Our troops don't need a different voting system; they need more body armour' and 'To change the voting system would cost the country £250 million – this is money better spent on our NHS'.

Referendums are not general elections. In referendums, people vote on emotion more than, say, the state of the economy. They also feel more inclined to vote freely as they generally see it as voting for a change in policy that either main political party could implement. In voters' minds, it's almost like a free vote and much more emotive and less tribal for them.

The key to winning a referendum is to appeal to people's emotions. There's no point in a politician saying 'We need to invest in our economy' to win a referendum. If you say 'Stop wasting money on silly things and give the money instead to our troops or our NHS', emotions run high and politicians generally have little or no response. Referendums are the kiss of death to normal political campaigning.

As Matthew and I ramped up our campaign and we raised more and more money to do more things, the PM, I understand, got a bit of flak from the Lib Dems over some of our slogans and advertising. But he could always say No2AV was an independent campaign that was not run by CCHQ, which was entirely true. Now the removed tone of our conversations at No. 10 Downing Street was making sense.

Anyway, our team – including Matthew, Rodney and me and many others – nailed it and we won a massive majority. If there was any political fallout that could be dealt with later but for now, it was time to celebrate.

On Saturday 7 May 2011, my wife and I were walking along Park Lane from our house to go for a drink at the Dorchester Hotel and then dinner at San Lorenzo. I noticed I had a missed call on my phone. At first, I didn't recognise the number or the message, which said, 'Please call this number, No. 10.'

Fiona said, 'You'd better call it.'

I sat down at a quiet table at the Dorchester and I called the number. Immediately, the receptionist said, 'Good evening, No. 10 Downing Street.'

I said, 'Hi, can I speak to the Prime Minister, please? This is Peter Cruddas.'

The receptionist said, 'Just a moment please,' and within a few seconds the Prime Minister came on the phone and said, 'Ah Peter, so nice to speak to you, thanks for calling back.'

I nearly wet myself with laughter as I couldn't believe that I had just rung the PM and he took the call. It was funny and surreal at the same time.

David Cameron said, 'Well done, Peter, you did a great job on the AV campaign and you have taken alternative voting off the political agenda for a generation.' He also said, 'I understand that you will shortly be stepping up to be treasurer of the Conservative Party and you have my full backing.'

I said I was glad to be of service and I hoped we hadn't upset too many of his Lib Dem friends. I said that as PM he had my full support and now, he could get on with running the country.

I also told him that I was going to drink a glass of champagne to celebrate with my wife and then we were off to San Lorenzo for dinner and I would send him the bill. He laughed and said that his salary was meagre and best to drink beer instead of champagne. Suddenly, we were the best of buddies and I was the golden boy for a few days. Unfortunately, this was not destined to last.

Chapter 35

RUBBING SHOULDERS
WITH THE TOP BRASS

I became Conservative Party co-treasurer alongside Stanley Fink in the summer of 2011. Stanley had already been in the job alongside Michael Spencer for two years so was well experienced.

Apparently making me Conservative Party treasurer was a reward for the good job I had done on the No2AV campaign, although it didn't feel like much of a reward as I had to pay for the privilege. However, I accepted the job and felt honoured to have it.

There was never an official appointment date, although there was a press release. I just rocked up at the Conservative Party offices on Millbank on my way to work every Wednesday morning. I also had to attend various events that were worked out around my diary and the treasurers' team at CCHQ.

When I attended the Wednesday weekly treasurers' meeting, I often had to leave my silver Rolls-Royce parked around the corner as the then head of events, Kate Rock (the CCHQ queen bee and Andrew Feldman's assistant), always said it was bad for the party's image to have millionaires seen going into CCHQ and parking their flash cars outside. I thought how ironic it was that the party didn't mind accepting a millionaire's cheque, but they didn't want to be seen with them.

I couldn't see the problem. After all, I was a working-class boy 'done good' supporting the Conservative Party. I hadn't been to Eton or Oxford. I was always proud that I had achieved so much despite not having a privileged upbringing. Therefore, I saw no reason to hide who I was and what I had achieved. Anyway, my appointment and my donations were made public as they were published quarterly on the Electoral Commission's website.

On most days, it suited the party to have me associated with them because of my upbringing. To keep the peace, I did comply with parking the car around the corner – it wasn't worth the grief. However, every now and again I would park on purpose out the front as an act of defiance. It probably didn't help me make friends with Kate, but I didn't lose any sleep over it.

Kate was always worked up about it. She thought I just didn't get it and that I was politically naïve. Of course I got it. But the party knew what they were getting when they offered me the job and cashed my cheques. I think it bordered on snobbery, but I am sure she had the party's best interests at heart.

One of the first meetings I had in mid-2011 was at CCHQ with the treasurers' team. Andrew Feldman asked me to sponsor the Conservatives' summer party at the Natural History Museum, which was happening a month later. I did this, but I said it would have to be the official launch of me becoming treasurer and it would be good if I was introduced at this event.

I sponsored the event for £150,000. I had two big tables and I invited the No2AV team onto one table including Matthew Elliott and Sarah Southern. On my table, I had some potential big donors and I sat next to Samantha Cameron, who was lovely and very charming. The PM was also on my table and was flanked by a couple of my rich friends who tried to outbid each other for an auctioned picture of Margaret Thatcher. The bidding stopped at £200,000, so my first event as the co-treasurer got off to a flyer – two new donors introduced within weeks of me starting.

I gave a speech that night and introduced myself, although I already knew many of the Cabinet from donating to centre-right think tanks like the Policy Exchange. I felt comfortable enough to joke about my daughter's boyfriend, who was sitting at one of my tables. I warned him to treat her well as I now had powerful friends. During the evening, the PM went up to him and said, 'You'd better look after her or you will be in big trouble.' It was a funny moment and nice of the PM to share the joke.

From the summer of 2011 until the end of the year I continued attending events and trying to raise money for the party, as well as putting my hand in my own pocket. I remember one meeting in August 2011 when the party was struggling to raise its normal monthly target. August is always a difficult month as most people are on holiday. Andrew had already indicated that I would be expected to donate around £750,000 a year as the senior treasurer, and I had accepted this when taking the job. At this meeting, I wrote a cheque for £100,000 and handed it to the team, which helped the party through a barren period. The party was in good shape financially, but it doesn't like to spend money it does not have, so I balanced the books for August. Then we all went off on holiday with the next meeting scheduled in October.

I enjoyed being co-treasurer. There were many good people working at CCHQ and I felt honoured to be invited onto the board. Being part of the Conservative Party board and treasurer was a proud achievement for me.

However, I never felt comfortable with Andrew, Kate and the inner sanctum of the CCHQ team. There seemed to be a clique that was not for outsiders or for me. Andrew and Kate would often travel together to CCHQ from their homes as they were near-neighbours and they were close. Kate was also good friends with the Chancellor, George Osborne, and she often talked openly about their families going on skiing holidays together. Kate and her husband owned a ski chalet and the Osbornes would join them.

Kate said she had known George all her life, and indeed she had. Once she and I went to Le Caprice for lunch and the team there, who knew her well, asked where George was. And Andrew was friends with the PM as they had gone to Oxford together, so it was all very cosy for him and Kate. They ran CCHQ and David and George ran the country.

I had no issues with any of this. It was their gig and I had only just joined the team. We would both need time to get to know each other. But I did feel that I wasn't really welcome at CCHQ. I just didn't seem to fit in. Certain social events – usually with big hitters and the PM or the Chancellor attending – were reserved for the clique and I was omitted from them. I didn't worry about it, but I decided that if I was not going to be invited to some of these exclusive events involving the PM, then I would make myself busy in other areas.

This didn't please the clique. However, my view was that I had been invited onto the board of the Conservative Party and I should contribute in the best way possible.

I decided to get out of the Westminster bubble and travel around the country to meet local party members and voluntary teams and just listen and learn. I went to the north-east and met the local party workers. I met Stockton South MP James Wharton, who became a good friend; and Hexham MP Guy Opperman.

I went to the north-east three times and, on one occasion, I hosted a dinner for young Asian Conservatives. It was at Wynyard

Hall, the hotel home of Sir John Hall, a long-time Conservative donor and former owner of Newcastle United Football Club, the team my dad had supported. Sir John asked me to speak at the event while he generously paid for it all. He felt that more young Asians should support the party and if I came up from London to talk to them it might make a difference.

Sir John put Fiona and me up at his magnificent home and we had a great time. Sir John was a marvellous host, a very friendly man, and I enjoyed his company immensely.

Sir John is a passionate, long-serving Conservative and he said that I was the first treasurer since Margaret Thatcher's days that had been up to see him. He appreciated the gesture so much that he slipped a nice cheque in my top pocket as a donation and thanked me for the respect I had shown him. Nothing like being a man of the people and getting out of Westminster. Being half Geordie I always gravitated to the north-east.

I also went to Manchester and Luton and I attended the party conference in Birmingham. But I was struggling with the closed-shop attitude of Kate and Andrew. So much so that during Christmas 2011, I talked to Fiona about resigning. I felt I was just being used (now there's a first in politics). I felt they just wanted me for money, and I would only get invited to events when it suited them.

After sleeping on it I decided to carry on but to cut back on working for the party – to just turn up when I was expected and to write the odd cheque. I felt I was not welcome, but the bigger issue was supporting the party and a Conservative government, which is why I joined in the first place. However, it was not easy as I was being undermined continually at CCHQ and the two perpetrators were either doing it on purpose or too ignorant to realise what they were doing – probably a mixture of both.

Here are two examples.

In his book *Dirty Politics, Dirty Times*, Lord Ashcroft wrote about when he was Conservative Party treasurer and how he attended the Conservative Party spring conference, which was an annual meeting of Conservative Party volunteers and senior politicians. Traditionally the Prime Minister attends the spring conference as it shows support for the people who do so much work unpaid for the party. Also, it gives the PM a chance to talk about strategy and engage with the people who do much of the campaigning.

One day in early March 2012, I picked up the newspaper and was surprised to see that the Conservative Party spring conference had gone ahead. It was the first I knew of it because I hadn't been invited. As a Conservative Party board member, I attended voluntary party board meetings to see if I could support and help the voluntary party in any way. When I pointed this out to Andrew Feldman, he apologised and said he should have invited me. He then said it wasn't necessary for me to attend but my response was that Stanley Fink when he was treasurer had been invited the previous year and at least he could have given me the choice.

On another occasion, in December 2011, there was a grand presentation at CCHQ by Andrew Feldman and Stephen Gilbert, the No. 10 strategy adviser. I was invited to the presentation and the invitation wording implied that I was expected to attend, and it was important.

I turned up at 5 p.m. at CCHQ and Andrew and Stephen gave a good presentation on how we could win the next general election, even though it was more than three years away. Their proposal was to recruit eighty part-time ground campaigners that would go around knocking on doors and gathering voting data that we could use when our general election ground campaign began. I thought it was an excellent idea and I was supportive.

But it was the first I had heard of it as it was presented to me with the rest of the staff at CCHQ. I felt undermined because I was expected to raise the £1.6 million needed to fund the campaign managers yet I was being treated as just another team member. It was also embarrassing for me as many of the treasurers' team at CCHQ had only learnt about it at the presentation. They were asking me about it, because they assumed that I had been part of the process. But unfortunately, I only knew as much as them: what we learnt at the presentation. Kate Rock seemed well-informed and answered a lot of staff questions, but that only further undermined my position. I had not been briefed, consulted or asked, and yet as senior treasurer I was expected to know and plan future funding requirements, especially as it is part of the treasurer's role to fund any shortfall at the end of the financial year.

Indeed, a few weeks later at our year-end treasurers' meeting I wrote another cheque for £100,000 to balance the year-end accounts. This was in addition to the £100,000 I donated in August 2011 to balance the books then. It felt as though the party were writing cheques on my account and informing me after the event.

There were many more occasions of me being undermined and they are not worth bothering with here because it is all water under the bridge. However, I felt that there was an undercurrent at CCHQ that I didn't fit in and it seemed primarily to emanate from Andrew and Kate as I got on well with most of the team at CCHQ.

I felt that I was paying £750,000 for the privilege of being treated like I was a nobody. To me it felt like snobbery.

Kate and Andrew were secure in their roles as they had the party's number one and number two backing them, so they must have felt they could not be challenged. They went back a long way with Cameron and Osborne, they had all been on a long political journey together. Andrew was backing David Cameron long before he became leader and Prime Minister and long before I was on the scene. I had no problem with this unless it undermined my position, which it did frequently. There was no justification to treat me with contempt.

However, I always felt it was wrong for the PM to have one of his best friends running CCHQ. I was worried that in the long term it would damage the Prime Minister. It was not personal to Andrew, it was just the situation.

I thought Andrew was good at raising money for the party, but I felt that, at times, his advice was not impartial. It was as if his major role was to watch the PM's back regardless of what was the right thing to do for the party. Time would tell and it did.

In 2012, Stanley Fink had told me twice that he was ready to step down so I could be the senior treasurer instead of co-treasurer, and on at least one occasion he asked me if I was ready to take over on my own. My response was, 'You have to speak to Andrew Feldman about this, but I am ready to step up.'

Andrew approached me and confirmed that Stanley was ready to step down. Stanley had done more than his bit for the party and is one of the most loyal Conservatives I have ever met.

The party had already asked me to step down from two charitable roles that I had – director of the Prince's Trust and chairman of Youth United. Their argument was that there was a conflict of interest because the Prince's Trust was receiving government donations. I did not agree with this, but I accepted it. I was not happy about it, especially as I was one of the biggest private donors to the Prince's Trust and I enjoyed the role and I loved the charity.

I explained to Andrew that once Stanley had stepped down, I wanted to be treasurer solely on my own. Andrew said he would discuss it with the Prime Minister. A few weeks later, he said that he had done this, and David wanted two treasurers along with two chairmen.

What Andrew may have actually said to the Prime Minister I simply do not know. I said I was disappointed with the decision but 'what David wants, David gets'. Mike Farmer stepped up to be co-treasurer with me. Mike was good to work with, a thoroughly decent bloke and I liked him.

I wasn't sure if the decision to appoint Mike Farmer was Andrew's or the PM's. I suspect it was Andrew's decision alone. But that was okay because it was Andrew's job to keep the money rolling in and having Mike Farmer on board made good financial sense.

However, I had my concerns about having two chairmen and two treasurers. I always felt that the PM needed a strong, independent person running CCHQ because it was the job of the party chairman to look out for the party and feed back to the Prime Minister any concerns. Andrew was not perceived to be independent by most of the party faithful, including some of the parliamentary party (MPs).

On many occasions in the past, the chairman has stood up to the party leader for the good of the party and its members. I couldn't imagine Andrew doing this and I felt this was bad for the PM.

At conference, for example, candidates and constituency chairmen would dance around being nice to Andrew hoping that it would curry favour and get passed onto the Prime Minister. They saw Andrew as a direct route to the PM and, although this might be helpful sometimes, mostly it meant that people were just sucking up to Andrew for political gain.

This to me is not how the party should run itself, because people need to be honest with each other around important party issues, not to use meetings as an opportunity to be nice to the PM's friend. While the PM had one of his best friends in control at CCHQ, the system between the party and its leader was, I felt, dysfunctional.

As a businessman, I see this type of dysfunctional structure all the time. That was why I was concerned while working for the party – to me it stuck out like a sore thumb. If I had become sole treasurer, I might have been able to change this, we will never know. I would not necessarily have tried to get Andrew doing another job, but I would have given him advice, support and guidance on some issues around how the party was run daily.

My major concern was for David Cameron and keeping him as PM for as long as possible. I felt things would come to a head sometime in the future, as they always do in business. Often in business, people are building up their own support mechanisms by promoting their friends. This leads to an atmosphere of 'who do you support to avoid being sacked', rather than promoting people on merit and being open to challenge on issues. Effectively you must pick a side to support regardless of the merits of one side or the other. It is all about building a friendship for protection and nobody wins if you surround yourself with sycophants.

In this scenario, often there is a lack of challenge at key moments and for me in business (and in life) meritocracy wins every time. Anything else eventually fails as performance levels drop and businesses under-perform.

The structure at CCHQ and the friendship between Cameron and Feldman was storing up trouble for the future. Trouble usually comes at the moment you least expect it – when you are riding high, and in time I was proven to be right. But little did I know the first bit of trouble from party dysfunctionality would put me on the front line between the Prime Minister, David Cameron, the co-chairman, Andrew Feldman, and a major accusation by the *Sunday Times*.

Chapter 36

TALK ABOUT A STITCH-UP

In early March 2012, I was on a business trip to Sydney and speaking to my PA, Sofia, in London when she said there was a request from Sarah Southern for me to meet two big potential donors who wanted to donate to the Conservative Party. I was still Conservative Party co-treasurer, alongside Mike Farmer.

Sarah and I worked together on the No2AV campaign, and she was one of the senior people on the team. Sarah was young but politically savvy and we got on well, even though she is a bit feisty. She can hold her own on any subject and does not suffer fools gladly. But she is a nice person with a big heart, and I liked her. We were also kindred spirits because she is a Geordie. But since the No2AV campaign, we had lost contact and I had no idea what she was doing.

Sarah wanted to bring the two big donors into my offices in the City of London as they were financial people and they were talking about million-pound donations. I thought this was good news as Sarah was a Conservative, she knew the party well and she was bringing two big potential donors to me directly. However, I was not dazzled by the potential of a big donation. I knew not many people would match what I was donating to the Conservative Party, there was no need for me to chase donors.

Also, other potential donors could see that I was a big donor, as it was all public knowledge. All political donations above £7,500 must be declared to the Electoral Commission. They are then published every quarter on the commission's website, so it was easy for me to show potential donors how much I had given. It's hard to ask a donor for, say, £100,000 when you are only giving £5,000 yourself. Big donors must be met by other big donors to be on the same level. Or at least that was the thinking at CCHQ.

I told Sofia that I was not prepared to see anybody unless it was cleared specifically by CCHQ and their compliance team. I asked her to discuss this with Sarah Southern and to email CCHQ for compliance checking. Once cleared, I would see the two potential donors in my role as party treasurer when I returned to London a few weeks later.

By the time I returned to London, there was a message from Sarah that it had all been cleared with CCHQ and that I was free to see the two new potential donors. This was the first contact I had had with Sarah since our No2AV days around a year earlier.

All I knew before seeing the two potential donors was that they had been cleared by CCHQ and they were potentially big donors. Regarding their background, I had two names that meant nothing to me. I didn't know they were supposedly representing a big hedge fund of Middle East investors and they were working out of Liechtenstein. Their company was said to be called Global Zenith. This turned out to be fictitious. But none of that made much difference at the time because I had been informed that they had been cleared by CCHQ and wanted to help the Conservative Party and assumed that the appropriate checks had been made.

However, it turned out that the two donors were not donors at all. They were undercover *Sunday Times* investigative journalists and they were out for a story, come what may. CCHQ knew I was meeting these people and they believed they were potentially big donors. Sarah had told me that she had cleared it all with CCHQ. But in fact, CCHQ hadn't bothered to compliance-check the two individuals and didn't even ask for their names and addresses.

A simple check by the compliance team would have shown that the two supposed donors were not on the electoral roll and they didn't exist in the UK because, in fact, they were using false names. They could have been donating in a company's name but all CCHQ had to do then was check to see if the company was UK registered. It was simple and the message I got was that I was clear to meet them.

Sarah Southern had worked at CCHQ for a few years herself and she knew the rules and regulations around donations. Sarah was still close to the compliance team at CCHQ and she spoke to them about bringing in the two donors. The Cameron family trusted Sarah; her party piece was to tell people how she used to babysit for Samantha and David Cameron when she worked at CCHQ and the Conservatives were in opposition.

To be fair to CCHQ, it wasn't necessary for them to completely compliance-check anybody until a donation was pledged or received. However, I would have been reasonable to expect them to check for any potential non-compliance donations by doing some very basic and simple tests, for example establishing the name of the donors or the company that was donating. During my time at CCHQ, there were a few occasions when cheques were not cashed because the donors could not donate due to residency issues; or they were not on the electoral roll; or they were politically sensitive. Also, some had dubious connections and one had a criminal record overseas.

The Conservative Party were always very diligent around who they took money from and strict around compliance check-ing. They always maintained high standards and even though they didn't bother to compliance-check the people who came to see me, there was logically no need to do it until a cheque or pledge was received. Kate Rock and Andrew Feldman were always strict about this and if there was anything remotely suspicious, they said no. They were, after all, there to protect their friends over at No. 10 and No. 11 Downing Street and they were fiercely loyal.

Anyway, on 15 March 2012, Sarah Southern and the two 'potential donors' turned up at CMC Markets and we met in my office to chat about donating. The meeting was relaxed, and we chatted about lots of things including football, business and the current political situation.

The two donors explained that they worked in Liechtenstein for an investment company and that they wanted to go to events where they could meet David Cameron and other senior party members to 'put across their points of view'.

I could write a whole separate book on this meeting – about what was said and what was meant. But to make sure there was no confusion about what they could and could not do, I explained to them the rules of donating.

I handed them a copy of the Conservative Party brochure that said: 'The Leader's Group is the premier supporter group of the Conservative Party. Members are invited to join David Cameron and other senior figures from the Conservative Party at dinners, lunches, drinks receptions, election result events and important campaign launches. Annual membership is £50,000.' The brochure was signed by David Cameron himself. The two donors asked if they could keep the brochure and they left with it.

During the meeting, there were lots of requests from them about being top donors. Keeping on the football theme that we had discussed before, I told them that to get into the premier league they would have to donate in the region of £250,000. I made it clear that all donations above £7,500 would appear on the Electoral Commission website and be public knowledge and that, before they could donate, they would need to be compliance-cleared by CCHQ. Whether donations were accepted or not was completely out of my hands.

I said I would always look after them at events and they would be able to have their photograph taken with the PM and Chancellor. They would get a chance to bid for auction prizes at our big events like the Black and White Party. That was all I could promise them as everything else was beyond my control.

I also explained that their British company could make a donation as many businesses donate to the Conservative Party. For example, at its annual conference, there is a business day for which all UK-registered businesses can buy a ticket and attend speeches and fringe group meetings with politicians and senior party members. There is a grand dinner in the evening attended by the Prime Minister or the Chancellor. Usually, the Prime Minister hosts a lunch as part of the business day ticket which for the past few years has been sponsored by Bloomberg. I have been on a few of them myself. These tickets are available to everybody, whether you are a party donor or not. Journalists attend these events and pay for a ticket. We even get trade unions buying tickets for some of their officials.

It was a normal thing within the party for me as treasurer to meet potential donors. What is not allowed is political lobbying by donors, but that was all academic as the two individuals had not yet donated and I didn't even know if they would be found to be fully compliant when CCHQ carried out their final complete compliance checks.

Some readers of this book will have seen the headlines later that month – 'Tory treasurer offers access to Prime Minister for

£250,000' – and drawn their own conclusions at the time. However, as the story broke it was clear that I had been being filmed covertly and the viewers only saw about thirty seconds of a cut-and-pasted video that had been recorded over a one-hour meeting.

What the video didn't show was the meeting ending with me telling the two individuals to meet with Mike Chattey (compliance officer) at CCHQ to get their company cleared for donations and I would follow up with them once CCHQ had cleared their donations. The thirty-second video also didn't show me explaining they couldn't make third-party payments or anything that could potentially be illegal or not allowed under electoral law.

Of course, there will always be sceptics around my version of events and whether there was any intention to offend on my part or whether I committed an inchoate offence. So here is what the Electoral Commission and the police made of the allegations after watching the full video recording of the meeting.

Electoral Commission decision on *Sunday Times* allegations
The Electoral Commission has concluded its assessment of allegations that Sarah Southern, Peter Cruddas or the Conservative Party breached donation law.

The Commission found no evidence to support the allegations and will not be opening an investigation into the matter.

During our assessment, we looked at comments made by Sarah Southern and Peter Cruddas in a meeting on 15 March 2012 with *Sunday Times* journalists, posing as representatives of a fictitious company based in Liechtenstein.

The journalists discussed making donations to the Conservative Party. For an offence to be committed under the Political Parties, Elections and Referendums Act (PPERA), a real arrangement to assist the making of impermissible donations has to be in place, as opposed to a fictitious one.

We will not be opening an investigation into the matter; however, the police are assessing whether any other criminal offences, outside the Commission's remit, have taken place.

The police sent the following letter to me on 3 September 2012.

Detective Inspector (name withheld) Special Enquiry Team Metropolitan Police.

An allegation of crime was recently made to the Metropolitan Police Service concerning the contents of an article published by the *Sunday Times* on 25 March 2012. This allegation referred to the activities of yourself and Ms Sarah Southern.

I elected to conduct a proportionate assessment of this allegation based on the material generated by the *Sunday Times* newspaper.

Having now reviewed this allegation, I conclude there is no evidence of any criminal conduct on the part of yourself or Ms Sarah Southern, either directly or by implication during the course of the *Sunday Times* investigation. I also conclude that no inchoate offences have been committed. My assessment is now complete unless further evidence comes to light.

The police were compelled to investigate the matter because a character called Mark Adams, who was a former aide to Tony Blair and John Major at No. 10 Downing Street, had turned up at Scotland Yard the day the article had been published and complained to the police that I had committed a criminal offence.

I have never been in trouble with the police apart from the odd speeding ticket and it was horrible to see Adams standing outside Scotland Yard telling the waiting press that he had just complained to the police to add effect and throw more fuel on the fire. Why the press was there in the first place is a mystery. I am sure it was pure coincidence.

Also, on 25 March 2012, the day the article was published, Adams had published another article in the *Sunday Times* alongside the main one, saying that the Conservative Party was rotten to the core and so was I. But that was not the end of Adams's exploits, because he began writing blogs saying that I was a criminal and I should be banged up and he would be calling me a criminal every day until I sued him. Once I got the letter from the police, that is exactly what I did and I won my case and I was awarded damages of £45,000 and costs.

He refused to pay, and the amount kept building up due to interest charges and more legal fees. Eventually he owed me over £240,000, which I recovered through the sale of his home. It was £241,981.15 to be precise.

I have no sympathy for Adams because he had plenty of time to apologise and withdraw his accusations against me after the *Sunday Times* filed a defence that claimed that I had not done anything criminal and they were not accusing me of criminal behaviour. My lawyers even sent him a copy of the letter from the police. I said if he withdrew his remarks and apologised then that would settle it. However, Adams persisted in calling me a criminal. He could have avoided losing his home by apologising and withdrawing his remarks. But he didn't so he paid the price.

Now, before the reader gets too teary-eyed about some rich, hard-nosed businessman evicting an ex-civil servant who served two Prime Ministers and was awarded an OBE – Mark Adams was convicted on 16 January 2019 of raping a teenage girl. He was then convicted on 26 February 2019 of raping a young lady in her twenties. In both cases the victims were asleep. Following these two convictions Mark Adams was stripped of his OBE in disgrace.

He was convicted twice for rape within one month and is serving at least seven years in prison – and he called me a criminal!

He was not the only person to come out on the losing side of this sorry event.

Chapter 37

LET THE STITCH-UP BEGIN

Following the meeting with the two journalists, I emailed CCHQ and told them of a pending £250,000 donation and that I had sent the two donors away to arrange a meeting with Mike Chattey, before they sent their money. Sarah said she would arrange the meeting with Mike as they were ex-colleagues. In my email, I asked Mike to contact me once the donors had been cleared, so I could follow up with them in the next week or so.

On Saturday 24 March 2012, nine days after my meeting with the undercover journalists, around 4 p.m., I was just about to leave my home in Park Lane to feed my daughter's cats, when my mobile phone rang. The voice was vaguely familiar, but I didn't twig that it was one of the potential 'donors' I had met the previous week.

The caller said she was Heidi Blake, a journalist with the *Sunday Times*, and that they were running a story the next day claiming that I was facilitating illegal payments to the Conservative Party. She said I had met two employees of a Liechtenstein company, called Global Zenith, the previous week and that I had told them about ways of circumventing the Electoral Commission rules on donating to the Conservative Party. She asked if I had any comments.

My response was, 'You must be joking. I did no such thing and I have no idea what you are talking about.'

I immediately emailed Andrew Feldman at CCHQ about the phone conversation and then went out to feed the cats. My two youngest children were by then twenty-four and twenty-six and they were living in their own places. My youngest had two darling little cats called Poppy and Tippy that I needed to feed as the girls had gone to Rome for the weekend with my wife.

While I was on my way to the cats, I rang Fiona and told her what had happened. She was worried and asked me if I was in trouble. I said, 'Absolutely not. I haven't done anything wrong and why would I do something illegal when the money involved is nothing compared to our wealth? Let's see what the article says but I am sure it will be a load of nonsense.'

She joked, 'Well, that may be the case but don't count on anybody at CCHQ backing you up. You are not part of the clique.'

This did cause me a moment of concern. Anyway, I said, 'Don't worry about it and I will watch the news tonight at 9 p.m. to see what is being said.'

We then exchanged pleasantries and I told her I was off to take care of the cats and I would give them a kiss from her and the girls.

Shortly afterwards, my phone rang, and it was Mike Chattey. He asked what was going on and I told him that I met the two potential donors. Mike said, 'Ah, those must be the two people Sarah Southern called me about.'

I said to Mike that I was not in the least bit worried as I had played it completely straight at the meeting and I had explained everything to them and, anyway, I asked them to come to CCHQ before they donated.

Mike said, 'Yes, I got your email and I have been waiting for them to get back to me.'

I told Mike I had given them the brochure and left it that they were going to see him before they made any payments. Mike said that Sarah had already been in contact shortly after the meeting and she was trying to pin them down to a day and time.

Andrew Feldman also called and asked what happened. I told him what I had told Mike Chattey and his response was, 'Well, we are digging around but we're getting nothing out of the press so we will just have to wait and see.' He said, 'Let's talk around 9 p.m. when the story breaks,' which is how we left things.

That was it, I wasn't at all worried, but then I got a call from the No. 10 press officer, who asked me what had happened. I told him what I had told Mike Chattey. He confirmed that nobody was saying anything, they were all tight lipped. He said we would have to wait until nine o'clock that night to see what the story was. He finished the conversation with 'Good luck'.

I thought, 'Bloody hell, talk about being on your own when you get involved with politics.' He didn't even know the story and was already sending out signals that I was on my own. It would have been nice if he had said, 'Don't worry, Peter, we know you are a straight guy. If it's bad, we can see what we can do to help you to sort any mess out.' But all I got was 'Good luck'.

I pottered around for a few hours waiting for the 9 p.m. news headlines, thinking, 'I am glad Fiona and the girls are outside the country because it looks like there will be some flak flying around, but hey, that's politics.'

Little did I know that the shit was going to hit the fan and at 9 p.m. it hit it hard and it was flying everywhere!

Chapter 38

WHY LET THE FACTS GET IN THE WAY OF A GOOD STORY?

On Sunday 25 March 2012, the *Sunday Times* headlines read: 'Tory treasurer charges £250,000 to meet PM'; '200 grand, 250 is premier league … it'll be awesome for your business'.

There was a picture of myself and David Cameron posing together.

The article said, 'The offer was made even though he [Cruddas] knew the money would come from a fund in Liechtenstein that was not eligible to make donations under election law.'

Further on in the paper there was another headline, 'Cash for access to PM'.

Later that day on television, David Cameron was stopped on a fun run in his running gear. He said, 'We do not raise money in the Conservative Party this way, it is quite right that Peter Cruddas has resigned.'

I have often wondered why the press gave so much credence to a story that was based on a one-hour meeting and nothing else. The story was weak because there was no donation made and there were no follow-up meetings by the journalists. I was not a government official; I was a volunteer that worked for free and donated UK tax-paid money to my political party.

Also, if there was some illicit activity by me and the headlines were true then there were much bigger fish to fry, especially if the Conservative Party was complicit in some way – that would have been bombshell stuff. If true, it could have brought down the Prime Minister and maybe the government, because it would have meant that the ruling party were indulging in criminal activity to fund their political ambitions and the buck would stop with the leader. It would have led to a crisis of confidence in the Conservative Party, who were the government.

What I also found strange, at the time, was that I was expecting my phone to ring off the hook from the media trying to pin me down and get me in front of a television camera and hear my side of the story. I was expecting some photographers to be outside my home but there was nothing. I also didn't receive one phone call on Sunday 25 March after the story broke from any journalist, or television or radio station.

Around 12 noon, I left my apartment in a bit of a daze. I walked across Hyde Park and sat in Harrods at the Italian restaurant with the singing pizza chef. I was surrounded by people, as it was standing room only. Apart from messages from friends and family and speaking to my wife and a few friends on the phone, I didn't get a call from anybody. It was all a bit surreal.

The Conservative Party didn't want to hear my side of the story. The previous evening, as the headlines broke, ahead of the publication of the *Sunday Times* story the next day, Andrew Feldman, the Conservative Party co-chairman, had called me at around 9.30. His first words were 'This is bad' and 'David is not happy'. My immediate response was, 'I suppose I have to resign,' and Andrew said, 'Yes, I am afraid you have to.' That was our first conversation after the story broke. Andrew Feldman did not once ask me for my version of events and he still hasn't to this day.

I said to Andrew, 'I will resign. Please put together a statement and issue it.' Which is what he and the Conservative Party did.

While I was speaking to Andrew, my wife was holding on the other line upset. She was wanting to speak to me from Rome where she had just finished dinner with the girls and was watching Sky News in their hotel room.

On the Sunday morning, Michael Fallon, a Conservative Cabinet minister, appeared on the Dermot Murnaghan show on Sky TV. Fallon was toeing the Prime Minister's line that my actions were inappropriate and unacceptable.

Murnaghan asked Fallon if he had ever met me and Fallon replied 'Not knowingly', which made me laugh because if Fallon had asked Murnaghan the same question, he would have had to reply, 'Yes, I met Cruddas as he invited me into his box at Arsenal Football Club a few months ago to watch the Manchester United game.' It did make me smile on an otherwise gloomy day.

As Sunday 25 March wore on, my head began to clear, and I was starting to think about the meeting I had with the journalists. The more I thought about it, the more I felt I had not done any of the things the newspaper claimed, and I was starting to feel less upset and confused and more angry. Here I was, a successful businessman, working for the Conservative Party, that I supported, meeting people who they were supposed to make sure were compliant. The next thing I know, the Prime Minister is on the television criticising me and defaming me vicariously for something I didn't do. I started to think about my next move.

That was the moment I decided I was going to do something

about it. I wasn't going to take this whole thing lying down and my first instinct was to go on television and be interviewed. But before I did anything, I rang a lawyer friend to get his advice and I am glad I did.

He said if I was going to sue the *Sunday Times* and the Prime Minister then I should say nothing to the press and media. I should keep my powder dry. He was worried that if I declared I was going to sue the *Sunday Times* for libel, the tape recordings of the interview might be 'accidentally' deleted.

He said without the full tape recordings of the meeting, it would be my word against theirs and much harder to prove. Also, as the paper had already published the story it would be hard to swing momentum in my favour. The best thing I could do was write down as much as I could remember of the meeting. Then we would meet the following week to discuss what happened next.

My lawyer friend also said that, if my version of events was true, I would have a claim against the sitting Prime Minister for libel – that would be explosive and I should not discuss this with anybody except my legal team. So, I kept my head down and said nothing while I decided what to do next. It was not easy being criticised without any chance to defend myself in the media. Nobody wanted to hear my side of the story anyway, but it was still hard.

Things were to get worse. The next day, there was an emergency debate in the House of Commons to discuss specifically my so-called illegal activities of raising funds in contravention of electoral law and selling access to the Prime Minister in return for donations. David Cameron stood aside from this debate and Cabinet minister Francis Maude represented the government.

I remember sitting in my office watching the MPs debating the *Sunday Times* story. The debate was like a feeding frenzy of politicians ready to give the Conservatives and me a good kicking regardless of whether the story was true or not. I found the whole thing ridiculous because not one person from the House of Commons had asked me for my version of events. It was just assumed that because it was in the *Sunday Times* the story must be true.

It would not have been difficult for the political elite, especially the Liberal Democrats, to try and find some evidence around the credibility of the story and in particular the credibility of one of the journalists. The Liberal Democrats had already complained to the Press Complaints Commission about Heidi Blake's behaviour back in 2010. Now they were supporting her story, apparently satisfied that she was a credible reputable journalist.

Heidi Blake was one of the journalists whose conduct had been the subject of a separate adjudication and upheld complaint by the Liberal Democrats when she worked for the *Daily Telegraph*. The complaint was lodged in late 2010 by Liberal Democrat president Tim Farron MP after undercover reporters from the newspaper secretly recorded Business Secretary Vince Cable claiming that he had 'declared war' on News Corporation owner Rupert Murdoch. At the time, Cable was responsible for deciding whether News Corp should be allowed to take full control of BSkyB.

The Liberal Democrats had complained about Cable being filmed covertly. Yet here were the same Liberal Democrats attacking the government for the things that were alleged I had said while being covertly filmed by the same journalist. What hypocrites! You couldn't make it up.

I couldn't understand why politicians, especially the Liberal Democrats, were wasting taxpayers' money debating a story that with the minimum of digging would have found its credibility under question and certainly not worth debating until more evidence had been found. Clearly, there was political capital in embarrassing the Prime Minister and they regarded it as fair game, regardless of the facts and what damage it did to me. They didn't care that they were trashing my reputation. At the same time, I couldn't help thinking that David Cameron had poured fuel on the fire for his knee-jerk reaction and for not establishing the facts before his comments on television the day the story broke. He laid the foundations for this frenzied attack on my character. He later told me in an 'apology' meeting at No. 10 that he hadn't thought about the consequences when he made those comments.

As the story and the attacks on me and the Conservative Party rumbled on, the Prime Minister decided to set up an 'independent' inquiry – called the Gold Inquiry. Lord Gold, a lawyer who was a Conservative peer, headed the inquiry to get to the bottom of the facts – more about that later.

During the rest of the weekend, I kept thinking about the conversation I had with my lawyer friend. He said to me that he didn't understand why the right-leaning press were jumping all over the story alongside the left-leaning press. He said, sure, the left-leaning press always had plenty to say about the Conservatives, especially if it was bad news. But why were the *Telegraph*, *Daily Mail* and *Times* all jumping on the bandwagon? More specifically, why was the *Sunday Times* trying to damage David Cameron and the Conservative Party?

His point was that this seemed to be a cross-press campaign to discredit the Conservative Party and the Prime Minister. He said it was like the brethren were sticking together and closing ranks. All any half-decent journalist had to do was pick up a Conservative Party donors brochure and they would see, written in black and white – if you join the Leader's Group for £50,000, you can have dinner with the Prime Minister and other senior people.

My friend said if it was the *Sunday Mirror* having a pop at the Conservatives, he could understand it. But surely the right-leaning press should be trying to play it down, not stick the knife in. I had my own theory about this, and my lawyer friend tended to agree.

Chapter 39

LET THE FIGHTBACK BEGIN

Fiona returned on Sunday evening, 25 March, and it was not a pleasant evening. I was feeling embarrassed and upset and I didn't feel like facing my wife and kids. The girls had gone back to their own apartments and Fiona returned home minus a gift for me.

I wanted to get away from it all to clear my head and decide what to do next. I had a cunning plan – one I thought Fiona would not be able to resist. How wrong could I be!

I offered to take her away for a few days to her favourite place, the Hotel Splendido at Portofino, Italy. I thought Fiona would jump at the chance, but I was totally wrong. She was very firm and looked me straight in the eye and said, 'Peter, did you do anything wrong and did you do what the journalists accused you of?'

My response was instant, I said, 'Of course not.'

She said, 'Well then, you can go to work tomorrow and walk into your office with your head held high. Show your staff that you are strong and that you will not be running away from any of this. This is not just about you; this is also about your company and the people that work for you.

'You have thirteen offices around the world, a charitable foundation and 800 staff. If you don't show up on Monday morning, they

LEFT 85 Bracklyn Court, Hoxton, where I lived up until the age of six.

BELOW Twins on the beach, on holiday in Jaywick Sands. Stephen, the elder by ten minutes, is on the left; I'm on the right.

LEFT 14 Vince Court, Brunswick Place, N1, where I moved when I was six.

On a Hoxton Market Christian Mission day trip to High Rocks, Tunbridge Wells, aged eleven, with my oldest friends, the Hill brothers. I am in front of Roy Hill, who is at the back wearing glasses. John Hill is in front of me. John and I were making funny faces. William is the tall person in a white shirt next to the tree.

My first trip abroad, to Lloret de Mar, Spain, aged eighteen. I am on the far left.

With Brunswick Albion – the Invincibles – on Hackney Marshes, 1973. I am second from right, standing. Stephen, my twin, is the goalkeeper. John is on the far right, crouching down in the front.

Amsterdam weekend, aged twenty. I'm on the far left, with John Hill next to me.

ABOVE With the beautiful XJS, my first really powerful car. Outside TOTS nightclub in Southend-on-Sea, looking super-cool in my mid-twenties and single.

LEFT In black tie and with hair, aged thirty-two. At Harrods restaurant for an American Express charity event.

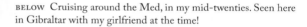

BELOW Cruising around the Med, in my mid-twenties. Seen here in Gibraltar with my girlfriend at the time!

My first holiday with Fiona, a Caribbean cruise in 1986.

Winning Golfer of the Year 1990 at Orsett Golf Club.

A trip to Wall Street to visit our office, 1996. Looking relaxed in my Giorgio Armani suit and tie.

The early days of CMC Markets, 1997, my first office. Note the old phone systems and the size of the computer monitors.

On holiday with Fiona and the girls, chilling on a speedboat, mid-1990s.

A trip to Egypt with Salem Chalabi, who is taking the photo. Salem is a cousin of Hussein Chalabi.

ABOVE Off to Australia for business but dressed down in a T-shirt ready for the long flight, 2003.

LEFT My 50th birthday weekend in Monaco, with CMC's board of directors holding in their stomachs.

ABOVE LEFT AND RIGHT *Management Today*'s Entrepreneur of the Year 2007.

ABOVE 19 September 2019 after meeting the Prime Minister at 10 Downing Street, who offered me a peerage. I gratefully accepted.

RIGHT Our home in Mayfair.

will worry about you and their own future. Some of your people have been working for you for twenty years and they will want to know that you are alright and that you will not be going away any time soon.'

I thought, 'Bloody hell, she's right.' From that moment on, I was on the front foot and I began the fightback.

The next day I got up early, showered, put on my best suit, went into work with my head held high and carried on as normal. There was no way I was running away from all this.

As I got back to normal, my head started to clear, and I began to answer some of my own questions about what really happened at that meeting with the two journalists. One thing nagging away in my mind was that the press was united in its condemnation, all based on the allegations published by the *Sunday Times*, and a thirty-second tape recording of a one-hour meeting. It was almost as if other newspapers were plagiarising the *Sunday Times* story and heaping as much pressure on David Cameron as possible. So much so that the Prime Minister had been forced to make a statement in his running gear on the day the story broke, effectively causing him to endorse the story and defame me at the same time.

The story went way beyond the normal politics of attacking somebody from the other side of your political viewpoint in the press. This was a concerted campaign by all sides of the press, regardless of their politics. Then one word popped into my head – Leveson – and it all made sense.

Wikipedia describes the Leveson Inquiry as 'a judicial public inquiry into the culture, practices and ethics of the British press following the News International phone hacking scandal, chaired by Lord Justice Leveson, who was appointed in July 2011. A series of public hearings were held throughout 2011 and 2012.'

It felt like there were wider reasons for the press to report my story collectively and show a united front. David Cameron had already told Milly Dowler's family that he would implement the Leveson recommendations. Plus Hacked Off, the campaign group headed by actor Hugh Grant, were also trying to get press reform and pressuring ministers to implement the Leveson findings. The press needed to fight back ahead of the PM's planned evidence to the Leveson Inquiry in June 2012, just a few months after my story broke.

My feeling at the time was that if the press could dish some dirt on the Prime Minister ahead of the Leveson Inquiry and before the PM gave evidence, they could say to him, 'Don't tell us to get our house in order when you cannot even keep your own house in order. Look at your treasurer, he is raising money from dubious sources and you appointed him.' Across the front page of the *Sunday Times*, there was a picture of Cameron and me sitting together as if we were good mates and drinking buddies. It looked contrived as I do not remember having that picture taken with David Cameron, I certainly do not have a copy of it. It could have been a cut-and-paste job for all I know.

It also made sense to me as to why the press didn't want to hear my side of the story and dig a bit deeper. If I had spoken to the press, denied everything, and said I was going to sue, the story would have taken on a different meaning.

Once I had said that I was going to sue the *Sunday Times* for malicious falsehood and defamation, the press would have had to say 'Cruddas denies the allegations and is suing', so the story would then have become an 'alleged act of impropriety'. It could not have been reported in the same way and it would have become less of a weapon to use against the Prime Minister.

I have often thought should I have come out and defended myself when the story first broke in March 2012. I am still not sure if I should have but it probably wouldn't have made much difference at the time because the press were on a mission and I was just the stick to beat the Prime Minister with ahead of his evidence to the Leveson Inquiry.

Eventually, when I had my day in court and the journalists were found guilty of malicious falsehood and libel, it was barely reported by the media and what little coverage there was, was effectively designed to just embarrass David Cameron. Also, at the time my story broke, Cameron was already under pressure from his appointment of Andy Coulson as No. 10 communications director.

Coulson, who was previously the editor of the *News of the World*, was later jailed for conspiracy to intercept voicemails, known as phone hacking. Cameron had done his best to defend him after it was reported in the press that Coulson was working at the *News of the World* while phone hacking was going on. Cameron stuck by Coulson. That all backfired when, in January 2011, Coulson resigned because he said he couldn't do his job properly with all the media frenzy around phone hacking.

As soon as my story broke, I think No. 10 made a quick decision and decided that they couldn't have any more controversy and they just had no appetite to stand by me. They didn't even have the appetite to hear my side of the story. The decision was made quickly and delivered within minutes of the story breaking. Of course, I could be stretching my imagination around the events but that was my overriding feeling at the time.

Once I got on the front foot and I made it clear I was suing the *Sunday Times*, Heidi Blake and Jonathan Calvert for malicious falsehood and libel, things started to go my way. In February 2013,

Lord Ashcroft wrote this blog for ConservativeHome, the blog site which supports the Conservative Party but is independent of it:

Former treasurer Peter Cruddas wins another victory in his bid to clear his name

Peter Cruddas, the former Conservative Party treasurer, has received yet another boost in his ongoing legal battle to clear his name. Mr Cruddas was awarded, earlier this week, £45,000 in damages (plus costs) against Mark Adams, the lobbyist and blogger, whose original tip to the *Sunday Times* led to their undercover investigation against him.

Mr Adams has publicly apologised for wrongly – and repeatedly – accusing Mr Cruddas of breaking the law relating to political donations.

The comments from the High Court judge presiding over the hearing must have been music to the ears of Mr Cruddas, who is fighting a determined campaign to restore his name.

However, the same comments from Mr Justice Eady are embarrassing for the Conservative Party, which dumped its treasurer with great haste within hours of the paper's 'revelations' last year.

Mr Justice Eady said: 'The allegations of criminality against Mr Cruddas were false and he is entitled to have his reputation vindicated in that respect.'

The judge added: 'It emerges clearly from the transcript that Mr Cruddas did not suggest that donations could be made from a foreign source, or that the law could be circumvented by means of a "front" company, but rather he emphasised that it would be necessary to be above board and that any donations would have to be compliant with English law.'

I [Ashcroft] disclosed in my blog of 25 July 2012 that Mr Cruddas, a wealthy self-made businessman, was suing Times Newspapers Ltd and two of its journalists, Jonathan Calvert and Heidi Blake, over stories that alleged he had offered access to David Cameron in return for large donations to the party.

Mr Cruddas had been the victim of an old-fashioned newspaper sting after walking into a carefully laid trap: the journalists set up a fake organisation, with a fake website and other subterfuge, to meet him in the guise of being prospective donors to the party.

Later, I questioned whether the party had been a little too hasty in forcing Mr Cruddas to resign within hours of the newspaper hitting the streets on the evening of Saturday 24 March. In addition, I suggested the party hierarchy had been amiss in not thanking him for his many years of hard work and substantial donations that he had given to the party.

David Cameron, no less, was one of those who had been quick to criticise Mr Cruddas in March last year. The Prime Minister said: 'This is not the way that we raise money in the Conservative Party, it shouldn't have happened. It's right that Peter Cruddas has resigned.'

In the aftermath of the *Sunday Times*'s story, the party set up an internal inquiry under Lord Gold to look into funding, in general, and the allegations against Mr Cruddas, in particular. This inquiry has since been put on hold.

Belatedly, Mr Adams has now apologised for his actions. In a public statement, he said: 'I have to accept that I made an allegation that I could not then prove and, under the laws of the land, I am liable to pay damages to Mr Cruddas and bear the costs of his legal action. I'm sure you will understand that I won't comment much on the case. It is however clear from his evidence in open court that Mr Cruddas is aggrieved to have been told by the Prime Minister that his actions were "completely unacceptable".'

Mr Cruddas has now been cleared of wrongdoing by the Electoral Commission, the Metropolitan Police, and a leading High Court judge. The *Independent* newspaper has also apologised for its follow-up stories that accused him of acting illegally.

It will be up to a jury to determine whether the *Sunday Times* libelled Mr Cruddas. The paper will face allegations – which it is contesting – of 'selective' editing and distorting the facts. The paper will insist, interestingly, that it never accused Mr Cruddas of breaking the law.

However, I would suggest that if the court does find in Mr Cruddas's favour, he will be entitled to substantial damages for the very considerable suffering he has received at the hands of the paper.

Also, the Conservative Party may have to investigate and analyse its actions on the night of 24 March 2012. For, by forcing Mr Cruddas to resign without properly establishing the facts of what had happened, it increased the harm to his reputation, and effectively gave the green light to the media and to individuals like Mark Adams to wade into him.

Was the party guilty of abandoning – even betraying – one of its most loyal supporters in his time of need? These are legitimate questions that, in time, may require measured answers.

Chapter 40

TAMPERING OF EVIDENCE?

The starting point in clearing my name was to get a copy of the tape recording of the entire meeting between myself and the journalists. I appointed lawyers Slater and Gordon to act on my behalf and they wrote to the *Sunday Times*. The paper refused to let us have a copy of the tape recording. We wrote twice and both times we were denied a copy of the tape on the spurious grounds that it was private.

So we tried a different tactic – we wrote to the Press Complaints Commission (PCC). At the time, the PCC was also under pressure due to the ongoing Leveson Inquiry. There were question marks around the PCC's independence and whether it was fit for purpose.

This worked in my favour as obviously my case was very high profile. The *Sunday Times* had made very serious accusations in its articles which forced me to resign. Parliament had an emergency debate on cash-for-access and the *Sunday Times* story. There was also the pending 'independent' Gold Inquiry. The *Sunday Times* would have to supply the Gold Inquiry with a copy of the tape recording, otherwise it could be accused of obstructing the inquiry.

The Gold Inquiry wanted to speak to me about the meeting, so at the very least I would be entitled to see a copy of the tape recording before I spoke to them. There is no way the Gold Inquiry could have spoken to me if they had seen the tape and I hadn't. It would have made a complete mockery of the inquiry and my lawyers would not have allowed it.

Therefore, following my complaint to the PCC, the *Sunday Times* was instructed by the PCC to let me see a full copy of the tape recording of my meeting with the two journalists. This was effectively to see if I had a litigation case against the newspaper. The *Sunday Times* had little choice and allowed me to see the video but there were conditions. One was that we were not allowed to make a copy of the tape recording, just notes, and another was that the recording could only be viewed at the offices of the *Sunday Times*. However, I could take my lawyers, so we agreed a date.

On 14 June 2012, my team and I sat alone in a small office at the *Sunday Times* building in east London with access to a television screen and a video recorder where we watched the recording of our meeting.

Now, call me old-fashioned, but if a journalist records a meeting with me without my permission, I think I can do the same to them. So, I stuck my iPad under the television screen and recorded the soundtrack of the meeting. This was a breach of the terms of the *Sunday Times* permission. My covert recording was useful because it meant that we could issue a writ with over 100 pages of particulars of claim. The *Sunday Times* and the two journalists were furious that I disregarded their conditions, but my response was 'So sue me'. Of course, they never did. During the trial, Heidi Blake brought up the fact that I had broken the conditions, but the judge just smiled and ignored her. Also, my QC, Desmond Browne, just said 'Tough' and 'Did that man tape you without your permission? Ah diddums.'

Before viewing the tape for the first time, I wrote down everything I thought I had said at the meeting. I wanted to write down my version of events, and to do this before I saw the tape recording because it meant that I had my own recollection of the meeting without being influenced by the recording.

I entered the room with a view that the journalists had lied and completely distorted the facts of the meeting in their articles. I knew what I had said.

I wanted my lawyers to view the tape of the meeting so they would advise me if I had a case against the *Sunday Times* and the two journalists. Their job was to listen to the recording and compare it to the articles that were written.

Once we left the *Sunday Times* building, they said to me that I had a strong case and they would get my audio recording written up and would begin the legal process against the *Sunday Times*. They said that I had been completely stitched up by the articles.

When I was listening to the tape recording with my lawyers at the *Sunday Times* building, I kept stopping the main tape and saying to my lawyers, 'There is something missing from this bit of conversation.' I said they had cut out part of the sentence. I was shocked because I knew what I had said for the most part and I could tell instantly that the tape was not the full unedited tape. There were important things I had said that were missing from the tape we were watching.

If you listen to my iPad recording you can hear me stopping the main tape and speaking to my lawyers at various points as the iPad recording was running the whole time. I was telling my lawyers that the tape had been edited, and this was before I had compared the audio to my written notes.

Remember this was the first time I had seen the tape recording since our meeting and my thoughts of the meeting were still very fresh. Of course, I couldn't remember all the contents of a one-hour meeting, but I didn't need to. I could remember the important points, and these were the points that I thought were not reflected in the audio recording I was listening to in the *Sunday Times* offices.

When I got back to my office with my own copy of the audio recording on my iPad, I started checking it against my written notes.

The first thing to say is that in the discovery phase of the litigation, I learnt that the two journalists were both wired up with video recording cameras. I understand this is part of the editors' code of conduct, so a copy of the recording can be given to the victim if there is a court case. Also, a copy could be sent to the police, unedited, if there were criminal proceedings. It's also a good backup for the journalists, in case one recorder does not work.

In my case, the journalists claimed that they had accidentally deleted one copy of the taped meeting. Which was unfortunate for me but very fortunate for them because it meant that I could not compare the two tapes to check for tampering. There is no way you can edit two tapes so they match up exactly, because of the digital data that is recorded in the background. You can see the numbers via the tape device and on the tape.

Nevertheless, I thought, that's fine because I could compare the one remaining tape with the machine it was recorded on to check for possible tampering. However, the two journalists had hired the machine and returned it to the hire company after the second tape had been accidentally deleted and apparently it had been hired out again and they did not have access to it. Again, very unfortunate for me.

However, there was still another way of checking the last

original tape with the digital data. But when we tried to check the tape that was sent to me, it was not the original tape recording. It was a copy that had been uploaded onto a computer. It was a video recording of the tape recording of the meeting without any of the original digital data. This recording had its own digital data, but it was not from the original taped meeting. I can remember at the time thinking it was as if they were washing the original recording to erase the digital data and there was only one copy when there should have been two.

When we asked for the original tape, the response was that they didn't have it as all equipment had now been returned to the hire company with the original (deleted) tapes. It was therefore impossible to see whether the one recording we got was the exact unedited recording of the original meeting or just a video of an edited version of the meeting. I protested to my lawyers that I should be supplied with a copy of the original tape, but the lawyers said the journalists didn't have it so there was nothing we could do.

Now I remembered the advice of my lawyer friend on the night the story broke, when he said, 'Say nothing as the newspaper could easily delete the tape recording and then it is your word against theirs.' I am glad on reflection I took his advice.

However, we still had a video copy of the meeting, so we had one last chance to see if the tape recording submitted as evidence was edited. So, I commissioned a forensic expert to look through the tape and try to see if there were distortions that could prove that it was edited from the original.

The expert did find distortions and one was exactly at the spot where I had said something, but it was not on the tape. Instead, there was a distinct distortion and garbling of the conversation at this point. The sentence does not make sense because it appears some words are missing. I thought I had the smoking gun, but the expert said that without the digital data and the original tapes he could not swear in court that the tape had been edited even though he felt that there was clear evidence of tampering in his opinion.

I can only imagine why the original tapes were not submitted as evidence. I am not sure how easy it is to accidentally delete something like that because you always get a message along the lines of 'Are you sure you want to delete this?' When this point came up in court, I glared at Heidi Blake and she just smiled at me and looked away.

If I could have proven that the original tape had been tampered with, we would never have ended up in court. I tried hard to prove this point but, in the end, since I could not prove the original evidence had been deleted due to a washing of the recording, I was left with an uploaded tape recording and the word of the two journalists.

What I would say is that five separate judges found Heidi Blake and Jonathan Calvert guilty of malicious falsehood, after giving their evidence.

Chapter 41

SHOULD I SUE THE
PRIME MINISTER?

Once I saw the recording, my legal team and I had no doubt that I had been libelled by the article and it was an easy decision to sue the *Sunday Times*. I also sued the two individual journalists because they were there at the meeting and they had knowingly lied in the articles about me.

The less easy decision was whether I should sue the Prime Minister at the same time for defaming me with his comments on television. I thought about this a lot and I couldn't see much upside to suing David Cameron. I could only see it creating more publicity for my family and me. I also felt that suing the Prime Minister would be a gift for the press to deflect the attention away from my case against the *Sunday Times* to my case against him.

My view was that it was the two journalists that were to blame, and they should be the ones in the dock. The Prime Minister was just dealing with events after they occurred, even though he handled them badly. I also thought that my family and I had had enough press for one decade, so I decided to let the issue go and just concentrate on the *Sunday Times* litigation. I let the Prime Minister off the hook.

At the time, when I was thinking about all this, I felt that

Andrew Feldman, the party chairman, should have stepped forward and taken control of the situation. This would have allowed the Prime Minister to distance himself from the story and focus on more important issues. If Feldman had done this then Cameron could have taken the line that it was a party matter and that the chairman would deal with it and see Cruddas first thing the next morning. There would have been no need for the PM to get further involved. By not doing this it meant that he was pursued by the press to make a comment which could have led him to being implicated in a defamation trial.

Even if this is stretching things, the party chairman should have had a role to play as I reported to him, not to the Prime Minister. Feldman then could have gone on television and said something like, 'I will be asking for a full copy of the tape recording from the *Sunday Times* because there are wider accusations here of illegal funding, which is not just a Cruddas issue but also a party issue. I want to get to the bottom of the allegations.

'However, I can say categorically that the Conservative Party is fully compliant with donations and that we have not accepted any donations from any overseas companies. For the moment, Cruddas is suspended pending our viewing of the tape.'

It would have been nice to get some support from the people I had helped so much. Instead, they abandoned me completely, and the Prime Minister was effectively put into a very difficult position by not having the right structure operating at CCHQ. If ever there was a time when the chairman should have stepped forward as a shield for his Prime Minister, this was it.

When Andrew Feldman called me on the evening of Saturday 24 March, I offered my resignation there and then. I could have dug in and said I had done nothing wrong, but if the PM wanted me out and the chairman wasn't supporting me, then what was the point of carrying on?

I get that Cameron was angry and upset and wanted it dealt with straight away, especially as he had taken a lot of flak over the Andy Coulson affair. But this was a time when we needed clear heads and experienced thinking from the top of the party – if only to assess the situation and decide what the next move was. This should have been basic stuff.

It was not the time for a knee-jerk reaction. A bit of joined-up thinking from the chairman and the PM would have led them to realise that I was well capable of suing the newspaper and, if I did that, I would need to be kept onside. It was just binary thinking from the party without any contingency planning. The PM was left in a vulnerable position by the chairman's handling of the situation and his lack of basic logic. By not thinking laterally about any future outcome or fallout from what could happen.

Of course, this is my version of events and David Cameron and Andrew Feldman will have their own version of events, and at the end of the day Cameron did apologise to me. But I think it all probably boils down to the fact that Andrew Feldman did not like me, or he didn't think I was the right sort, and it was an opportunity to get rid of me. It might have been snobbery for all I know. But, by doing this, he left the party and more importantly the Prime Minister in a vulnerable position. It also underlined the dysfunctional nature of the party chairman being a close friend of the Prime Minister.

Because of the actions of Feldman and Cameron on the night the story broke, I became isolated from them. They cut me off almost instantly and made it difficult for them to find a way back and try to control the ongoing events as it became clear I was going to sue the *Sunday Times*.

There was an attempt to reach out to me a few months before the trial in July 2013 when I got a call from the queen bee herself, Kate Rock, Feldman's right-hand woman at CCHQ. Kate was all friendly and said she was speaking from the Cabinet Office, and would I like to attend the funeral of Lady Thatcher at St Paul's on 17 April?

I couldn't believe my ears because I had been completely cut off from CCHQ. Even the staff were sent a message asking them not to contact me.

Lady Thatcher was my hero and I immediately accepted the invitation. I was proud to attend the funeral. It was very kind and much appreciated but I was not invited for drinks afterwards with the Cabinet and the team from CCHQ. Still I felt honoured to be there and pay my respects to the great lady herself.

There were no other attempts to reach out to me before my trial.

Chapter 42

AGENTS PROVOCATEURS FACE THE MUSIC

My litigation trial for malicious falsehood and libel against Times Newspapers and the journalists Heidi Blake and Jonathan Calvert (the defendants) began at the Royal Courts of Justice on 2 July 2013 and lasted until 12 July with judgment handed down on 31 July.

The trial judge was the Honourable Mr Justice Tugendhat. The defendants' QC was Richard Rampton and my QCs were Desmond Browne and Matthew Nicklin.

As the trial got going and we were all in court, my QC and I bumped into Blake and Calvert on the stairs. I said to them, 'Where are you going? Don't you want to see your boss John Witherow squirm in the witness box?' Desmond added, 'Don't be long because you will miss the best bit.' They were not amused and quickly moved off, but it was a funny moment for my QC and me and we both laughed.

For me it was my time to fight back, for Blake and Calvert it was their time to face the music. I am quite sure they were not looking forward to the experience. There was every reason for them to feel uneasy as there was a lot worse to come for them. My QC's off-the-cuff remark would be nothing compared to what Mr Justice Tugendhat thought of them.

Here are extracts from the judge's summing up and conclusions after he handed down his judgment on 31 July 2013. If you want to read the full case you can find it under case number HQ12D03024, citation number [2013] EWHC 2298 (QB).

The judge said:

> I have set out what in my judgment is the true meaning of what was said at the meeting, which I have found after viewing the audio-visual recordings.
>
> As to the oral evidence, I accept the evidence of Mr Cruddas. Where it conflicts with his evidence, I reject the evidence of the defendants' witnesses.

Mr Justice Tugendhat said the use of the words 'awesome for your business' in the articles reflected the main thrust – for example, on the front page, the words '200 grand is premier league ... it'll be awesome for your business' appeared. The first article said: 'A co-treasurer of the Conservative Party was forced to resign early today after being filmed selling secret meetings with the Prime Minister in return for donations of £250,000 a year and boasting: "It will be awesome for your business."'

'To succeed in a claim in malicious falsehood, unlike libel, a claimant has to prove that the defendants were malicious,' said the judge. 'I have found that they were.'

The judge said the journalists entered the meeting, not with an open mind, but intending to prove a case. 'In their evidence to the court they were claiming that Mr Cruddas had given them encouragement that as donors they would get what they had been asking for, in cases where, in my judgment, what he had been doing was lowering their expectations, not assenting to what they asked.'

He continued:

> Mr Cruddas confirmed that, as members of the Leader's Group, they would not have a long meeting with Mr Cameron, except in the context of a social dinner, and in the presence of at least ten or so other donors ...
>
> Mr Cruddas made clear that they would not be able to influence policy which affected Global Zenith's business specifically, e.g. as a prospective contractor with the government.

The transcript demonstrates beyond doubt that, at the meeting,

> Mr Cruddas was describing how the Leader's Group works, and [that] the access he was offering to Mr Cameron and to other senior ministers ... was the kind of access which Mr Cameron was advertising in the brochure ...
>
> Mr Cruddas made clear what was not permitted at the private occasions on which donors met ministers. He said it was not permitted for them to attempt to obtain commercial benefits specific to their particular businesses. He said (in a passage from the transcript omitted from the [*Sunday Times*] articles): 'If you've got someone who's got a big government contract coming up and they want to talk to the Prime Minister about the contract terms, that ain't gonna happen ... There's no cash for access, there's no cash for honours, the party is really clean.' ...
>
> The false impression conveyed to readers by the articles was accentuated by the way in which the Leader's Group was referred to, and by the omission of statements which Mr Cruddas had

made at the meeting, which would have made clear what he was explaining to the international financiers, and that he was not contradicting himself ...

The articles do not explain that the fact that such meetings took place was public knowledge, as are the identities of large donors, and that what was secret was the identities of the particular donors who attended particular meetings, and what was said at those meetings.

The judge said that

in fact Mr Cruddas used the words 'premier league' to refer to those members of the Leader's Group who contributed six-figure sums. He did not say that there was a separate 'premier league' that a donor could join.

And the things that he explained would 'open up' were not information from, or private access to, the Prime Minister, but opportunities to buy tickets for expensive events where hundreds of other people would be present ... [Mr Cruddas] did not say that anyone could lobby the Prime Minister directly on issues that would give his business an unfair advantage.

'The articles mislead the readers by conveying the meaning that the benefits for their business will be benefits that come from meeting and lobbying Mr Cameron and other ministers,' said the judge. 'But the word "insider" was not used in the meeting, and Mr Cruddas made no statement that there was "insider information up for grabs". It is the journalists' inference that Mr Cruddas was referring to insider information. The inference could be their opinion, but it is not fact.'

The judge went on:

[Mr Cruddas] said: 'Unfortunately donating to a [political] party is not the most effective way to get your voice heard ... If you're unhappy about something you can, we can, we'll listen to you and we'll put it into the Policy Committee at Number 10. We feed all feedback into the Policy Committee ... But just because you donate money it doesn't give you a voice at the top table to change policy, that doesn't happen.'

No one could interpret that answer as Mr Cruddas saying that feeding their feedback into the Policy Committee would be awesome for their business. He was lowering their expectations, not raising them.

The journalists could

have an opinion as to the value of feeding donors' feedback into the Policy Committee, which is different from what Mr Cruddas said. But in quoting the words 'awesome for your business' they were not telling the reader that that was their opinion. They were falsely attributing to Mr Cruddas an opinion which he had not expressed on that topic.

The short video compilation of the undercover footage which the defendants sent to broadcasters at about 6 p.m. on Saturday 24 March, and to which they referred the reader of the articles by giving a web address, makes the same false point. In the first seconds it shows passages in which Mr Cruddas is shown to link the £200[,000]–£250,000 donation, the information, the confidential dinners with Mr Cameron and Mr Osborne, and the feedback to the Policy Unit. These quotes are followed by the video of Mr Calvert provoking Mr Cruddas with the words 'And it's good for business I mean'. Mr Cruddas answered 'It'll be awesome for your business.' The video goes on to show the viewer that Mr Cruddas said that the donor would get a photograph with David Cameron. But the video omits the next sentence in which Mr Cruddas made clear that the photograph was 'part of the ticket' which the donor would buy to get an invitation to a charity or fundraising event.

Conclusion

Mr Justice Tugendhat said:

For these reasons I find that, in relation to the first meaning, the corruption meaning, the defence of truth fails. The articles are untrue in relation to this meaning ...

The defendants have expressly stated that Mr Cruddas is a man of 'total integrity'. Apart from the matters which are the subject of this action, it has not been suggested that Mr Cruddas has ever broken any law or regulation, or that there has ever been any grounds to suspect or believe that he might have done that, or might have been willing to do that.

An unblemished reputation for honesty and integrity is, as is well known, of considerable importance to anyone engaged in providing financial services in the UK and elsewhere.

The judge noted that

Mr Cruddas has been a lifelong supporter of the Conservative Party ... He has established a charitable foundation and has stated that his intention is ultimately to give £100,000,000 to charitable causes. Some of those causes, and the sums he has donated, are set out in his witness statement.

The reputation of a deputy treasurer of the party is of critical importance and Mr Cruddas was informed that his background had been checked and nothing adverse had been found.

Mr Cruddas's reputation was, of course, also of importance in connection with the other charities and national institutions with which he became associated as a large donor. This is particularly true of his position with the Prince's Trust, in which role he had been invited to attend the Royal Wedding in 2011 ...

Mr Cruddas's evidence is consistent with what he wrote to Lord Feldman, Mr Chattey and others on 23 March. At that time he was expecting that a donation by a British company would be given clearance by the Compliance Department. He had no reason at that stage to say anything other than what he truly believed.

Mr Cruddas had repeatedly emphasised in the meeting that if a donation was to be made by a company it had to be a bona fide company. With his experience of establishing his own company's international operations, he was well placed to judge whether a bona fide British operating company was likely to be part of Global Zenith's structure. He was better placed to understand the implications of the journalists' cover story than they were.

Jonathan Calvert and Heidi Blake

The judge said:

There was no evidence or suggestion at any stage of the case that Mr Cruddas had ever considered a donation to the party from a foreign source before the meeting. The case included evidence as to how the journalists had obtained editorial approval for the use of subterfuge, in accordance with the PCC [Press Complaints Commission] code. If the journalists had had such evidence, and had not been merely fishing for evidence of a possible offence under PPERA [the Political Parties, Elections and Referendums Act] Section 61, then they would have been expected to produce that evidence in order to obtain approval of the proposal to use covert methods to investigate Mr Cruddas ...

The subsequent use of the foreign origin of the fake company to suggest a breach of PPERA Section 61 was not planned until late into the investigation. It was opportunistic.

Mr Calvert said in his witness statement that 'as co-treasurer of the Conservative Party ... [Mr Cruddas] had a duty to ensure all donations are within the law and I expected him to ask more about this secretive and complex web of international money we proposed to use for the donation, but he did not do so.' However, this simply demonstrates that Mr Calvert did not know what were Mr Cruddas's duties, and what were not. Mr Rampton did not challenge Mr Cruddas's evidence that checking compliance was the duty of CCHQ, and not part of his duties ...

Mr Calvert said in cross-examination that he did not know what the editor meant when on 30 November 2011 he said to the journalists to be mindful of not being in any way an *agent provocateur*. I did not believe that answer, and Mr Calvert did act as an *agent provocateur*, in relation to ... Mr Cruddas ...

Later, in his cross-examination, Mr Calvert declined to state whether he believed that Mr Cruddas was willing that the international financiers should make an illegal donation. When Mr Browne asked: 'Are you saying, yes or no, that Mr Cruddas demonstrated on 15 March a willingness to commit an offence under Section 61?' Mr Calvert replied: 'I've just explained, I don't want to answer that question yes or no.' ...

Mr Browne, and I myself, had asked the question a number of times before Mr Calvert finally said he did not want to answer.

In her witness statement Ms Blake wrote that: 'Given that electoral law is designed to prevent foreign money entering the British political system at all, I was surprised that he did not rule this out altogether as the Treasurer of the governing party ...'

Her summary of the law is consistent with her being under the same misunderstanding of the law as Mr Calvert admitted that he had been until 23 March (namely that UK subsidiaries of foreign companies could not lawfully make donations). She wrote in her witness statement that she did not realise at the time that the requirement for a company to make donations only using money generated from profits in the UK had been omitted from PPERA.

Ms Blake went on to write that when Mr Cruddas told them that they should talk to Mr Chattey in the party's compliance team that 'I took him to mean that the compliance process was a box that we had to tick but was not going to present us with a major obstacle ...'

She made clear that she was accusing Mr Cruddas of treating the compliance process as a sham. The necessary implication of this is that she was also accusing Mr Chattey and others in his department of operating a sham. Although this would obviously be a very serious breach of electoral law, if Mr Cruddas, Mr Chattey and others were all treating compliance checking as a sham, Ms Blake nevertheless wrote in her witness statement that the 'Cash for Cameron' memo that Mr Calvert emailed to her on 19 March was jointly written by herself.

John Witherow, editor of the *Sunday Times*

The judge said:

> Mr Witherow had been equally clear in his witness statement exchanged in May that he was not seeking to prove the case that was first raised on 26 June by the amendment to para 7(2) of the Defence. He had written: '[Mr Cruddas] explored ways by which the party could accept the donation from a foreign fund which, although not illegal, undermined the spirit of the electoral laws ...'
>
> Pressed by Mr Browne, Mr Witherow recognised that this was inconsistent with his saying at trial that Mr Cruddas was willing to commit an offence under Section 61. He chose to resolve the inconsistency by stating that his witness statement was inaccurate ...
>
> The suggestion that Mr Cruddas might have been offering to arrange for the party to receive a donation from donors engaged in an illegal transaction is all the more surprising and improbable in that there was no suggestion that he had ever done such a thing before, and because there was no plausible motive suggested as to why he might have been willing to do that on 15 March 2012. He told the journalists that he had made a number of six-figure donations himself, and that there were other people who were accustomed to doing the same, all of them lawfully. He had not sought the meeting with the international financiers, and, as he told them, he did not normally have people come to him as they did ...
>
> Mr Cruddas had made it abundantly clear that third parties could not lawfully make third-party payments. That would apply just as much whether the person purporting to make the donation was an individual or a company. He had made it equally clear that

a bona fide operating company could lawfully make a donation, even if it was the subsidiary of a foreign company. He also made clear that any question of whether a proposed donation could be lawfully accepted would be a matter for CCHQ to decide, and not himself. I do not accept that he failed to make these matters clear to the journalists at the meeting.

The judge concluded: 'The defence of truth to the Electoral Law Meanings ... is without foundation and I reject it.'

Malicious falsehood

In his summary and conclusions, Mr Justice Tugendhat said:

Mr Cruddas claims that the articles and video extracts published by the *Sunday Times* bear the same meanings for the purposes of the claim in malicious falsehood (with one exception) as they do for the purposes of the claim in libel. He claims that these meanings are all false, and that they were published maliciously, and that they were calculated to cause pecuniary damage to him in respect of his profession and business as executive chairman of an FSA-regulated online trading company ...

However, it is the experience of judges in practice that the burden of proof is very rarely decisive of the outcome of an action. In the present case it is not because of the burden of proof that I have decided that the defence of truth failed for the purposes of the libel action. I would have reached the same conclusion if the burden of proof had lain on Mr Cruddas. Mr Cruddas has more than satisfied me that the three meanings were all false.

So Mr Cruddas has succeeded on the first stage of his case in malicious falsehood, that is, in proving the falsehoods.

The two remaining issues on the question of liability in the malicious falsehood claim are whether the journalists were malicious, and if so, whether (since Mr Cruddas does not claim that he suffered any actual damage) he can satisfy the requirement of the Defamation Act 1952 Section 3.

The judge went on:

I find that the journalists knew that Mr Cruddas had not suggested any breach of electoral law or shown himself willing to commit an offence, or to provide benefits to them if they committed an offence ...

The evidence of Mr Calvert and Ms Blake was not frank. In relation to the Breach of Electoral Law meanings, I have not found credible their denials that they understood the meanings of what they wrote ...

Mr Cruddas pleaded his case in malice on a number of bases. The first is that the journalists knew that the articles were false in the meanings in which a substantial number of readers would understand them (as I have already found). In addition Mr Cruddas submits that there is other evidence that the journalists intended to injure him.

This evidence included:

(a) the delight that they manifested when Mr Cruddas resigned immediately upon the publication of the articles;
(b) the way the articles had been edited through at least five different drafts, including the omission of passages from

the transcript that made clear that what Mr Cruddas had been doing was in accordance with the party's public stance, and in accordance with what was stated in the 13th Report of the CSPL [Committee for Standards in Public Life] ... and the omission of Mr Cruddas's statement that a donor company had to be 'bona fide';

(c) the association of the quote 'Awesome for your business' with other statements made by Mr Cruddas which they knew were not in fact associated by him with that quote;

(d) the unsuccessful attempts by the journalists to provoke Mr Cruddas to make compromising statements, during the meeting, and to provoke Sir Christopher Kelly [then chairman of the CSPL] in a telephone call after the meeting to make statements supporting the allegations in the articles;

(e) the statement at the end of the third article that it was 'unclear what [Mr Cruddas's] view was' on a suggestion that the international financiers make individual donations by falsely claiming that the money was their own, when Mr Cruddas had made clear at the meeting that donations had to be compliant and could not be made through proxies, and when they did not offer him an opportunity to comment upon that particular allegation before publication of the articles;

(f) the editing of the video extracts sent to broadcasters to make it appear that Mr Cruddas was guilty of the conduct alleged against him;

(g) the covert recording of Mr Cruddas when the journalists knew that there was no justification for doing so, and no evidence that Mr Cruddas had ever done any of the things that the journalists alleged in the articles that he had done;

(h) the knowingly false statement made by the journalists made to the editor ... in order to induce the editor to give to them authorisation (in accordance with the PCC Code) for the use of subterfuge, namely the statement '[Sarah] Southern says Cruddas will also advise us on how to get round rules which ban foreign companies', when Ms Southern had not said that to them at all;

(i) the decision not to give Mr Cruddas the opportunity to comment upon the allegations until after 3 p.m. on the Saturday afternoon preceding the publication at about 10 p.m. that evening of the edition of the *Sunday Times* dated 25 March 2012, and what they did tell him about the articles at that time was too vague to enable him to comment effectively;

(j) the decision not to give an opportunity to Mr Cruddas to state his position was motivated by the desire of the defendants that he and the Conservative Party should not have the opportunity to correct the falsehoods in it, and so spoil the story;

(k) the failure to discourage [Mark] Adams from asserting, as he did, that the articles demonstrated that Mr Cruddas had committed criminal offences (Mr Cruddas had to sue Mr Adams to make him stop making allegations of illegality ...);

(l) the failure by the *Sunday Times* to publish ... that they were not alleging that the corruption that Mr Cruddas had engaged in was criminal;

(m) that in the issue of the *Sunday Times* dated 2 September 2012 there was an editorial comparing Mr Cruddas to Lance Armstrong. Mr Armstrong had successfully sued [Times Newspapers], but subsequently had been proved to have lied in denying that he took drugs to enhance his performance as a cyclist.

The greater part of the trial was devoted to a detailed investigation of the matters relied on to show that the defendants intended to injure Mr Cruddas by publishing what they knew to be false.

The judge said that, since he had already decided that the claim in libel had succeeded, it would be disproportionate to make findings on each of these many allegations of malice. He therefore limited his findings to the following.

On 1 March the [Cruddas] meeting was arranged ...

On 6 March the journalists wrote a memorandum for Mr Hymas [the *Sunday Times* managing editor for news] headed 'Update on Insight Investigation of Sarah Southern, a lobbyist selling access to the Prime Minister'. It included: 'The purpose of the meeting is to discuss what we will get in return for a six figure donation, in terms of access to ministers, influence over policy and membership of networking clubs. Southern says Cruddas will also advise us on how to get around rules which ban foreign companies from donating.'

The last sentence referring to Mr Cruddas was false. Ms Southern had said nothing of the sort.

Continuing his summing up and conclusions, the judge said it was

very surprising that the journalists should so consistently and seriously have misled the editor as to the basis on which they sought authorisation for the use of subterfuge. Whether and if so how much Mr Hymas was misled is not something on which I can make a finding. The journalists claimed in evidence that he had been kept fully informed. But since I find much of their evidence incredible, I doubt that too.

Chapter 43

VINDICATION

Mr Justice Tugendhat said that, in the case of Heidi Blake, it should have been all the more surprising that she had misled the editor, since she had been one of the journalists whose conduct had been the subject of a separate adjudication made upholding a complaint by the Liberal Democrats. 'But in her evidence Ms Blake showed why I should not be surprised.'

She said: 'I actually don't personally agree with that judgment by the PCC.' This answer was typical of her manner in giving evidence. This was a prolonged demonstration of self-assurance and unwillingness to accept that anything she had done would have been better done differently or not at all …

This case for the defendants is built on what are said to be the journalists' assumptions and impressions, instead of on facts. However, errors, however careless and irresponsible, are not proof of malice. Malice is a form of dishonesty.

There certainly have been errors on the part of the journalists. As noted above, both Mr Calvert and Ms Blake recognised in their evidence that their understanding of the law was mistaken until after the meeting, and was only put right between the meeting and publication …

I have no doubt that Ms Blake was out of her depth on other matters too, such as whether a company such as Global Zenith could be expected to set up a bona fide British subsidiary in order to carry out or facilitate the carrying out [of] the UK investment strategy which she was pretending that it wanted to do.

But ignorance of electoral law, and of how financial services companies operate, is not an excuse or justification for recording in reports to her superiors as facts matters which were not facts, but were in truth only her impressions and assumptions.

If she had wanted to inform her superiors what were her impressions and assumptions, and what were facts, she could easily have done so. She knew what she was doing in confusing the two. She was not being honest with her superiors.

For a court to find that a witness has been untruthful, it is not necessary to find a motive. But a motive, or its absence, may support a finding. The judge said he had 'noted the absence of any plausible motive that could explain the very serious allegation the defendants have made against Mr Cruddas'.

Heidi Blake made several remarks which

suggest she did have a motive to injure Mr Cruddas. She expressed strong disapproval of the present system of party funding. She said it was 'quite shameful for the Prime Minister to tout himself to businesses who pay to have their photograph taken, it's demeaning to his office'. She also expressed the scepticism of the motivation of donors which, according to the 5th and 13th Reports of the CSPL, is a scepticism shared by many members of the public. But disapproval of the present system of party funding is not an excuse for misreporting impressions and assumptions as facts. Ms Blake is entitled to express the opinions which she did express, if she honestly holds those opinions. But such opinions are not facts.

The judge continued:

I have not found a motive why Mr Calvert did what I have found that he did. He is an experienced investigative journalist. So far as the telephone conversations were concerned, he was not a party, and was dependent upon what Ms Blake told him Ms Southern said, at least until the transcripts of those calls became available. The investigation was also a project initiated by Ms Blake, and her first project in her new job. She may well have been very enthusiastic and persuasive. Her evidence was not persuasive under cross-examination, but she was very persistent and self-confident.

By 15 March 2012 the journalists had no evidence upon which to suspect Mr Cruddas personally of impropriety or of misleading the public, whatever views they held about the present system of party funding. The information that they had received from Mr Adams about Ms Southern, and which had led them to start their investigation in November 2011, had not been supported.

It is difficult to prove a negative, but all that Ms Southern had said to them in meetings and phone calls prior to 15 March 2012 came as near as possible to proving that she was not making the claims which Mr Adams had alleged that she was making. So it is impossible to understand why the journalists persisted in the investigation for as long as they did. By 15 March 2012 it had become a fishing expedition.

Mr Witherow had not read the transcript or watched the audio-visual recording. It is far from clear whether Mr Hymas had either. Anyone who read the transcript and did not listen to and watch what had actually happened could easily be misled as to what Mr Cruddas was really saying. However, that does not apply to Mr Calvert because he was at the meeting.

Finding on malice

The judge said:

In my judgment, for the reasons stated above, Mr Calvert and Ms Blake did know that the articles were false in the meanings which they knew them to bear. They did have a dominant intention to injure Mr Cruddas, and they expressed delight when they learnt that they had caused his resignation. Mr Calvert nominated himself for a prize with *Private Eye*, and did so in terms which led the editors of *Private Eye* to report the matter in terms that caused further damage to Mr Cruddas, saying that he 'was even prepared to receive a donation illegally from a Liechtenstein fund'.

The journalists have done nothing to limit the damage to his reputation by making clear that the Corruption meaning was not intended by them to impute criminality, until after my 5 June judgment in which I had found that that was a meaning which a substantial number of reasonable readers would understand … It soon became clear that many readers had understood the Articles in that way.

I find that Mr Calvert and Ms Blake were malicious, and the Third Defendant is vicariously liable for their malice.

The facts

The judge said:

As already recorded, Mr Cruddas issued a resignation letter immediately after the first edition of the *Sunday Times* had appeared late on Saturday 24 March. Lord Feldman had called him to say that the Prime Minister was 'very upset' and that he had 'destroyed seven years of good donor relations'.

Mr Cruddas said he was in a state of shock, and more concerned for his wife and children than anyone else ... On the Monday he wanted to go away, but his wife told him that he had 700 people working for him with mortgages and children to support and he had to go to the office to hold his head high ...

Mr Cruddas describes in his witness statement the distress and embarrassment he and his family have suffered as a result of the articles. These included humiliating remarks made to his adult daughter. This was the incident that upset him more than anything to do with his business.

He also described in his oral evidence that he became disillusioned with his charity work. He would have felt embarrassed to be meeting people like Prince Charles, who he had been meeting through the Prince's Trust ... and he did not wish to bring embarrassment on such a person by appearing in public with him. He is still not as active in his charity work as he had been. He was also angered by the decision of the defendants to re-amend in June to seek to prove true the allegations of criminality which, until then, they had not alleged to be true.

The circulation of the *Sunday Times* both in the print edition and online is very large. The readership of the articles was probably in millions. The story had been trailed by the video extracts which the defendants sent to broadcasters for the purposes of advertising the articles. The articles were not taken down from the defendant's website until 6 June, the day after my 5 June judgment ...

There was a media storm over the weekend and the following week ...

On the Sunday the Prime Minister gave an interview on TV in which he said that 'what happened was completely unacceptable. This is not the way we raise money in the Conservative Party.' On the Monday the Prime Minister was due to give a speech to the Alzheimer's Society. He took the occasion to state ... 'Yesterday I said that what the former treasurer of the Conservative Party, Peter Cruddas, said was completely unacceptable and wrong.' ...

The Prime Minister did not know what Mr Cruddas had said. All he knew was what the *Sunday Times* had reported. This speech by the Prime Minister was a massive public humiliation for Mr Cruddas.

On *The Andrew Marr Show* David Miliband said: 'The idea that policy is for sale is grotesque. I think David Cameron is going to have to, if not today, then in the next few days publish the list of policies that have been sent from these dinners ...'

On 26 March Ed Miliband raised the matter in Parliament: 'It is illegal to solicit donations through overseas companies and illegal to disguise those donations, yet there are allegations that this was exactly what Mr Cruddas was suggesting ...'

The defendants did nothing to inform the public that this was a misrepresentation of the articles, and that they had made no such allegation. This is to be contrasted with the Saturday morning, when Mr Adams had sent an email saying the Conservatives may have broken electoral law and suggesting that he should make a complaint to the police. Mr Calvert replied, with a copy to Ms Blake, telling him to wait and read the articles. He explained: 'We are not going as far as alleging anything.'

Mr Adams did report the matter to the police on the Sunday, with as much publicity as he could generate, giving interviews on Radio 4 and Radio 5 Live, and saying he thought a crime had been committed. The only comment Ms Blake made was a text saying 'You were great' referring to his appearance on TV. As already noted, Mr Adams continued with the allegations of illegality until Mr Cruddas sent him the transcript, following which, on 2 November 2012, he said he did not defend the action Mr Cruddas had brought. Judgment was entered against him by default.

On 29 March Mr Cruddas's solicitors asked the defendants for a copy of the covert recording. The next day the defendants refused on the spurious ground that it was confidential. It was over two months later, on 14 June 2012, and after Mr Cruddas's complaint to the PCC made on 5 April, that the defendants allowed him to watch the covert recording. Even then they would not provide him with a copy until 14 June. The defendants have complained that Mr Cruddas had himself covertly recorded a copy when he viewed the video on 14 June.

In delaying that, the Defendants prolonged the period during which Mr Cruddas was unable to demonstrate what he had said at the meeting, and this increased the injury to reputation and his feelings.

The Defendants had given a viewing of the covert recording to the Electoral Commission and to the police, who cleared him on 3 September 2012. And Mr Cruddas provided a copy to Mr

Adams, as recorded by [Mr Justice] Eady, as a result of which Mr Adams ceased to defend that action. But they did their best not to provide a copy to Mr Cruddas ...

On 29 June Mr Cruddas sent a detailed letter before action. On 13 July the defendants wrote that if he sued 'a number of substantive defences would be available' ...

On 2 September they published [an] editorial ... The editorial referred to the remarkable record of achievement on the part of the Insight team of the *Sunday Times* in the field of investigative journalism. But the editorial went on to compare Mr Cruddas with Lance Armstrong. Mr Armstrong had undoubtedly taken performance-enhancing drugs, and had lied to the court and many others in denying it (Mr Witherow said the defendants were expecting to recover money from Mr Armstrong on account of that). They wrote that they would 'robustly defend' Mr Cruddas's action, but they did not say that they would defend it on the basis that they had not alleged against him any criminality, or anything more than a breach of the spirit of electoral law.

On 3 September the police wrote to Mr Cruddas a letter clearing him, which he sent to the defendants, and which the defendants did not report, in spite of the fact that Mr Cruddas's solicitors requested that they publicly state that Mr Cruddas was not guilty of any criminal conduct. The police wrote there was 'no evidence of any criminal conduct on the part of yourself or Ms Sarah Southern, either directly or by implication during the course of the *Sunday Times* investigation. I also conclude that no inchoate offences have been committed.'

Asked why the defendants had not publicly stated that no criminality was alleged, Mr Witherow said he was no longer the editor of the *Sunday Times* and the journalists said they had nothing to correct. They were not responsible for what so many readers had said they understood the articles to mean.

The cross-examination of Mr Cruddas was as robust as it could be. Mr Cruddas found it offensive, and it was. He was strongly challenged on the truthfulness of his answers. Although Mr Rampton started by acknowledging that Mr Cruddas was a man of integrity, he made no allowance for that in his cross-examination. Mr Rampton, instructed late as he was, said he had not found the time to look at the whole of the audio-visual recording. He accepted that Mr Cruddas appeared sincere, but submitted that that was only an appearance.

Conclusion on damages for libel

'The articles received the maximum possible publicity,' said the judge. 'They go to Mr Cruddas's personal honour and integrity.'

Mr Cruddas has suffered great personal distress, both directly, and through his family and the employees of his company. He has suffered public humiliation from the Prime Minister. He had a high standing in society, both for his business success and his charitable work, all of it earned by him personally through his own efforts, and from a disadvantaged start. The conduct of the defendants in contesting the action both before and at the trial has been offensive.

It may be a small consolation to him that the trial has received almost no publicity in the media, so far as I am aware. So the damaging allegations against him have not received wider circulation in that way, as often happens in libel actions that go to trial. But that makes it all the more important that the award of damages should be one that will receive publicity.

In my judgment, the sum which is necessary and proportionate to mark the vindication that Mr Cruddas is entitled to, and compensate him for his distress and humiliation is £180,000. That includes £15,000 for aggravated damages.

Chapter 44

DRINKS ALL ROUND

The trial finished with my complete vindication, winning all my claims. I won substantial damages and costs and the judge found the two journalists to be guilty of malicious falsehood.

To me, the journalists committed the cardinal sin of writing and publishing a story that they knew was not true. Surely for any journalist at any level, integrity and honesty around a story must be the starting point. Otherwise they might as well just make up stories as they go along.

However, I suppose Times Newspapers Ltd were in damage limitation mode, especially with the Leveson report due to be published. They also had to consider an appeal and if they did appeal, they would need the two journalists onside to go through the appeal process.

That was all for later but for now it was time to celebrate my victory. It was August 2013 and I was just about to leave for a holiday with my family in the south of France and a welcome rest. But before I jetted off, I had lunch with my legal team and drinks were on me.

We had a nice lunch in the City, but their mood was not as jovial as mine. Their attitude was that I should not go out and spend all the £180,000 damages just yet. Times Newspapers were bound to appeal because the judgment handed down was so damning of the newspaper, its processes, and the integrity of two senior journalists as well as the editorial team. My legal team felt that an appeal was inevitable.

They were also surprised by the size of the damages awarded to me because it was way above what they expected, and it equalled one of the biggest payments for libel they had seen in decades.

We were all expecting the journalists and Times Newspapers to appeal and that is what they did.

Chapter 45

A PANDORA'S BOX

The first application for permission to appeal by Times Newspapers, Blake and Calvert was based on the trial transcripts and taped meeting, but without an oral representation from our barristers. There had already been a trial where both sides could have their say. The first appeal was effectively another judge reading through the transcripts of the trial, watching the taped interview, and deciding whether the trial judge got it wrong. The first appeal judge was Dame Victoria Sharp.

On 29 November 2013 Lady Justice Sharp's judgment was handed down. She robustly rejected the appeal and it was dismissed. Within her judgment she said:

The assessment of the honesty of the journalists' evidence – on this and every other aspect of the case – was quintessentially a matter for the [trial] judge who heard and saw them give evidence.

I do not think there can be any doubt about his conclusions on their honesty or intentions in relation to the false meanings as the judge found them to be. As to the criticisms of his reasons, the judge was doing no more, it seems to me, than evaluating the credibility of what [the journalists] had to say in the factual context of the case.

On malice and the electoral law/foreign donations meaning Sharp LJ further said:

> There are no arguable grounds in my view for impugning the judge's reasons for his conclusions as to what the defendant journalists knew to be the true position, what they nonetheless knew was conveyed by the articles, and therefore as to their honesty.
>
> I am not persuaded either that there are grounds for concluding the judge erred as to the correct approach on the law and/or therefore on his approach to the facts.

This was a further endorsement of the trial judge's findings and underpinned the trial judgment. This judgment completely undermined the honesty of the articles and the credibility of the two journalists.

My damages remained at £180,000 and all that was left for the defendants was to appeal one last time.

This time it would be an oral appeal in front of three judges, Lord Justice Jackson, Lord Justice Ryder and Lord Justice Clarke. Barristers would be able to argue for both sides. It was in effect a mini trial but without the journalists and me giving evidence. It was argued between all the legal people, namely the three judges and barristers from both sides.

The Court of Appeal sat for three days and their judgment was handed down on 17 March 2015. This time it was not as conclusive for me as in the trial and the first appeal.

Lord Justice Jackson, handing down his appeal judgment, commented that 'the defendants have failed by a wide margin' to prove the two defamatory meanings of the articles, that the claimant made the offer, even though he knew that the money offered for such secret meetings was to come, in breach of the ban under UK electoral law, from Middle Eastern investors in a Liechtenstein fund, and ... in order to circumvent and thereby evade the law, the claimant was happy that the foreign donors should use deceptive devices, such as creating an artificial UK company to donate the money or using UK employees as conduits, so that the true source of the donation would be concealed.

He held that 'the allegation that the claimant was countenancing criminal conduct is a serious matter and of a different character to the "cash for access" allegation'. In this judgment, the Court of Appeal ruled that the two journalists had lied in the article and they knowingly knew they were lying, accusing me of serious breaches of electoral law, which are criminal offences. Now we had five judges all confirming that the two journalists were guilty of malicious falsehood. However, the court upheld the defendants' appeal for the cash-for-access aspect of the story, effectively accusing me of offering access to the Prime Minister at dinners and events and thereby the chance to influence government policy.

I won my claim on the two counts for malicious falsehood and defamation and my damages were reduced from £180,000 to £50,000.

I thought, you have got to be kidding me. I found this decision completely bizarre, because the two journalists were guilty of malicious falsehood and yet they could be believed on the cash-for-access aspect of their articles. And this was all based on the three Court of Appeal judges reading the trial transcript and viewing the taped recording of the meeting. They came to their decision after a 'thorough' reading of the transcript of the trial, but without ever speaking to or cross-examining the journalists or me.

Lady Justice Sharp in the first appeal process did not rely on the trial transcripts to ascertain who was telling the truth. She was not the trial judge, Mr Justice Tugendhat was, and as noted earlier it was a matter for the trial judge as he had heard and seen them all give evidence.

Following this judgment Inforrm.org commented:

This appeal did not turn on any substantial legal issue but on an analysis of what the Claimant said when he was secretly recorded by *Sunday Times* journalists. After analysing a large quantity of material, the Court of Appeal, unusually, took a different view of the facts from the trial judge.

I thought, what was the point of a trial and hearing what both sides had to say, the very people who were at the meeting? We could have all saved ourselves a lot of time and money and just gone straight to the Court of Appeal to read a transcript of our meeting.

Following this judgment, on 16 March 2015, with incredulity, I sent the following message to my supporters via email:

A Pandora's Box

You might have thought it was all over but the saga of my case against the *Sunday Times* ('*ST*') continues. It is becoming a bit like a Tolstoy novel. Since I last updated you another couple of chapters have been added. In my opinion the most recent development raises much wider and dare I say it profound questions for not just political parties but for those, particularly senior individuals, involved in political fundraising. I believe this goes beyond my own personal position and is relevant to others – hence my observations and questions below.

As I reported after the judgment in the High Court in July 2013 the trial judge found in my favour on my three assertions as to the meanings of the articles in the *ST*. Months later the *ST* applied for permission to appeal – in fact on the last day available to them ...

The appeal was heard before Christmas. This time a different set of judges in the Court of Appeal have found in my favour on two out of the three assertions in my pleadings as to the libellous meanings of the *ST* articles and have awarded me damages. I am very pleased that the Court of Appeal also upheld the finding of malicious falsehood in relation to those two meanings. These related to the *ST*'s allegations about my approach to overseas do-nations and my alleged willingness to breach electoral law. These false allegations had the most serious implications for me. My third claim on the meaning of the articles related to access to and influence on senior members of government. Although not supporting the findings in my favour on this point, it seems to me that the approach taken by the judges to my third claim is potentially opening a Pandora's box!

Unlike in the earlier court hearings, on this occasion the judges said they ought to consider issues which are appropriate or not to the funding of political parties. To that end they referred to a book entitled *The Funding of Political Parties* by Professor Keith Ewing and others ...

The judges pointed out that the above book states that different

considerations come into play when one is dealing with donations or funding which political institutions provide to political
parties compared to individuals. They quote a line from the book
which says that institutional donations from political parties
'may be more democratic'. But they then say they don't comment
on that distinction or address the different considerations (if any)
that might apply between institutions and individuals but ... will
just focus on individuals.

The judges soon thereafter say that on a number of occasions
in the *ST* recording I had stated that 'you cannot influence government policy or buy access to the Prime Minister'.

In spite of that statement ... acknowledging my 'health warnings' and no criminality or breaches of electoral law by me the
judges accepted the *ST*'s contention that what I had offered was
'inappropriate, unacceptable and wrong'. Their view of the transcript was that I was offering influence and unfair advantage.

It is a pity that, unlike the case before the trial judge, the nature
of this appeal didn't require either me, the two journalists or their
editor being cross-examined in open court by each QC.

In similar actions will judges now look at the wider issue of
the funding of political parties from different sources and how
should that be weighed up? They seemed to imply (even though
they didn't say what it was) that there is a distinction between the
types of donor where it is promoted as leading to access to senior
politicians.

Of course, donating at any level doesn't mean you influence
policy, that is determined by the response! But is there now not
a danger that a distinction could be developing between how
donations are viewed depending on whether one is a political
institution or, say, a trade union or an individual?

Is there going to be a presumption that the former is generally appropriate, acceptable and right and the latter, particularly when from individuals, is generally 'inappropriate, unacceptable and wrong'?

And in deciding that, who is the right person or persons to say so and what different considerations, if any, need to be taken into account? I am not suggesting that these issues or questions are not legitimate, but I am left with the clear impression that this is getting into the realms of public policy.

The most recent chapters have not been all grim. There have been moments throughout this process, and not without a touch of a little irony, which have brought a smile to my face. It is clearly stated in the Conservative Party's Leader's Group brochure, signed by the Prime Minister, that Leader's membership will lead to you meeting him. Is that cash for access? Is it 'inappropriate, unacceptable and wrong', even where other parties have similar funding inducements? This is the big question. Food for thought.

So, future budding treasurers of any political party be warned!!! There is a real risk that even when, as in my case, not acting contrary to any laws and making numerous 'health warnings' in connection with promoting various levels of membership and benefits for party donors, one can end up on the wrong end of articles from some sections of the press who have their own agenda.

Although my two most serious claims have been upheld, becoming a potential football in a wider political/legal debate, about what in effect is a policy matter, as to when is access 'inappropriate, unacceptable and wrong', doesn't particularly enthral me ... I would rather stick to business where the rules are clear and there are no political agendas.

I am also very happy to be involved in philanthropy through the Peter Cruddas Foundation. So, despite all the turmoil over the last three years, I am happy and fulfilled and my business is thriving, and my foundation is benefitting.

As always thank you for your support.

Chapter 46

PRINT AND BE DAMNED

The original trial judgment was a damning verdict on Times Newspapers, Heidi Blake, Jonathan Calvert and the editorial team for their lack of diligence and process checking. It demonstrated all that was wrong about the press at that time, printing malicious falsehoods, lack of integrity, lack of process, covertly filming me without having any evidence to suspect that I would do anything wrong. Fishing expedition journalism without due cause.

The Leveson Inquiry was set up to investigate issues like these – bad press behaviour, complaints and how they were handled, procedures, processes, and criminal activity like phone hacking. It's fair to say the press were under pressure as editors, journalists and owners were all scrutinised by the Leveson Inquiry.

The worst example was the accusation against the *News of the World* of hacking into murdered schoolgirl Milly Dowler's phone. This gave her parents false hope that she was alive because the phone messages were being listened to by the press. They hoped that it was Milly who had listened to the messages. This was a criminal offence and eventually some editors and journalists would go to prison over phone hacking.

It was reported in the *Guardian* on 15 July 2011 that Rupert Murdoch had made a 'full and humble' apology to Milly's family at a private meeting held at a central London hotel. The global head of News Corporation (owners of the *Sunday Times* as well as the *News of the World*) 'held his head in his hands' and repeatedly told the family he was 'very, very sorry', according to the Dowlers' lawyer, Mark Lewis.

My case was a very high-profile one for obvious reasons. I was working alongside the Prime Minister to raise money for the Conservative Party. The Prime Minister had been forced to make a statement on the day the story broke. And on the Monday Parliament was called to debate the cash-for-access story and illegal political donations from overseas donors. To say it was front-page news was a bit of an understatement. It was everywhere.

With all this backdrop going on, if the Court of Appeal had upheld in full the trial judgment it would have been another black mark against the press and the two journalists, alongside all the other issues coming out from the Leveson Inquiry. The stakes were very high for the press at this time and the worse the news that came out about them, the more pressure it put them under.

The Leveson Inquiry was in two parts. The first part looked at the culture, practices, and ethics of the press. The second part was meant to be an investigation into the relationship between journalists and the police. At the time of the appeal by Times Newspapers, this second part was pending, but it had been delayed while criminal proceedings against various newspapers were ongoing.

In his report Lord Justice Leveson called for a new independent press watchdog underpinned by legislation. The 2,000-page report into press ethics found press behaviour was 'outrageous' and 'wreaked havoc with the lives of innocent people'. Also, the Hacked Off campaign, which demanded a public inquiry into phone hacking, was gaining momentum in the media as its famous spokesperson, the actor Hugh Grant, was appearing on political television programmes.

The pressure was building on the press and my case was so high profile at the time that they had to fight hard to try to overturn the verdict. Especially as I had already won the first two judgments. Also, the police and the Electoral Commission said I did nothing wrong and there were no criminal charges hanging over me.

It was all to play for at the final Court of Appeal.

At the original trial, Times Newspaper and the two journalists never called their immediate boss as a witness, the managing editor of the *Sunday Times* (at the time) Charles Hymas. The trial judge commented as follows:

> Whether and if so, how much Mr Hymas was misled is not something on which I can make a finding. The journalists claimed in evidence that he [Hymas] had been kept fully informed ...
>
> On the other hand, he has not been called to give evidence, notwithstanding that he gave a witness statement, and attended the first day of the trial. Since he is not a party the decision whether he would give evidence was not his, but the defendants' to make.

My first thoughts when I heard Hymas was not being called as a witness at the original trial was that he didn't want to tell his side of the story. According to the judge he was there for the first day of the trial, so he was available, and this was an important trial.

I do not know why Hymas did not appear as a witness for the defendants, only they and their legal team know why. But it was easy to think that his version of events might differ from the journalists' and undermine their defence. If Hymas agreed with the journalists' version of events why not give evidence and help them out in the legal process? By giving evidence he could have supported the two journalists and added weight to their evidence. It was only the two journalists, Heidi Blake and Jonathan Calvert, who were in court to face the music. They were the ones carrying the can for what was printed. They were the ones found guilty of malicious falsehood along with the paper. The managing editor was nowhere to be seen. Sure, it was Blake and Calvert's story, but it only got published because somebody signed it off.

My barristers wanted to ask Hymas on whose authority the story was printed. What checks were in place to see the evidence that the journalists claimed was the reason for covertly recording me? Also, journalists cannot decide what stories appear in a national newspaper and where. That is the decision of the managing editor or the editor.

More importantly, Blake and Calvert's story had to be checked and cleared for publication by the legal department. This is normal practice in any newspaper. So, what was the verdict of the legal department, and who decided whether this story should be published? The point here is if it was signed off by somebody else, would they have been complicit in the publication of malicious lies by the *Sunday Times*?

Also, we wanted to know how far up the chain of command this story went. Did it go as high as the owner of the newspaper? It just didn't seem possible that two young journalists would be able to print such an important story without it being vetted, especially as one of the journalists had previously been censured by the PCC.

Was a decision made to print and worry about the consequences afterwards? Because if the editors had really checked out the story, seen the tape, they must have realised that it was highly likely that a rich businessman with deep pockets, being accused of criminal and illegal activities, would come out fighting. There was every chance that they would be sued, which is what happened.

But was printing the story worth the risk? Or was there an ulterior motive to print what proved to be malicious lies? Was that motive an effort to throw some dirt at the Prime Minister ahead of Leveson, given that David Cameron had said he would be implementing the Leveson recommendations? In other words, 'Get your own house in order before you tell us to get ours in order'?

A top lawyer said to me after the trial that the behaviour of the journalists and the newspaper was shocking. He said there was no way, having seen the tape and read the story, that as a lawyer he would have allowed the story to be published as it was. It would not have taken too long for an average lawyer to pick the story apart and see the massive holes in it compared to the taped meeting.

His view was that there were so many issues with the integrity of the story and what was said at the meeting, that it made him think that the *Sunday Times* knew that the story was flawed and wrong, but they published for another reason. What that reason was, who knows, but if Charles Hymas had given evidence, these are the questions we would have asked him.

The lawyer said, 'Peter, it cannot be in the public interest to print malicious lies so there must have been an ulterior motive. Either that or they are all a bunch of idiots at the *Sunday Times*.'

One other thing he said was that the decision to print this story must have gone high up the chain of command. We will probably never know how high, but somebody signed it off. He said it just didn't make sense for this story to be published without a higher authority's permission.

John Witherow, the senior editor who did give evidence, but conveniently didn't work for the *Sunday Times* when he was doing so, said that he had not read the transcript or watched the audio-visual recording. Also, during the trial Witherow had to change his evidence, as seen in Chapter 43.

The two journalists in my opinion were hung out to dry by the *Sunday Times*. They had no support from the newspaper. Maybe they deserved it because they lied about the reasons to covertly film me. Maybe the editor was unhappy with them for what they did. It's hard to know why the managing editor was not in court to give his side of the story and defend the journalists.

The two journalists were left to defend themselves. It was as if they were sacrificial lambs for the newspaper when others must have been involved.

Heidi Blake is no longer working for the *Sunday Times*. Jonathan Calvert is still with the paper. Charles Hymas has moved onto the *Telegraph* and John Witherow was promoted within the newspaper group.

Chapter 47

DARK ARTS

My overriding feeling about the Appeal Court's decision is that it didn't involve a full or dispassionate airing of the principles and involved a less than comprehensible reinterpretation of questions of fact by the trial judge. It appeared to be a decision that was arrived at by reverse-engineering the process to get to the result. I feel that the Appeal Court judges had to find a way to level the playing field and that was their mindset when they heard the last appeal.

Now the reader might think that it is sour grapes on my part because it was not a decisive victory for me like the first two judgments. But there is more to it than that and in the next chapter I will explain the judgment in more detail.

As with the original trial, I attended the Court of Appeal daily from start to finish so I could hear what was being said and arguments from both sides' barristers. It didn't take me very long to feel pessimistic about my chances even before the judgment was handed down, even though I had won on all counts at the trial and at the first appeal and received record damages, way beyond what I was expecting.

Before I began my libel proceedings against the journalists and Times Newspapers, I was discussing with my lawyer friend the costs of libel and what I could expect in damages. His view was that I should expect around £50,000 in damages if successful and around 70 per cent of my costs. We estimated my legal costs would be around £1 million so if I received around 70 per cent of those costs that would amount to approximately £700,000. So even if I was successful with my libel claim and I was awarded damages and costs I would still be out of pocket by around £250,000. This was in his opinion what I could expect, and I agreed with him. But we also agreed it wasn't about the money; it was about my reputation.

When I received £180,000 in damages, my legal friend and I were surprised. My legal team said it was one of the highest libel awards they had seen in a long time. My legal team advised me at our celebratory lunch not to go out and spend all the money because in their view the size of the damages left the defendants with little option but to appeal.

It was one thing to be stitched up by the *Sunday Times*, it was another to feel that the Court of Appeal were being swayed by the press push-back against Leveson. From the very beginning of the Court of Appeal process I could not believe how the judges tried to steer arguments with my QC, Desmond Browne, in favour of the defendants.

At one stage they told Desmond, 'You will have to hit it out of the ballpark to convince us of your argument,' before he even stood up. Which I thought seemed to pre-empt their thinking and their motivation. It gave me the impression that they were not totally impartial. I felt that the judges wanted to give something back to Times Newspapers to balance things up a bit, and attending the court in person just confirmed my suspicions.

It was not just the Court of Appeal hearing that concerned me but something that happened in the run-up to it. Lady Justice

Sharp, who dismissed the first defendants' appeal, had recused herself from being one of the three Appeal Court judges, in the interests of transparency. Apparently, her brother had been a donor to the Conservative Party in the past but had not donated for several years.

Sharp LJ's recusal was a surprise because in the Court of Appeal in 2014, she sat on almost every media law case (only missing the full set of the libel appeals by recusing herself from my case). There was no logical reason for her to recuse herself over something her brother did years before. She was either impartial or she was not. It was a ridiculous and flimsy reason to recuse yourself.

More significantly, if Sharp LJ recused herself from the Court of Appeal then why didn't she recuse herself from the first appeal? She was quite happy to adjudicate on the first appeal but not on the second, even though almost nothing had changed between the two appeals. Her brother had not made any donations to the Conservative Party in that time.

The only difference in circumstances between the two appeals was that an article by Nick Cohen had appeared in *The Spectator* magazine (motto 'firm but unfair') in March 2014 entitled 'Who judges the judges?' Was Sharp LJ spooked or pressurised by this article and did it prompt her to move aside? Only she can answer that. But I was disappointed that she recused herself on such a flimsy excuse.

It was clearly better for the Times Newspapers appeal if a judge that had rejected their first appeal was not on the second appeal panel, and I remember thinking, this is better for the paper than it is for me. Because it would have been hard for Sharp LJ to reverse her first decision having already dismissed Times Newspapers' first appeal after completely siding with the trial judge. It also reminded me of when one of the journalists 'accidentally' deleted one of the two identical tape recordings which made it impossible to see if the tape submitted to the courts had been changed or tampered with from the original meeting.

The big question is why Mr Cohen's *Spectator* article was published in the run-up to the Court of Appeal hearing. Were dark arts at play to try to shift the thinking of the Court of Appeal judges and to effectively smear the trial judge and the original trial verdicts, because of Sharp LJ's family connections to the Conservative Party? This, I presume, is why the title of the article was 'Who judges the judges?'

It is also very unusual for the Court of Appeal to override a trial judgment, on questions of fact and evidence presented in court. Because the trial judge hears first-hand oral evidence and he can assess the answers given. He can also ask his own questions. I found myself wondering whether Times Newspapers, having decisively lost through the legal process at the trial and then at first appeal, were hoping that the publication of this article might shift the thinking of the Court of Appeal judges.

When you read Mr Cohen's article, reproduced below, you should do so in the context that Times Newspapers, Heidi Blake and Jonathan Calvert had lost the trial judgment. They had lost the first appeal and the charges against them were malicious falsehood and defamation. My comments are in square brackets.

Who judges the judges?
[This is a provocative headline and is saying that judges are accountable too. But who is it directed at? The reader or the Court of Appeal judges before the appeal process has begun? It sets the

reader up to think that something is not right here, and here's the reason why.]

I like Jonathan Calvert and Heidi Blake of the *Sunday Times*. I will not pretend they are anything like close friends or family. I doubt if I see them more than once a year. But before you read any further you should know about our acquaintance. It is important for journalists to declare their interests.

Readers must be free to make up their own minds, even if I believe – especially if I believe – that a friendship or family bond could never influence my writing.

[This is setting the reader up to think the journalist is transparent and would never be influenced by friendships when he is writing an article. So, the article must be true, 'you can trust me on this'. I am not saying he isn't transparent, but there is a reason for this article and only the writer knows why he wrote it.

But there are suspicions because it came in the run-up to the Court of Appeal process. Also, the opening paragraph sets the scene as a good honest transparent journalist should, and the implication is that Blake and Calvert are the victims in this case. He likes them and he wants to help them even though he admits he barely knows them.

But if Mr Cohen is true to his word, he will disclose whose idea it was to write this article at this particular time.]

In a few days, the *Sunday Times* will apply for the right to appeal against a decision by Mr Justice Tugendhat from July last year. Peter Cruddas, a former co-treasurer of the Conservative Party, had sued the *Sunday Times* after it sent undercover reporters – Calvert and Blake – to interview him. The investigative journalists brought all their kit with them – concealed cameras, hidden tape recorders, the works. They pretended to be agents for foreign investors, who wanted to give money to the Tories, and covertly recorded as Cruddas talked.

[No mention here that the two journalists clearly failed to tell their bosses the truth to get permission to film me covertly. No mention here that their managing editor was not called as a witness to back up their story.]

The headline 'Tory treasurer charges £250,000 to meet PM' followed.

Tugendhat found the paper guilty of libel and malicious falsehood. It should not have said that Cruddas was a corrupt man, who offered opportunities to influence government policy and gain unfair advantage through meetings with ministers. It was also false, he continued, for the paper to allege that Cruddas accepted donations to the party knowing that the money was to come from abroad, in breach of UK electoral law. Tugendhat ordered the paper to pay £180,000 in damages – not least because the party leadership forced Cruddas out after the story broke.

Here is why I am dragging up this old case, and it is not because I am concerned with the details of the dispute between Cruddas and *Sunday Times*. [This may be true, but I have my suspicions.] What strikes me is Tugendhat's failure to declare an interest – in this instance his family connections to the Conservative Party.

[Is Mr Cohen trying to influence the thinking around the upcoming appeal? The suggestion is that the original trial decision was flawed due to family connections of the trial judge. Tugendhat didn't declare his family connection to the Conservative Party. In other words, there's more to see here than meets the eye.]

Michael Ashcroft, the Tory donor, congratulated his friend and ally Cruddas on his victory. [Why does Cohen assume that

Ashcroft is my friend and my ally?] While Tugendhat was a barrister, Ashcroft hired him. In his account of his life in politics *Dirty Money, Dirty Times*, Ashcroft describes Tugendhat as 'formidable' and 'arguably the greatest legal expert in the country on privacy'. [The writer is suggesting there is a possible link between the trial judge and myself through Lord Ashcroft. Which is a major slur and a smearing of the judge.] Lawyers compare themselves to taxi drivers because they will work for anyone. I always reply that they remind me of an older profession.

[Now Cohen is slurring and smearing the legal profession alongside the judge. It is insulting to compare lawyers to 'an older profession', by which I think he meant prostitution.

Also, why bring in things outside of the original trial to his article? Lord Ashcroft only wrote articles after judgments. I didn't know Ashcroft before the *Sunday Times* sting; I had only met him socially at political events on a couple of occasions. The writer has no idea about my relationship with Ashcroft, but now he's saying, 'Aha, here's the link, readers.'

It seems this article is building into an ulterior motive: that the judge was not reliable because of connections, and the link is Ashcroft. There is no evidence of this because there is no connection. But that doesn't stop the writer suggesting there is.]

The point remains that just because Tugendhat worked for Ashcroft may not mean much or indeed anything at all. Nevertheless, I'd have liked him to have declared the association.

[He doesn't want to get sued here so he mentions the connections and then says 'But I am not saying this was the reason'. The only person suggesting there is a linkage between the judge and myself through Ashcroft is the writer.]

More solid are Tugendhat's family ties to the Conservative

Party. His brother, Christopher Tugendhat is a Conservative peer and former MP. In November 2013, local Tories in Tonbridge and Malling selected his son, Tom Tugendhat, a former soldier, to be their parliamentary candidate at the next election for one of the five safest Tory seats in the country.

Tugendhat did not declare his connections and invite both sides to consider whether they wanted another judge. The *Sunday Times*'s lawyers might have raised them, but the paper says it did not know about [the] judge's son or the praise in Ashcroft memoirs at the time of the case.

[Is this an attempt to influence the Court of Appeal?]

I called Tugendhat's clerk and left a message asking to speak to the judge last week. No one got back to me, so I will ask you the question I would have asked him: should Tugendhat have recused himself, as the lawyers put it?

Tugendhat has not broken any rules by not declaring his family connection. But, in my view, he should have declared the connection and left it to others to decide whether he should hear the case. People always wheel out Caesar's long-suffering wife on these occasions.

[The writer is trying to be learned and articulate here. To impress the reader with his intelligence and thus be taken seriously about his points.]

But hackneyed though the emphasis on poor old Pompeia's virtue may be, hers is not a bad example to follow. Judges must be above suspicion.

[Judges *are* above suspicion, but he is trying to indirectly smear the trial judge with this sentence. Desperate times call for desperate measures.]

Meanwhile it seems to me that eventually a writer or publisher will need to challenge one part of Tugendhat's judgment. Most of it was devoted to why the *Sunday Times'* accusations were false. But some of the words he used are open to a dangerous interpretation.

[I wonder if Cohen read the full judgment or was he given a brief on any of this by a third party? Because these comments almost look like a message to the Court of Appeal judges: this is where you need to look. This is a good area of contention.

But this is selective interpretation of what was said at trial and ignores the oral evidence of myself and the journalists under cross-examination from both sets of barristers and listened to by the trial judge. This was the whole point of the trial: to understand what was said and what was meant.

The trial judge's job was to listen to all the evidence and decide who was telling the truth. The two journalists didn't get off to a good start because they had lied to their own bosses to get permission to film me covertly. Why would you believe anything they said after this? I know I didn't and neither did the trial judge.]

'In his speech of 8 February 2010 Mr Cameron explained that for him to give access to donors and to be influenced by them could be proper,' the judge said. Those words might be interpreted to mean that if the Prime Minister says it is proper to give access to donors in return for money, then it is proper, and the citizen cannot gainsay him. If so, it becomes very difficult if not impossible to call the swapping of influence for cash or the sale of peerages 'corrupt'.

[This is completely out of context to the trial and what the journalists wrote and published.

The writer is being selective and completely ignoring the conduct of the two *Sunday Times* journalists. There is not one bad word about their behaviour in his article. Even though he professes not to let friends influence his writing. Yet the writer compares the legal profession to an older profession than taxi drivers.

But what about the phone-hacking trials and investigation that were going through the courts at the time of this article? If lawyers are from an older profession than taxi drivers, where does that leave journalists?]

In fact, the Cameron speech Tugendhat quoted from was his famous declaration that lobbying would be 'the next big scandal'. Cameron acknowledged that it was proper for businesses to lobby government on occasion (which may have been the point that Tugendhat was trying to make). He did not say, however, that it was proper for rich men and organisations to pay for access to political power, not least because he would have been hounded from office if he had. It seems to me that Tugendhat's words create the opposite impression.

[Cohen has really tried to push the boundaries of what Cameron said by writing what he didn't say. He then draws in the association of rich men who pay for access. Of course, Appeal Court judges can easily look into this speech but if they want a way out from the original judgment, then why bother? Here is all they need to do. Just misinterpret what David Cameron said and use that to reverse-engineer a decision.]

Tugendhat went on to find Heidi Blake guilty of malice against Cruddas on the basis that she had told him that, like millions of others, she disapproved of the present system of party funding.

'Ms Blake made a number of remarks which suggest that she did have a motive to injure Mr Cruddas. She expressed strong disapproval of the present system of party funding. She said it was "quite shameful for the Prime Minister to tout himself to businesses who pay to have their photograph taken, it's demeaning to his office". She also expressed the scepticism of the motivation of donors ... But disapproval of the present system of party funding is not an excuse for misreporting impressions and assumptions as facts.'

Nor is it. But what does he mean here? If Tugendhat thinks that it is libellous to falsely accuse a party fundraiser of selling access to ministers, then of course he is right. If he means the English can no longer describe the selling of access or peerages as 'corrupt' simply because that sale does not technically break any laws, then, in my view, he misunderstands how a free society works.

[No peerages or honours were ever mentioned during the taped meeting or during the trial. But, the writer is suggesting, rich businessmen, cash for honours, cash for access may not be illegal, but it is only for the privileged.]

His judgment is perilous [and, by implication, the judge is out of touch] because it seems to adopt the extremist position.

'The present system of party funding, whether desirable or not, is lawful and practical, whereas other possible systems, such as funding out of taxation, or mass membership of political parties, are either not provided for by law, or not in practice available to the parties, however much they might wish that they were. This court cannot declare to be corrupt, as a matter of fact, the system of party funding authorised by Parliament and adopted by the Conservative and other parties. That may or may not be an opinion which people may honestly hold. It is not true as a matter of fact that the system is corrupt.'

As I wrote of his circular reasoning in *The Spectator* at the time:

'One of the many pernicious aspects of our libel law is that it allows judges to express personal prejudices that have no place in a courtroom.

[Libel used to be tried by juries and was changed in 2013. For centuries prior to that, it had been a constitutional right to have a defamation trial decided by a jury. However, in recent times there was a growing emphasis in favour of trial by judge. This ultimately led to Section 11 of the Defamation Act 2013, which abolished the right to jury trials in a defamation action. A jury trial will only now take place if the court exercises its discretion in favour of such method.

The press tends to prefer a trial by jury in libel cases. I will leave you to decide why. My opinion is that the press is easily able to sway some jury members by playing the victims as they are only in court in the interests of the public. They are on the side of the people.

But a judge can easily see through this because he or she is only interested in the facts and the truth. Not playing on people's heart strings.

In a trial by a judge, both sides give their evidence. Both sides are cross-examined, and an experienced trial judge who has seen and heard it all before can make a reasoned decision. An experienced judge tends to get it right as there is no hiding place in a courtroom unless you can back up your facts with evidence.

In my trial it was clear, listen to the tape, watch the taped meeting, and compare it to what was written.]

'It is not up to a judge to start pontificating on the practicality or otherwise of state funding. These are political questions that ought to be beyond his brief. Meanwhile his statement that "this court cannot declare to be corrupt, as a matter of fact, the system of party funding authorised by Parliament and adopted by the Conservative and other parties" manages to sum up everything that is wrong with British complacency in one sentence.'

[The above is disingenuous. The trial was not about political funding and whether trials should be heard by judges or juries. The trial was about the honesty of two journalists and a newspaper publishing something the truth of which needed to be decided.

My name and reputation were dragged through the mud and I wanted a chance to clear my name. That was and is my right and the right of any citizen.

I suspect the writer had some legal advice here because the writing style now doesn't appear to match the style in the first part of the article. But I could be wrong. After all it is not for me to pontificate on the writer's thinking.]

I might have added that in a free society the citizen is perfectly entitled to call cash for access 'corrupt' or the 'behaviour of a banana republic' or any other insult he or she wants to deploy. Free societies are boisterous places. It should be for the public to decide whether a writer or speaker has gone too far, not the courts.

[Cohen is really going to town here. He is calling cash-for-access akin to a banana republic and it looks like it is his own writing now. He is good, trying to plant words and phrases into the minds of the people reading his article.

It is ridiculous to suggest that if somebody is libelled it is up to the public to decide via a jury. Here it goes to undermine the process of libel through the courts in front of an experienced judge.

Whenever the press used to lose a high-profile case against a celebrity like, say, Elton John, the press was calling for a trial by judge. The suggestion was that the jury had stars in their eyes. You can't have it both ways.]

If we keep on having rulings like Tugendhat's, the danger for the future will not be that writers go too far but that they will not go far enough.

[The writer just couldn't stop himself in kicking Judge Tugendhat for his decision.]

But the real question is, why was the article written in the first place and whose idea was it? Did Mr Cohen decide to write it himself on his personal opinions, or was there a more sinister reason? Was he encouraged to write the article by somebody else, somebody connected to the case, to try to influence the Appeal Court judges before the appeal? Did he read the full trial judgment? In the interest of public interest journalism, I think we have a right to know. But don't hold your breath.

I have no idea if Sharp LJ would have recused herself if the article had not been published. But it didn't feel right to me.

It was fortuitous for the *Sunday Times* that such an article should appear before the Court of Appeal sat in judgment. It was also fortuitous that the judge that had ruled against the *Sunday Times* in the first appeal process was not one of the three judges that would hear the second appeal. By recusing herself Sharp LJ had completely changed the makeup of the Appeal Court judges. The three new judges would have to start from the beginning and read through all the transcripts.

Once the second Court of Appeal process was over, I issued this statement.

The court has said that the newspaper failed 'by a wide margin' to justify their suggestion that I was prepared to break UK electoral law by accepting foreign donations. What is more, they have confirmed that, based on the judge's assessment of the oral evidence from the *Sunday Times* journalists, there is no basis for overturning his decision that they were malicious and knew that suggestion to be untrue.

It is a sad day for honest journalism when a trial judge finds it very surprising that journalists should so consistently and seriously have misled their editor as to the basis on which they sought authorisation to use subterfuge against me. It is telling that the *Sunday Times* did not try to challenge that finding in the Court of Appeal.

Not long after the appeal process, Heidi Blake left the *Sunday Times*. But before she went, she and Jonathan Calvert had one more job. However, that didn't go well for them either.

The pair did an overseas investigation posing as a married couple trying to buy a baby in Bulgaria. However, they were exposed as fakes by two Bulgarian investigative journalists, who set them up in a reverse sting operation and exposed them on Bulgarian television. If you would like to see them, watch 'The Stingers Get Stung' on YouTube, https://youtu.be/8_8csduQFCo. It's worth a view.

Chapter 48

WHO JUDGES THE COURT OF APPEAL JUDGES? (NOT BY NICK COHEN!)

I asked a very good lawyer for his thoughts on the Court of Appeal judgment when writing this book. His view was that the third aspect of the appeal wasn't a good judgment. It troubled him. He felt important aspects of principle in respect of the policy considerations were dismissed and swept aside without proper scrutiny. Had they not been swept aside then the policy question would probably have had a very different outcome with a materially different result.

He also thought that on the factual aspects of the appeal, it felt as if there had been some contortions to try and reinterpret the trial judge's interpretations on questions of fact. Which was my earlier point about the reverse-engineering of the Court of Appeal decision.

His view was that this was

highly unusual as the trial judge had heard the oral evidence in a wider context than the Court of Appeal had. The Court of Appeal had only read a transcript of the trial. This was even more unusual given the trial judge's (Tugendhat J) renowned wisdom, perception of people and insight in libel trials.

His reputation was based on being a leading libel QC when practising as a barrister before joining the High Court and unquestionably being the most pre-eminent libel judge for some time since joining the Bench.

The lawyer commented as follows:

It is firstly necessary to explain why the policy question is material because it has a significant effect on the outcome of the successful part of the appeal verdict.

The second part of the judgment is more focused on the factual aspects of the libel against you as Jackson LJ saw them. But the statement he makes about a reinterpretation of the facts doesn't really align on close scrutiny with the facts.

The lead judge's (Jackson LJ) judgment is broadly in two parts. The first part of the Court of Appeal judgment is in fact a policy issue and question. This was simply because the journalists' defence to the libel action was that the current funding of the Conservative Party by wealthy donors and access to senior members of the government was morally unacceptable.

Further, the more substantial the donation then access to more senior members of Parliament could follow. This was in [the Appeal Court judges'] view 'inappropriate, unacceptable and wrong'. This, they argued, [is what] was meant by the articles in the *Sunday Times* and is key to the policy issue.

Jackson LJ says that in answering the policy question above, the question the court is being asked to decide is, what type of relationship between a political party and its individual donors is acceptable and what type of relationship is 'inappropriate, unacceptable and wrong'.

Very significantly he says in his judgment that on several occasions during the hearing he expressed his concern that the judges were not being given sufficiently wide material from counsel to decide a policy question of such wide import.

For example, they had seen nothing about the funding activities of the Labour Party. This is a reoccurring theme in his judgment. Reliance was being placed, he said, on general knowledge ...

Jackson LJ then refers to a book, *The Funding of Political Parties* by Professor Keith Ewing and others. He says he came across it. In other words, it was not submitted in evidence by counsel.

He follows this by making a strange and defensive comment. Namely, his reading of it didn't alter his views. He says he had provisionally formed such views before reading the book. It appears as if he is saying evidence he introduced, and which was not more appropriately introduced by counsel, didn't sway his opinion.

Then he adds that he had found it useful for two reasons. Firstly, helpful background material. Secondly, he says it shows that different considerations apply to (a) individual donations to political parties and (b) institutional funding of political parties.

But there is no further rationale for that statement. No explanation as to why that opinion is a good one or even one which is not just based on political considerations or even political sympathies instead of pure logic ... There is just no commentary in the judgment as to how acceptable or not that is as a bold statement. It is taken as read!

In the context of the appeal this is a highly important and significant statement to make. The importance of it and the defensive position taken in respect of its introduction is further illustrated by Jackson LJ then making the clearly defensive point in his judgment that counsel were given the opportunity to make any submissions they wished concerning Professor Ewing's book.

So, on the one hand Jackson LJ is downplaying its contribution to his reasoning as well as trying to exculpate his own conduct of introducing external evidence not submitted by counsel. As noted above he does so by saying counsel had the opportunity to challenge it.

It is quite extraordinary that the opinion in *The Funding of Political Parties* quoted by Jackson LJ (that institutional funding by for example trade unions of political parties is more democratic than individual funding) should not be subjected to more analytical questioning by the Court of Appeal.

For example, both an individual donor and a trade union may have an axe to grind or an agenda. Just because an individual may have an agenda that doesn't mean that agenda won't be of benefit to a great number of similarly placed people, and neither may the latter though its membership arrangements be particularly democratic ...

Jackson LJ then spends several pages referring to, more in a narrative style than analytically, the Committee on Standards in Public Life – an advisory non-departmental body; the Political Parties, Election and Referendums Act 2000; [and] speeches given by David Cameron and Lord Feldman (all of which led to the Transparency of Lobbying, Non-Party Campaigning & Trade Union Administration Act 2014).

He finishes this section of the judgment by referring in detail to the Conservative Party members' brochure and the various groups or clubs which donors may join. It does not explore in detail either the Labour Party['s] or Liberal Democrats' membership schemes and benefits.

The conclusion in effect drawn from this part of the judgment is that these committees and senior Conservatives acknowledge that the current funding of political parties and the ability to get access for cash is open to misconstruction by the public.

Notwithstanding ... Jackson LJ then says the conclusion he draws is that in reality it is indeed acceptable and indeed inevitable that donors will have access on social occasions to senior Conservative Party members and it may be on an intimate basis like a dinner party.

He specifically says that on such occasions it is 'inevitable and acceptable' that the conversation will range over political issues. But what he says is not acceptable on such occasions is that (a) politicians reveal confidential information, (b) the views expressed by donors on policy issues should carry greater weight merely because the proponents are donors or (c) politicians should give any form of preference to donors.

So what Jackson LJ is saying is matters discussed on such occasions could get into sensitive areas and that is not wrong. But what is wrong is if that results, in effect, in favouritism or a breach of confidential information by third parties, namely the politicians. It is for them as politicians to know when the line might be crossed because it is their conduct which makes something acceptable or not. The key is how the politicians react ...

Jackson LJ yet again further on in his judgment reverts to his concerns that he is not on strong ground.

He says that he has been worried in stating the above principle as to what is acceptable because he is trespassing on territory which has not been explored during the appeal. Namely the relationship between political parties and institutional funders such as trade unions.

Indeed so, as it is a big policy question and there are very good reasons why the courts are not the right forum for such a question.

Having raised what is obviously a problem in the approach so far taken by the court, Jackson LJ then seeks to absolve himself and the other sitting judges in the appeal by simply stating that his fears are misplaced.

And the source for that absolution he finds by referring again to ... *The Funding of Political Parties* ... and in particular Chapter 2 of the book written by Jacob Rowbottom. Namely the evidence he introduced as being authoritative of different reasons coming into play when dealing with funding of political parties by institutions.

He says that a donation from a political organisation to which members subscribe may be seen as part of a democratic effort of a group of citizens to collectively influence politics.

That is a sweeping statement to make and is made worse by being unchallenged for the reasons mentioned above.

The acceptance of principles relied on from the above book is predicated on the belief that such opinions are fair, balanced and not written by authors from a highly political angle of one sort or another. Yet the constitutional structure of many trade unions and members' rights and lack of them is not well known as being a gold standard of democracy!

What he has in effect just said is that a trade union making donations to a government and seeking influence cannot be said to be acting inappropriately, unacceptably or wrong[ly] as it is already part of the democratic process and so is bound by different principles.

Quite extraordinary!

The double standards in George Orwell's *Animal Farm* immediately came to mind! (Some animals are more equal than others.)

It is not immediately obvious why there appears to be a lack of intellectual rigour in the Court of Appeal in considering what are the applicable principles to be applied to an important part of the appeal. Particularly so when some of the underlying principles involve the court getting into public policy matters of a political nature. Basically, what conduct in the funding of political parties is acceptable, appropriate and not wrong and what isn't.

The second aspect of the appeal, namely factual matters, also surprisingly leaves a lot to be desired in terms of logic and reasoning. Compounded by the unusual selection by Jackson LJ of some points out of context of the evidence given by the witnesses (the journalists and yourself) under cross-examination in front of the trial judge, Tugendhat J.

In the policy issues question above we see in the Jackson LJ judgment sweeping unsubstantiated generalisations. By contrast on key factual issues discussed below we see a perversely very narrow and literal interpretation of some statements which ignores the wider context of what was being said and so is unrepresentative of all the evidence given before Tugendhat J.

Jackson LJ says that you said in the meeting with the journalists that 'You cannot buy access to the Prime Minister and that donations do not entitle you to influence government policy.' He then says you went on to contradict those statements. He summarised what he considered to be the contradictory statements. He lists six. They are as follows:

(i)   Donors to the Leader's Group will be invited to join the PM and senior ministers at large public events and also private dinners.

(ii)   At private dinners donors can ask the PM anything and they will pick up much useful information.

(iii) If donors are unhappy about something the government will listen and will feed their concerns into the Policy Committee at 10 Downing Street. But donors cannot change policy. Their views may be and sometimes will be rejected.

(iv)   At larger events if donors have paid enough they may be on the same table as the PM or a senior minister and if not then the PM or senior minister may come over to their table to meet them and have a brief chat.

(v)   There will be photograph opportunities with the PM and senior ministers.

(vi)   At both larger events and intimate dinner parties donors can meet captains of industry and other prominent people, which affords valuable networking opportunities.

Paragraphs (i), (iv), (v) and (vi) above are simply general summaries made by Jackson LJ of points you made in your meeting with the journalists about the level of possible engagement if you joined the Leader's Group level of membership. The summaries are taken out of context and don't acknowledge basic underlying applicable principles you made throughout the meeting.

You repeatedly said in the meeting you cannot influence policy or be guaranteed access. Donating doesn't buy you access.

It was clear from your meeting as recorded and in your cross-examination that should a donor meet the Prime Minister or a senior minister that is all. You cannot expect to be even listened to, let alone influence things ...

Paragraphs (ii) & (iii) simply make clear that whilst you can ask anything and may pick up useful information you cannot expect to influence policy.

As Jackson LJ said (as I have noted above under the policy question) as a matter of realpolitik it is indeed inevitable and acceptable for donors to have such access and have conversations about political issues but what he said isn't acceptable is for the politicians to reveal confidential information, give weight to donors' views on policy matters or give a donor an unfair commercial advantage.

It is quite a leap of deductive reasoning for Jackson LJ to move from his summary of the points you made in the course of the meeting to say that contradicts the statement you made not just early on in the meeting with the journalists but also later in that meeting.

He did acknowledge that you began by saying 'When you give to the Conservative Party it doesn't buy you access to anybody'. This was clearly understood by the trial judge (Tugendhat J) as being an underlying point of substance you were making. This Tugendhat J concluded, from seeing yourself being cross-examined rigorously, as well as all the other evidence produced to the court, including the recording of the meeting. But Jackson LJ wishes to interpret that differently.

The above are the independent views of the lawyer on the Court of Appeal verdict, and they are hard to argue with. He said he thought it was a superficial judgment which didn't require a great deal of scrutiny to be taken apart.

After this last partial appeal success by the *Sunday Times* and the two journalists, my lawyers asked me whether I wanted to appeal the decision on the winning third aspect of the *Sunday Times's* appeal. It would have gone to the Supreme Court.

I decided not to as I thought, what was the point? I had lost confidence in the Court of Appeal in the way they dealt with the policy issue and the factual evidential aspects of the original trial, in respect to the third element of the final appeal. I had lost confidence in the process because the Court of Appeal had decided that despite all my warnings to the two journalists that you cannot influence policy, you cannot buy access to ministers, they decided that I meant the opposite.

Also, to get to that verdict the Appeal Court judges decided to overrule the trial judge's verdict based on the oral evidence he had heard from all the witnesses and the cross-examination of the oral evidence.

Additionally, the Court of Appeal decided to overrule the first appeal based on a 'thorough reading of the trial transcript'. It seemed to me as if there was a concerted effort to be seen to be making some findings in favour of the *Sunday Times*. I thought it felt contrived. As if some other motivation was in play. I felt there was possibly more going on here than just my case. Meanwhile, the *Spectator* article was clearly challenging the impartiality of the original trial judge and that of the first Court of Appeal, while at the same time ignoring the conduct of the two journalists and the editorial team.

Of course, judges are meant to be above such matters. I hope they were, but it didn't feel like it. I had my doubts; the third aspect of the *Sunday Times* appeal wasn't strong. It doesn't withstand proper analysis.

That was disappointing for me and it was the basis for me not to pursue the matter any further. It just didn't feel right. Better to move on with my life. It proved to be the right decision.

Chapter 49

PROFITS, POLITICS, PEERAGE

After the original *Sunday Times* sting operation against me and the subsequent legal proceedings, I felt like I was the main victim. But then I started to think that actually I was the main winner in all of this.

Sure, I could have done without all the grief, the mockery, the insults, the criminal accusations and all the court cases. I most certainly could have done without the Prime Minister, David Cameron, vicariously defaming me on national television. But, as events moved forward, my life took a different track and led to a lot of successes. In business and in politics.

In fact, just a few days after Lord Feldman said that I should resign as co-treasurer of the Conservative Party on Saturday 24 March 2012, my life started to move in an upwards direction. I quickly realised that eventually this would all die down and I have a great family and a great business. I was not dependent on a job from the Conservatives or the government.

It was about managing my reputation – not politically, because I was not a politician, but through business. There was a remote chance that there could be criminal proceedings, but I knew that

I hadn't done anything wrong, and no crime was committed, so eventually that would die away as well. Which it did!

I had been on the cusp of resigning as party treasurer on at least two occasions, something I had discussed with Fiona more than once. Fiona was the first person I called when the story started to unravel during the day on 24 March 2012. She was always full of calm and great advice and always kept my thinking on track.

She was the one that told me to hold my head high and turn up for work the next day as I had done nothing wrong. She said my future now was the business and the family would always love and support me. She said, 'You can count on us, now get on with what you are good at, running a business, and that starts first thing Monday morning.'

The moment I was forced to resign, I got control of my life back. I was no longer running around doing political things to raise money for the Conservatives and having to deal with being undermined at CCHQ.

In the first six months after my resignation I had to deal with all the turmoil of getting lawyers, preparing my legal documents and so on. But then I took back control of the company by becoming chief executive in January 2013. That's when things really started to take off and I got back to doing what I do best.

Profits

At the end of December 2012, CMC Markets was losing money for a nine-month period. This covered the period I was chairman and Conservative co-treasurer and was the first and only time in its history the company ever lost money. Losses were approximately £20 million.

By the end of March 2013, my first full quarter as CEO, we had our best profits quarter for the year and our loss year to date was almost wiped out. Since I became CEO, I have generated approximately £550 million in profits over an eight-year period, with every year being profitable.

Alongside the improved financial performance, in December 2016, we signed the largest partner's technology deal in our history when we agreed to service ANZ Bank Australia's stockbroking business through a white label technology agreement. As part of this transaction, overnight we acquired around 1 million retail stockbroking clients and 103 intermediaries' relationships.

Within three years of taking over as CEO and after resigning as treasurer, I listed the company on the London Stock Exchange on 6 February 2016 for a valuation of approximately £700 million, from a losing position three years before. As of 2021 the market valuation is approximately £1.5 billion. In 2020 we were the second-best performing share in the FTSE 250, rising approximately 200 per cent.

Since I took over as CEO, the average profits per annum have been approximately £65 million for eight years, with a record year of £100 million in 2020 and another record profit the following year of approximately £224 million.

The total dividends for this period paid to shareholders of March 2018 was approximately £235 million. My family and I, as owners of 62.5 per cent of the company, received £180 million in the IPO listing proceeds plus 62.5 per cent of all dividends paid. As a result, I am in the top fifty taxpayers in the UK.

Politics

I became a Eurosceptic over several years, primarily because the European Union was moving into a more centralised and integrated system with less control in Westminster and more control moving to Brussels. There is no need to list all my concerns here about the EU but it's fair to say that I thought that political and financial integration by the EU was outside of the original Common Market concept, which I supported.

Since the first EEC referendum in 1975, we have seen all sorts of changes to the EU project and not once were the British people asked if that was what they wanted. It was certainly not what I wanted. I wanted our general elections to mean that we appointed a government and they were accountable to the electorate.

Brussels was becoming less accountable as its controls grew. To me it was back-door socialism.

Now I was no longer on the Conservative Party board and their treasurer I was free to take on any political jobs and roles I wanted. I was so glad that I could do this because I was passionate about leaving the European Union. One might even say that it was my destiny to be involved in the EU referendum. I already had experience from the No2AV campaign, where I had worked with Matthew Elliott, and we would team up again on Vote Leave, which I co-founded. It was almost as if No2AV was a warm-up event for the main EU referendum event, which would come a few years later.

Call it fate, call it destiny, who knows, but I played a major role in the running of the very successful Vote Leave campaign, working alongside Boris Johnson, Priti Patel, Michael Gove, Dominic Cummings, Matthew Elliott and Gisela Stuart, our chairperson. I became a board member, treasurer and one of their biggest donors in the run-up to the EU referendum. I campaigned on the red battle bus with Boris Johnson and Priti Patel in Preston.

Everything happens for a reason and without the *Sunday Times* sting I would not have been part of Vote Leave. If I had still been Conservative Party treasurer, there is no way I could have gone against the Prime Minister's Remain stance. I could not have campaigned or donated to Vote Leave because of my position within the party. I would have just stayed in the background and let others work for Vote Leave.

It was an amazing and victorious campaign, and today we have a Brexit government with Boris as our Prime Minister, Priti as our Home Secretary and many other Brexiteers in Cabinet and the House of Lords including me as Lord Cruddas of Shoreditch.

Peerage

Boris Johnson became Conservative Party leader in the summer of 2019 and on 9 September there were treasurers' drinks for supporters and donors to the Conservative Party in London.

Even though the referendum was in 2016 we had still not left the European Union. Primarily because the Conservative government led by Theresa May could not agree on a withdrawal agreement that Parliament would vote for. There was stalemate in the Commons and the Conservative Party elected Boris Johnson as a prominent Brexiteer to lead the party and to find a way forward.

I have various pictures of Boris and me hugging on the referendum result day, 24 June 2016, which hold pride of place in my office. These were taken at the offices of Vote Leave in Westminster, on the morning of the results. I also have a surreal photo of Boris watching the television as his father, Stanley Johnson, a Remainer, gave an interview.

At the drinks event, I chatted with Danny Kruger, who was Boris's political secretary at the time. Danny said I would be coming in to see the PM at No. 10 Downing Street soon, as he wanted to discuss a few things with me. A meeting was set for 19 September at 4.45 p.m., which I happily attended.

The reason for the meeting was that the Prime Minister said he wanted to elevate me to the House of Lords, as he was extremely grateful for all that I had done for the country in supporting and working for the Vote Leave campaign. He also wanted to recognise my charitable work and support, not least for the Conservative Party, over many years.

He said:

You have supported three different Prime Ministers, you have worked as treasurer and been on the board of the Conservative Party. Also, you have been a major part of two important referendums. You have contributed greatly through business, creating jobs and revenues for the country. Peter, you are a hero for this country. Your business success and experience and political successes will be an asset to the House of Lords, and I want you to continue to beat the drum of capitalism and Brexit.

I told the PM that I was extremely honoured by his recommendation and I gratefully accepted. I said I would keep everything confidential until it was officially announced. I did ask when the appointment would be announced, to which one of Boris's aides replied he wasn't sure because various checks needed to be made, and I should just be patient.

The meeting ended after about thirty minutes and it was great to catch up with Boris. Ben Elliot, the Conservative Party chairman, who was at the meeting, took a lovely photo of me standing outside No. 10 on this very special day.

I was next invited to No. 10 on 31 January 2020, marking the day we finally left the European Union. This time Fiona was with me and we were there for a Brexit party. I should make it clear that Fiona was there to support me and not necessarily as a Brexit supporter. I am not sure if Fiona voted Leave or Remain as I try to keep politics outside our home, and I wouldn't dream of asking her. That's her business and nothing to do with me.

We celebrated with many fellow Vote Leave workers including Dominic Cummings and Gisela Stuart. I estimated over 100 people were there. We were even drinking Brexit beer which had been supplied by Vote Leave director Jon Moynihan. Jon had commissioned a special brew from a Reading brewery, and it had a special Brexit label. I wore my Vote Leave badge for the evening. There was a great speech from the Prime Minister and Dominic Cummings said a few words, which was a bit emotional.

Fiona and I left around midnight and there were masses of people in the streets around Parliament Square. As we were walking home, I thought, not many people can say they spent the moment the UK left the European Union with the Prime Minister at No. 10 Downing Street. As a prominent Brexiteer it felt amazing.

Eventually the peerage announcement was made on 22 December 2020. As the announcement was made, the Prime Minister published a letter alongside the press release, because the House of Lords Appointments Commission (HOLAC) did not support my nomination.

HOLAC's role is to undertake vetting of all nominations to the House of Lords. The Commission is an independent non-statutory body. It provides advice, but appointments are a matter for the Prime Minister.

The Commission stated that it had completed its vetting in respect of all nominees. The Commission advised the Prime Minister that it could not support one nominee – Peter Cruddas. This may have caused a delay in my elevation to the Lords, because in September 2020 No. 10 had released a list of new peers and I was not on that list, although I had expected to be.

I was surprised that HOLAC had not supported my nomination, primarily because the police and the Electoral Commission had said quite categorically that they found no evidence of wrongdoing in the *Sunday Times* affair. Also, I had already been through a thorough vetting process before my nomination had even got to HOLAC as I had to give permission to the Lords compliance team to conduct various checks on me.

As part of that process, I had to list all political donations past and any more that I would make in the run-up to my introduction to the Lords. I was even asked to supply a biography for my introduction. I also had to sign a legal document declaring that I did not have any personal financial relationships with any politically exposed people including senior government ministers, either directly or indirectly.

Further, I had a clean Criminal Records Bureau (CRB) check, and my tax status and payments were all up to date. I had no tax investigations. I had no business black marks around regulatory breaches and investigations over a thirty-year period.

Everywhere you looked my record was clean. So, it came as a complete surprise to me that HOLAC would not support my nomination.

HOLAC's mandate is not to reject anybody for political reasons. So, all I could surmise was that it was because of the limited successful appeal by the *Sunday Times* at their Court of Appeal hearing. But I felt that was not a valid reason for HOLAC not to support my nomination.

So, I came to the conclusion that my nomination was in effect not supported by HOLAC because I was doing what every political party was doing: raising money for their party through a perfectly legal system that everybody used. Therefore, HOLAC were not supporting my nomination for doing my job. I wonder whether the totally out-of-context reporting by some sections of the media influenced HOLAC? I would hope not.

However, No. 10 Downing Street took the time and effort to look at the facts and establish exactly the outcome of the Court of Appeal findings. They did their homework and found that actually it was the perfectly legal system of raising funds that was being criticised extensively.

This was important because there has been a lot of lynch mob journalism around the limited appeal success by the *Sunday Times* and the journalists, with non-existent reporting of their malicious falsehoods. There has been little or no balance to the appeal outcome in the press. It is reported out of context and is misleading, without fairness to what was the final outcome.

By establishing the facts No. 10 did not endorse the lynch mob journalism, which I am grateful for. It also explains why they felt they could bypass the HOLAC decision to not support my nomination.

As for HOLAC, not only do they ostensibly appear to support lynch mob journalism, but they also cast doubt on my reputation and character, and that is very serious. Their own processes should not be above scrutiny and challenge if they do not want to look like a local lodge of the Freemasons.

This is the letter that the Prime Minister published alongside my nomination on 22 December 2020, addressed to the chair of HOLAC, Lord Bew:

Dear Lord Bew,

I am grateful for your letter of 18 December and to you and your Commission Members' careful and thoughtful advice in respect of the most recent nominations for appointment to the House of Lords.

It is my expectation that we will publish a Political Peerage List on Tuesday 22 December. This will include the public service Crossbench nominations that your Commission has also considered and supported.

I have previously invited the Commission to consider a nomination for Peter Cruddas. The Commission has confirmed that it is unable to support the nomination. This relates to historic concerns in respect of allegations made during Mr Cruddas' term as Treasurer of the Conservative Party, and the judgment reached by the Court of Appeal in subsequent libel action.

It is vital that we give due weight and consideration to your scrutiny of these matters. There are, however, a number of wider factors which must also play into the consideration of this case. Firstly, the most serious accusations levelled at the time were found to be untrue and libellous. In order to avoid any ongoing concern, Mr Cruddas resigned from his post, and offered an apology for any impression of impropriety, and reflecting his particular concern for integrity in public life.

An internal Conservative Party investigation subsequently found that there had been no intentional wrongdoing on Mr Cruddas' part.

The events in question date back eight years, and the Commission has found no suggestion of any matters of concern before or since that time. Mr Cruddas has made outstanding contributions in the charitable sector and in business and has continued his long track record of committed political service. His charitable foundation, which supports disadvantaged young people, has pledged over £16 million to good causes through over 200 charities and he is a long-standing supporter of both the Prince's Trust and the Duke of Edinburgh Award.

I have given very careful consideration to the points raised by the Commission and have weighed these alongside the mitigating and wider points I have set out here.

Mr Cruddas was born without the advantages of many of those in the House of Lords and has gone on to become one of this country's most successful business figures. His broad range of experiences and insights across the charitable, business and political sectors will, in my view, allow him to make a hugely valuable contribution to the work of the House and on this basis, it is my intention to recommend his appointment to Her Majesty in light of that benefit to public service.

I would like to reassure you and your colleagues that I see this case as a clear and rare exception. Whilst the Commission's role is advisory, I continue to place great weight on your careful and considered opinions.

It will, of course, be important to ensure the position is transparent and well understood. I will make clear when we publish the List that I have, after careful consideration of the issues, reached a different conclusion to the Commission on this particular case; in the interest of transparency, I also will place this letter in the public domain.

Yours

Boris Johnson

Prime Minister

After the announcement was made and the list published, I was very grateful to the Prime Minister for writing this very supportive letter and placing it in the public domain.

I also got quite a few friends calling me, some from within the Lords. The overwhelming response was that there was no reason for HOLAC not to support my elevation. It was good that Boris overrode their decision.

The feedback I was getting was that I should be in the Lords because I was more representative of the electorate as a prominent Brexiteer. Apparently, the House of Lords is two thirds Remain supporting, and it is quite right that, since the UK voted to leave the European Union, more Brexiteers should be elevated to the Lords.

Also, quite a few of my friends said that the Lords should welcome me with open arms just for my success in business and the entrepreneurial experience I could bring to the Lords. They said HOLAC's reluctance was down to snobbery because of my background.

Whether any of this was true or not I do not know or care. However, with these points in mind I gave my maiden speech on 12 March 2021. Time was tight and I was only given two minutes along with other new peers, but I enjoyed the speech as it was a very proud moment for me.

My Lords, it is a great privilege and honour to deliver my first speech to your Lordships' House. First, I will quickly thank Black Rod and her team, and the many helpers and support staff who have been so helpful to me. I also quickly thank Garter [King of Arms, the senior officer of the College of Arms], who I found very helpful. I have a special thank you for the noble Baroness, Lady Stuart, and my noble friend Lord Leigh of Hurley, for introducing me to your Lordships' House ...

In Easter 1969, I left Shoreditch Comprehensive School, Hackney, with no qualifications and no job. I was fifteen years old. I had no choice; my mum needed the money. I got a job as a telegram operator with Western Union. I would give all my weekly wage to my mother. I have not been out of work since. At eighteen I joined a bank in the City as a money market dealer's assistant. In 1989, at the age of thirty-six, I started my own financial services company, which I still run today and which is listed on the London Stock Exchange. In 1996, I launched Europe's first online trading system to allow people to buy and sell financial products.

Off the back of this success, I started my Peter Cruddas Foundation to help and support disadvantaged young people. To date, my foundation – which is funded entirely by me – has donated to over 200 charities. I also had some political successes, namely No2AV and Vote Leave; I was a director and treasurer for both campaigns.

I will do my best to support your Lordships' House with my experience and expertise. I will do so freely and with an open mind. My objective is to be an asset here.

With roaring profits, political success with Vote Leave and a peerage, if there was a loser after the *Sunday Times* sting and legal processes, it didn't feel like it was me. However, that doesn't mean things have been easy, especially with the continuous disingenuous reporting by the press on my case.

Lynch mob journalism

What has been personally very disappointing and quite sad from a wider perspective is the clear disrespect sections of the media and press have for the public.

It is their job and duty as journalists or media commentators to properly inform the public about current topics of interest. Yet, as was apparent in December 2020 when my nomination to the Lords was announced and again, when my continued donations to the Conservative Party were quite correctly in the public domain, sections of the media went into overdrive. They continued to report out of context extracts from the Court of Appeal judgment, as I have shown in earlier chapters.

The out-of-context reporting has been seriously misleading and to me clearly shows in a very bad light those sections of the media that continue with it. Because it fails to address a key point in my case against the *Sunday Times*, namely that the paper and its two journalists were malicious liars.

The reporters are misinforming the readers or audience whom they seek to address. There is neither balance nor judgement. No insightful editorial comment. To continue to quote out of context comments ten years after the event simply confirms that what they have to say is more driven by vitriol than anything else. It demeans them, but they clearly cannot see that.

It must bring into question their judgement and the values of their reporting, as proper journalistic commentary has clearly gone out of the window. A strongly balanced, even polemical, piece on the real policy issue in the case – by whom and how should political parties be funded – or proper commentary on the malicious falsehoods the judges found the journalists guilty of would raise their professionalism and esteem. It would also show some respect to their readers. But their manner of reporting, so long after the case, continues to display a malice which the judges commented on when they referred to the malicious falsehoods of the *Sunday Times* journalists.

It seems to be endemic, in the DNA of those in the media who continue to report as they do. By doing so they are beginning to look like characters in a Western – a bunch of self-important small-town empty vessels drowning out reason to incite a lynch mob.

As either a reader or an owner I wouldn't want to be associated with lynch mob journalism. There should be no place for it in a civilised society. But sadly, over these last few years there are many high-profile people from all sorts of worlds (business, entertainment, politics) who have been subjected to inaccurate and in some instances highly deliberate and damaging and even malicious reporting.

I am grateful that the Prime Minister and his office clearly spent the time to check out the facts and did not rely on inaccurate reporting or pay attention to tweets from certain people who are more interested in their own profile than in what is actually accurate and correct, who jump on any bandwagon just to get their name in the public domain.

Says more about them than anything else.

Chapter 50

THE 'INDEPENDENT' GOLD INQUIRY

Before the appeal process and after I won my judgment in August 2013, I went to the south of France for a holiday. As soon as I landed at Nice airport, my mobile phone rang. Lo and behold, it was the chairman of the Conservative Party, Lord Feldman, wanting to have a chat. This was the first time I had heard from Feldman since that fateful night in March 2012 apart from a short call from him on 23 April 2012.

Before my trial with Heidi Blake, Jonathan Calvert and the *Sunday Times*, Feldman and David Cameron had set up an 'independent' inquiry headed by Lord Gold to investigate the allegations made by the paper. I was to be invited to speak to Lord Gold to put my side of the story. However, when Feldman called me on 23 April 2012, he effectively pre-empted the Gold Inquiry outcome as he told me to forget politics and concentrate on business. I thought, bloody hell, at least let's wait to see what Lord Gold has to say.

It would have been difficult to discuss anything with Andrew Feldman while this inquiry was ongoing. But that didn't stop him ringing me, to say, 'Time to move on, old boy, your services are no longer required.'

I shrugged this off because I thought I would have my day in court, and we will see how this all pans out. I knew a victory for me would put Cameron and Feldman in an invidious position. But that was all for later.

Also, at this time I was still considering whether to sue the Prime Minister for defamation. But for now, I would bide my time. I took the knocks because I knew my day would come.

However, it didn't take long to form the view that the Gold Inquiry seemed more interested in protecting others rather than getting to the truth. The so-called 'independent' inquiry would soon unravel.

On 7 June 2012, around 7.10 p.m., I had a phone call from Stanley Fink, my immediate replacement as Conservative Party treasurer. It was a hot summer's evening and I was in my daughter's garden kicking a football with my grandchildren. I put the call on speaker so my daughter could hear what Stanley had to say.

Stanley said he had spoken to Lord MacGregor, a friend of his who had called him. MacGregor was one of the people on the Gold Inquiry team and he was assisting Lord Gold to get to the bottom of the story. MacGregor had told Stanley that he had seen the full video recording of the meeting between me and the journalists. Stanley had not seen the tape recording himself, because he was not part of the Gold Inquiry team.

Stanley also said that MacGregor told him that I had been completely stitched up by the journalists and they had been shockingly deceitful about the meeting. Stanley said it was clear that this was a stitch-up.

My first thoughts were that Stanley (who is a good friend and nice guy) was calling me up to give me the wink to sue the journalists. But I thought wrong. I quickly learnt that the reason for the call from Stanley was not for my benefit.

Stanley went on to say that if I sued the *Sunday Times*, I would only win £10,000 damages as that was the norm, but it would cost me £1 million in legal fees. He said the *Sunday Times* would simply be required to print a small apology on one of the back pages and it was not worth the effort. Especially as I would be massively out of pocket in exchange for a small one-line apology from the newspaper. If I sued the newspaper, Stanley said, it could create all sorts of bad press and it would reflect badly on the Conservative Party and there would be no way back for me. But if I didn't sue, when things quietened down there could be a way back.

Then Stanley said that the best thing for all concerned was, when it was my turn to view the tape recording as part of the Gold Inquiry, that I should take with me the Conservative Party lawyer, because my own lawyers would be keen to sue so they could make their fees.

Firstly, I thought, 'What the hell is going on?' The Gold Inquiry was meant to be an attempt to establish the facts and was there to find out the truth, then print an open report on what happened. That's what David Cameron promised on television.

I realised Stanley was not calling me for my own benefit, it was obvious. Which made me instantly angry. Also, if this was correct, it was troubling that Lord MacGregor appeared to be involving Stanley, who was not part of the Gold Inquiry. He seemed to have undermined the credibility of the so-called independent inquiry by discussing the tape with Stanley before I had viewed it, and they were trying to head off any fallout once I viewed the tape. What a disgrace. From that moment on, I had no intention of speaking to the Gold Inquiry.

I assumed that somebody on the Gold Inquiry team was worried that this could escalate, dragging the Conservative Party and the Prime Minister into litigation. The Prime Minister might even have to appear in court if I litigated against him personally. It would be clear to any lawyer that if I was going to sue the *Sunday Times* and I had a more than fair chance of winning, then I could drag the PM into the litigation at the same time.

I do not know whose idea it was to ask Stanley to call me, but it must have come from a high authority as the motive was to put me off litigating against the *Sunday Times* with the offer that there would be a way back for me in the future. Alarm bells must have been ringing because a few days later I even got a phone call along the same lines from a peer friend.

If the Gold Inquiry was not going to get to the bottom of the issue but seemed more interested in protecting the Prime Minister from all sorts of embarrassing situations, then Stanley's call was their first course of action to that end.

Of course, this is not the first time a political party has set up an 'independent' inquiry to investigate so-called misdemeanours. But this time, I was on the receiving end and I was not in the mood to roll over. I thought this behaviour was disgraceful because of the complete lack of consideration for the welfare of my family and myself. This was about as low as it gets.

It took me about ten seconds to explode into rage on the phone. Talk about shooting the messenger – I tore into poor Stanley, who thought he was only trying to do the right thing for everybody concerned. Stanley meant well but I had had enough.

I said, 'Stanley, you must be fucking joking. I do not care what fucking damage suing the *Sunday Times* does to the Conservative Party or the PM, they should have thought about that on the night the story broke. My only concern is for my family, myself and our welfare and that's what comes first.'

I said David Cameron and Andrew Feldman had never asked for my side of the story. They cast me adrift without any concern for the consequences and the damage Cameron's remarks had for my charities, my business and my family.

I told Stanley I was going to do what was right for my family and me. I was not going to speak to the Gold Inquiry, and I was definitely going to sue the *Sunday Times*. I said I was not bothered about costs of litigation as the £1 million it would cost me to sue the *Sunday Times* was money I was going to donate to the Conservative Party but now it would be better spent on my lawyers.

I quickly put the phone down on him. Later, after I had calmed down, I did feel a bit bad about the way I had spoken to Stanley, who is a friend and a decent man. Stanley was only trying to sort things out, I guess he was one of the few people from the Conservative Party at this time that could call me, and I would take the call.

The only leverage the Conservative Party had over me not to cause them lots of grief was to dangle the carrot of reintegration, at some stage in the future. But I would have to play ball now.

However, I was not in the mood to be conciliatory and Stanley got both barrels from me. Fortunately, I was with the grandchildren, who wanted me to kick the ball to them again, so I calmed down quickly.

Afterwards, discussing the call with my daughter, I realised that the call was a good sign. Because clearly other people who had seen the tape thought I was stitched up.

This was the first bit of feedback I had following the meeting with the journalists. I had not seen the video tape, and neither had anybody from my team. We were still waiting for permission from the *Sunday Times* to see it. So, all the information and comments about the meeting were coming from the *Sunday Times*. It was only their side of the story, until Stanley's call.

At the time of the call from Stanley my only record of the meeting was my own memory and notes. Now it looked as though others were agreeing with my recollection of events. This gave me a boost and effectively put me on the front foot. I viewed the tape a few weeks later and events unfolded as previously described in this book.

When the phone call came from Stanley, I was ready to sue the Prime Minister's arse off and drag him to court. In the end I decided not to, for reasons that are mentioned above. However, I kept the option open in case I had any more nonsense from Cameron and Feldman. I didn't want them to think that their actions had no consequences.

The cut-off point for suing the Prime Minister was one year after the *Sunday Times* story was published. A long time to wait for a knock on the door from my lawyers. I always had a vision of my lawyers presenting a summons in person to David Cameron at No. 10 Downing Street and the cameras filming it. But then I thought I would be lowering myself to the level of the journalists, so I let the Prime Minister off the hook.

It was probably the right thing to do although plenty of friends and family were pushing me to do it, because of the way Cameron had criticised me on national television. But ultimately in the end the trial judge's criticism of him would have more impact than anything I said or did as he was completely independent.

I rest my case.

Chapter 51

AN ETON MESS

When Lord Feldman called me in August 2013, after I won my legal case, he wanted a nice friendly chat. He said, 'David and I congratulate you on your well-deserved victory, we are delighted for you. David would like to invite you in for a cup of tea and a chat at No. 10 Downing Street.'

I thought, 'Yes, I bet he does,' but I had no appetite to meet him. David Cameron may have been Prime Minister, but he only wanted to meet me to try and repair some of the damage he had caused for himself in the media through his lack of judgement. It was a damage limitation phone call as far as I was concerned. I was not in the mood to be forgiving.

So I told Feldman, 'I am on holiday for a few weeks. When I get back, I will think about it but for now I am going to relax and enjoy my holiday.'

Feldman pushed me for a date on the phone. I could understand why he wanted to get something in the diary. On the steps of the Royal Courts of Justice, a journalist had asked me whether David Cameron should apologise to me for the way he treated me. My response was, 'Well, if it was me, I would apologise.' Feldman wanted to get a date in the diary so he could say something to the press along the lines of 'the PM will be meeting with Peter after the summer holidays'. But I knew what they were up to, so I just said I would think about it and let the buggers stew a bit.

At the time, there was a small campaign building in the press for the PM to apologise to me. Clearly there was potential political capital for opposition parties in showing the Prime Minister in a bad light. I thought he had done a good job of that himself, especially being criticised by a High Court judge that had seen the evidence. But anyway, it wasn't my problem. I was on holiday enjoying my well-earned break and victory.

Initially, I decided not to meet with Cameron and Feldman. I thought they had been sitting in the wings watching events unfold like Waldorf and Statler, without really paying attention and realising the potential fallout for them, if I won my case. So I would just ignore them. I thought these two had no real interest in meeting me, except to manage any fallout for themselves.

They didn't call me before the court case to wish me well. The PM had not thanked me for what I had done for the party, No2AV and his charities. So, the only thing that had changed was me winning the court case and the position it put them in.

However, in the end, I changed my mind and met David Cameron at No. 10 Downing Street. It turned out to be a lively meeting.

On Wednesday 4 September 2013 in the early evening, I walked through the front door of No. 10 and waited a few minutes for Andrew Feldman to greet me. I didn't know the meeting was going to be in the PM's private residence, although when I found out I presumed they wanted it there so that it did not have to appear in the No. 10 visitors' political diary. I immediately thought, 'Well, it wasn't private when the PM defamed me on national television.'

Andrew led me up the stairs and there was the Prime Minister with Ed Llewellyn, his chief of staff. This was the first time I had met David Cameron or even spoken to him since that fateful night in March 2012. They were all smiles and handshakes. I didn't realise that Llewellyn was going to be present at the meeting, but he said very little. He just sat and listened and poured the PM and me a drink.

I remember walking into the room thinking, 'Fuck me, am I at an Eton and Oxford reunion?' They were all posh boys together. Probably Llewellyn was there to make sure that the Prime Minister stayed on script and in case it got nasty and they needed someone to keep notes. Who knows? But I am sure it was a meeting they were not looking forward to because they just didn't know how I was going to react.

I think they were also a bit concerned because Lord (Michael) Ashcroft had been writing articles during my court cases and my various victories along the way. Ashcroft's articles had questioned whether the PM and the Conservative Party had acted too hastily, before establishing the facts.

At the meeting, the Prime Minister looked relaxed in an open-necked shirt, which slightly surprised me as the week before he had lost a Commons vote on bombing Syria and I had seen him on television looking a bit stressed. Here he was not stressed at all. I couldn't help thinking, this guy loves being Prime Minister. A few years later, as I watched his resignation speech, I thought back to this meeting and how much he seemed to enjoy the job. It must have hurt him deeply to resign.

The apartment was big and spacious and nice with a big mural on the wall and large windows onto St James's Park. I had been to

No. 10 on a few occasions before for functions, but I had only seen it from the front and the garden at the back. This was a beautiful apartment with stunning views. There was no sign of his wife and children.

The PM said I looked well and asked if I had lost weight. 'Too true, mate,' I thought. 'Of course I've lost weight, I've been fighting the press and putting up with shit since you slagged me off on national television last year.' However, I just thanked him and said I was fine. I was in a cordial mood and enjoying the moment as the posh boys looked uncomfortable and uneasy. As far as I was concerned, this was a victory for me, and the three amigos were on the rack ready to eat some humble pie or, more appropriately, Eton mess.

It was time for them to squirm a bit. I am sure they hated every minute of it as these three were used to people sucking up to them but that was not my style.

The PM kicked things off with what seemed to me to be a scripted and rehearsed apology. He said if he had known at the time how badly the journalists had behaved, he might have acted differently. I had to laugh because as he was delivering his so-called apology Ed Llewellyn was pouring him a pint of beer to show he was one of the boys.

I just asked for a glass of water.

The PM barely touched the beer, but at least good old Ed was doing his duty and fagging for Cameron. The Bullingdon Club would be proud of their boys mixing it with the plebs.

Once the scripted apology was delivered, the PM just sat there and waited for my response. I had promised Fiona that I would not lose my cool and I tried hard not to.

My first thought was, 'Well, is that it?' I was annoyed because I thought the apology completely lacked sincerity. I felt it was just meant to tick a box so the Eton boys could say to anybody that asked, 'Oh yes, we have seen Peter, and everything is fine.'

I am sure the Prime Minister had more important issues to deal with and I understood that, but this was an important issue to my family and me; and it was important that the Prime Minister made a sincere apology so that we could move on. I thought that was the least he could do. After all, I had agreed to meet him in private. I had not said anything in the press to the effect that I was waiting for an apology. I was quite prepared to accept an apology in private and let the matter rest.

It would only have taken a moment for him to say something along the lines of, 'Peter, I'm very sorry about all this, I got it wrong and I am sorry for the grief I caused you. I am glad you won your case and you sorted it all out. I want us both to put this whole episode behind us and see if we can find a solution for you.'

But he didn't.

He then went on to say he hadn't realised how badly the journalists had behaved and at least I had now cleared my name.

I could feel myself getting angry inside, but I tried to control my feelings and I said to the PM, 'Well, if this is your apology then I am not accepting it.' I said it wasn't good enough. His response was, 'Well, if you do not accept my apology how can we move forward?'

He tried to smooth things a bit by saying, 'We want you back in the fold,' and he asked whether I would consider joining a Leader's Group dinner the following week, which he would attend.

I told Cameron that if he really wanted to put things right then I needed to be fully integrated back into the party in a senior position, like before. I said I would like my old job back. I wasn't sure if

I really wanted my old job back, but I thought I would push them a bit to see how far they would go to put things right.

Feldman interrupted and said, 'It doesn't work like that.'

'Well, it did when you asked me to take on the role of treasurer of No2AV.'

'But we don't have a vacancy for treasurer.'

'There was no vacancy as treasurer to the No2AV campaign,' I said. 'They already had a treasurer, but that didn't stop you, as the incumbent treasurer was just kicked to one side when you asked me to inject £500,000 as a fighting fund and become the new No2AV treasurer.

'You created the vacancy so why not now? You boys can do what you like, there's nothing stopping you.'

It was clear that they still had contempt for me, that Feldman didn't want me back in a senior role and that they wanted to get the so-called apology over with and send me on my way. If this was the case, that's fine, but I was not going to make it easy for them. I was beginning to think this meeting was a sham just like the Gold Inquiry.

The conversation continued but in my mind the PM was just going through the motions. So, I tried to make him feel uncomfortable by pointing out all the things I had done for him. I figured I would only have one shot at this and if all I left with was the scripted apology then at least I could give them an emotional kicking and feel better about myself and the whole situation. I was well rehearsed in what I was going to say as I knew what they were like.

I pointed out that I had given the National Citizen Service (NCS), David Cameron's pet project, a substantial donation of £600,000 to get it up and running. I had also been appointed a trustee of the charity. The donation included a £200,000 request for additional funds made when I was attending the NCS launch at No. 10 Downing Street on 22 July 2010. At this launch, attended by Michael Caine and other celebrities, the PM had stood up and said, 'If it wasn't for Peter Cruddas we would not be here today.' It was a nice speech telling everybody there what a great guy I was. Michael Caine gave me a big hug and a pat on the back and said, 'Well done, son'. A few minutes later, I got a tap on the shoulder from an MP who asked me to donate more.

Now I reminded the PM of the extra funds that had been requested, and that I had injected, following the event at No. 10. It was important because the NCS was running out of money and needed to survive a few more months, until it could expect to receive some money in the first round of government funding later that year.

The PM was beginning to squirm a bit, so I thought I might as well carry on. There was no sincerity coming from the other side of the pint of beer, which was getting a bit flat by now – as was the PM – but I was loving it. I said, 'Prime Minister, do you remember when you called me personally to ask me a favour, when you asked me to donate £20,000 to the Youth Adult Trust?' This donation was to close this charity, so they could start the NCS.

He replied, 'Yes, I do remember that.'

I also pointed out that, since he had become leader, I had donated around £1.2 million to the Conservative Party.

But I was just warming up now, so I decided to give the PM a bit more grief. I said, 'Do you know that I could have sued you personally for vicariously defaming me for what you said on national television about me?'

'Yes, I do know that, and I thank you for not doing so, but why did you not sue me?'

'Because I didn't want to put my family through any more stress. Can you imagine the headlines if I sued the incumbent Prime Minister?'

I said there were more important things in life and although I wanted to sue Cameron personally, I decided my family had had enough of all the nonsense and they were more important. It was better for them if this all went away, the quicker the better.

At last, this prompted some sincerity from the PM because he seemed genuinely grateful that I hadn't sued him.

After I had let off steam a bit, they asked me about things with Lord Ashcroft. I said Michael had been a good supporter of my cause by writing various articles. Then Cameron started swearing and saying things like, 'I don't know why Michael fucking dislikes me. I know he wants to get rid of me and maybe he will succeed, I don't fucking know.' Clearly the Prime Minister was rattled by Ashcroft and was swearing like a trooper. I couldn't believe my ears.

I was a bit shocked to hear the PM swearing, especially as I tried not to use any swear words myself during our meeting. But I remember at the end of the meeting thinking, 'Bloody hell, I don't know how or why but Ashcroft has got under the skin of Cameron.'

Towards the end of the meeting I said to Cameron that I am a loyal Conservative and I had put up with a lot of crap over the last eighteen months or so. But to move on I said that I not only needed to be integrated back into the party, but it had to be seen that I had been integrated back into the party. Cameron replied that he had a history of putting things right and I should trust him.

Eventually, I felt it was best to stop kicking them around emotionally and see what happened over the coming weeks. At least we were talking after twelve months of silence from them.

The meeting lasted for about forty minutes and ended with

Feldman offering to meet me a few weeks later to see if they could find a new role for me. I wasn't sure they were going to come back to me, but I thought, 'Well, I am in No. 10, I have had a sort of apology from the PM, so let's see what they come up with.'

The Prime Minister walked me down the stairs to the front entrance and as we went to the front door, we exchanged some small talk. It was the day before his trip to the G20 summit in St Petersburg. That is why I think he had time to see me the evening before he packed and prepared for his trip and probably why the family were not in the apartment. They had probably taken off to Oxfordshire while the PM was going to be away.

I wished him well and he said Putin was in a tough-talking mood, so he was not expecting it to go well. It was general chit-chat and he was not giving away state secrets, but I think the PM felt a bit bad about things and wanted to come across as friendly.

As I left No. 10 and walked down Whitehall, I called my wife. Her first words were 'How did it go?' I said, 'Well, I think I have said enough to get a mention in his autobiography,' and we both laughed.

I said, overall, I was disappointed with the apology and 'it's lucky that Larry the Downing Street cat was not around as I might have kicked it up the arse as I left'. Again, we laughed as Fiona knows I am a big cat lover so I must have been angry. It was a joke, but it broke some of the tension I was feeling.

I had a few more meetings with Lord Feldman at CCHQ but I felt they were just fobbing me off with meaningless offers – trustee of the NCS, or trustee of the Conservative Party Foundation, party-related fringe jobs. There were no offers to reinstate me to the main board of the party or as treasurer.

In my mind, to put things right after their bad behaviour, they had to fully integrate me back to where I was before with a high-status position. That would have shown real remorse and vindication for the way they treated me. I felt it could have all been managed. It was probably never going to happen because they never liked to admit their mistakes, but I thought, 'Well, those are my terms – take them or leave them.'

During one of my meetings with Lord Feldman he said, 'Well, Peter, you did say a lot during the meeting with the journalists.' I snapped and responded sharply with 'What do you mean? Like calling people swivel-eyed loons?' Feldman had been reported as saying this about party workers at an event, so he had little to talk about. I had had enough of these people treating me like a nobody, I wasn't going to put up with it anymore.

During my last meeting with Feldman, I said their offer to put things right was not good enough. Feldman asked me to reconsider but I said I felt the jobs on offer were below the status of the one I had been kicked out of by their mistakes and their lack of wanting to hear my side of the story. I said I found their whole behaviour since I won my case to be just as bad as it had been before.

As my meetings with Andrew Feldman were coming to an end, I kept on thinking of my time as treasurer and the way that Feldman and Cameron were running the party. I felt it was fundamentally flawed.

I have seen this a thousand times in business, where people promote their friends and cronies to give them a support mechanism in case one day the shit hits the fan. It is a safety-in-numbers thing. It has little to do with promoting people on merit and all to do with protectionism.

I knew that this nepotism at the top of the party would come back to hurt the Prime Minister. It always does in business. It was only a matter of time.

As I left our final meeting, I looked Feldman in the eye and said, 'Andrew, you need to put this right and if you don't put it right then I will.'

I could see confusion on his face and in his eyes. I am sure he was thinking, 'How's this bloke going to put things right? Who the hell does he think he is?' Well, he didn't have to wait long to find out that my warning would come true.

Chapter 52

YOU REAP WHAT YOU SOW

After my various meetings with Andrew Feldman following David Cameron's so-called 'apology' I had little appetite to donate to the Conservative Party under their leadership although I would have done so and moved on if they had put things right. Even though I had been a big donor in the past, the party was well-funded, so in their eyes they had no use for me.

As far as they were concerned, there was no need to find a (meaningful) role for me or to put things right. So, we basically went our separate ways. I was still a member of the Conservative Party and I would vote Conservative at the next election.

I thought David Cameron was a good leader of the party but inexperienced in life and commercial matters, although not politically. He was clearly a good politician and I always thought that he was a good speaker. He knew how to work a crowd and he was popular among donors.

However, I could always see a day when things would blow up, because the party structure was all wrong and they had had no interest in listening to me whenever I brought it up in the past. Whether Cameron would survive a blow-up or not I did not know, but I knew he was heading for some problems and those problems would manifest themselves through the party structure that he had created.

Andrew Feldman was too close to the PM, and too secure in his role as party chairman, I saw this as a weakness and a long-term area of concern. It also led to a conflict of interest between the leader and the chairman.

Being chairman of a political party is a very fine balancing act that requires great political understanding and experience but also a certain amount of detachment from the leadership, to be the bridge between the party and their leaders. The grassroots of the party need a senior person that they can talk to about any concerns and worries they are hearing when they go around the country knocking on doors.

This was difficult to achieve while the Prime Minister had his friend as chairman of the Conservative Party. The party understood this and chose to deal with it by creating dual chair roles, with Sayeeda Warsi working alongside Andrew Feldman from 2010 until 2012 as co-chairman.

Sayeeda was an excellent chairperson and a minister in the Cameron–Clegg coalition government, she was definitely politically savvy. I liked her a lot and had planned to go campaigning with her for a few days. But once the *Sunday Times* story broke, that was not possible. The party wanted to distance themselves as far away from me as possible, although I stayed in touch with Sayeeda, who was very supportive and a very nice person.

After Sayeeda, Grant Shapps took over for a few years. Another politically savvy co-chairman to work alongside Andrew Feldman. The people with the political nous may have changed but Andrew stayed and so did the dysfunctional structure.

The consequences of the dysfunctional structure were percolating down to the grassroots and I found a lot of discontent among the voluntary sector of the party. As treasurer and on my trips around the country, many party workers told me that they didn't like the fact that the Prime Minister's mate was party chairman. They felt that they needed somebody that they could trust and who could listen to their concerns without any conflicts around personal relationships with the Prime Minister.

I said, 'Well, why not speak to Sayeeda? She will listen to you.' But there was a growing feeling that it was the David and Andrew show and Sayeeda could only do so much. A lot of them said, 'But that's not the point. Why should we have to deal with these conflicts? Why should we avoid one chairman to speak to another?' They had a point.

We are not talking about major discontent within the party but Feldman's closeness to David Cameron at times was creating a disconnect between the party faithful and the leadership, which would normally be bridged by an impartial chairman, ready to listen to them. As an example of the disconnect, at the Conservative summer party they held an auction and the prize was taking on the Prime Minister and the chairman at tennis in a doubles match. This just reinforced the notion that it was the David and Andrew show.

What made it worse was that Feldman seemed to think that the closer to the Prime Minister he was and appeared to be, the easier it was to raise money. This was true for fundraising but it was not so true for the structure of the party and the relationship with the hundreds of ordinary people working hard, knocking on doors and trying to run a ground campaign.

They saw CCHQ as some sort of inner clique run by friends of No. 10 and No. 11 Downing Street that was detached from the many grassroots members and volunteers. Especially as queen bee Kate Rock was mates with George Osborne alongside the David and Andrew show.

In time David Cameron and Andrew Feldman would become victims of the dysfunctional system they created. The same system that cut me off from the Conservative Party and led me to pursue any political path I chose.

You reap what you sow.

Chapter 53

ANOTHER REFERENDUM, ANOTHER ROLE FOR ME

After my various meetings with Feldman and the Cameron meeting at No. 10 Downing Street, I felt that if they had found a role for me, they could have effectively put me back in my box, and the next part of this book would not have been written. But they didn't. They left me to my own devices.

I had won one successful referendum campaign with Matthew Elliott (No2AV) and appearing on the horizon was another much bigger campaign that had my name written all over it: the 2016 EU referendum.

Regardless of any position I would have had with the Conservative Party, I would always have been a Brexiteer. But if I had the backing of Cameron and Feldman and my old job back as treasurer, I would not have taken up a prominent position with Vote Leave.

As treasurer of Vote Leave, I donated more than £1.3 million to the campaign, money that, if I had been treasurer of the Conservative Party, would have gone to them instead. This was vital for Vote Leave and ultimately Brexit, because my donations helped Vote Leave to win the Electoral Commission nomination as the official Leave campaign for the 2016 EU referendum.

Prior to the nomination process, there were many different groups campaigning for Brexit but only two that really had any chance of getting the official Electoral Commission nomination. It was a two-horse race between Vote Leave and Leave.EU, which was fronted by Nigel Farage and backed by Arron Banks.

Leave.EU was a well-organised campaign group run by Banks. They were aggressive, well-funded and focused and there were times when we thought they might win the nomination. They had a good chance. But in the end, we won although it was a narrow victory and it went right down to the wire.

It was crucial that Vote Leave won because we did not want a campaign based on immigration issues. Vote Leave saw the NHS and the cost of being a member of the EU as its main focal points and the best chance of victory.

I do not know if Boris Johnson, Michael Gove, Priti Patel, Gisela Stuart and other prominent Brexiteers would have campaigned alongside Mr Farage. But I do know that a lot of prominent Brexit politicians were pleased that we won the nomination.

We had done lots of focus groups up and down the country, through the Business for Britain campaign group described in the next chapter and in the early days of Vote Leave. It was clear that the NHS and the cost of EU membership were the main concerns of people. Immigration had a role to play in all of this but that wasn't the main issue we came across.

Also, by winning the official nomination, it meant that prominent politicians like Boris, Michael, Priti and Gisela could align themselves to a campaign that was about supporting the NHS. There had been a concern that, if Leave.EU had won, some prominent politicians would not have backed their campaign. This was the worry at Vote Leave HQ at the time. It would have meant that the whole Leave campaign would have been fragmented and not as focused, with some prominent politicians on the sidelines. It would have meant Nigel Farage fronting the Leave.EU campaign, not Boris.

Boris made a massive difference to the Leave campaign and without him we would not have won. But my early support for Vote Leave, prior to our nomination victory, got us to the starting post. Like my donations to the National Citizen Service, it kept Vote Leave afloat long enough to win the nomination. Then the money started rolling in, including the grant from the Electoral Commission.

On the creation of Vote Leave I had pledged £1 million, not knowing if we would win the Electoral Commission nomination. I told the team that I would send them money when they needed it. Often, I would be sending instalments of £100,000 every week, to keep them afloat.

Many people claim to be the architects of the Leave victory. There were a few, at the heart of the Vote Leave campaign, that I think made the difference between victory and defeat. Of course, ultimately it was up to the electorate, but a good case needed to be presented on why we should leave the EU, so people could form an opinion and make up their own minds. To win the referendum, we needed a co-ordinated campaign, backed and supported by powerful politicians on issues that were relevant to the electorate. Vote Leave ticked all those boxes.

If there was a podium moment for those key people working for Vote Leave, then Boris Johnson, Gisela Stuart, Priti Patel, Michael Gove, Dan Hannan, Douglas Carswell, Matthew Elliott, Jon Moynihan, Victoria Woodcock, Dominic Cummings, Alan Halsall and Peter Cruddas would all be on that podium.

Chapter 54

THE EARLY SHOOTS OF
VOTE LEAVE

In the build-up to the referendum, some of the newspapers were
trying to create mischief by saying that I was out for revenge
for the way Cameron and Feldman had treated me. For example,
Daniel Martin of the *Daily Mail* wrote an article on 10 October
2015 headlined 'Revenge of the Tory donor as he funds EU no vote'.
Martin's article talked about the way Cameron cast me aside even
though the accusations in the *Sunday Times* article were proven to
be untrue, and how I would now be trying to get my revenge on
the Prime Minister for the way he treated me.

I never saw this as a personal revenge thing because there were
issues of much greater importance. I thought the UK should
leave the EU, regardless of whether Cameron was for or against
membership.

Matthew Elliott and I had worked together on the No2AV campaign and we had stayed in touch. We often had lunches together
and we would chat about our next potential project. We enjoyed
working with each other. For some reason, we just clicked, and we
did a great job together when we turned around the AV campaign
in 2011.

On 23 January 2013, David Cameron made his Bloomberg speech where he called for fundamental reform of the European Union and, for the first time, he called for a referendum on whether the UK should remain a member. This would be the first in/out referendum in over forty years.

Following this speech, Matthew, myself and others mobilised and created a campaign group called Business for Britain (BfB), and I became one of its seed funders. Matthew and his team were building the infrastructure of BfB during most of 2013 and we got lots of support from the business community. He and I saw a chance to work together on a referendum campaign – but only if the Conservatives won the 2015 general election.

With just over a year to the next general election in early 2015, we published the following press release:

> Business for Britain – the business campaign for a better deal from the EU backed by over 800 leading UK businesspeople – has today announced the names of eight business leaders who will join an expanded board.
>
> The board members bring a wealth of business experience and represent the full spectrum of UK plc – from finance to services, retail, and culture.
>
> One of the board members Peter Cruddas – chief executive of CMC Markets, the leading financial derivatives dealer, and former treasurer of the Conservative Party – is reunited with Business for Britain chief executive Matthew Elliott. The pair worked together when Peter was treasurer and Matthew the campaign director for No2AV – the successful campaign against the alternative vote.

The board will help guide the campaign and provide strategic and business oversight. The new names join the existing team who have helped establish Business for Britain as the leading cross-party business campaign for a fundamental renegotiation of Britain's EU membership.

Business for Britain will shortly be coming forward with a proposal for EU renegotiation that has been compiled following a lengthy consultation with its campaign signatories and wider business community.

So, the new board was up and running and our campaign team was fully funded by myself and others. The team had a broad reach of businesspeople from around the country and we were going public about our campaign.

We were lobbying the business community about their views on our relationship with the EU. But the BfB board always felt that, should the Conservatives win the 2015 election, Cameron's pledge of reforming the EU and offering an in/out referendum meant that eventually we would campaign to leave. We were Brexiteers. And so, following the Conservative Party election victory, the BfB board declared in October 2015 that it would support the Leave campaign.

The good news was that the Prime Minister had given us three years' notice of a potential referendum. His Bloomberg speech was in January 2013 and the referendum was eventually held in June 2016. So we had plenty of time to get organised, which we did.

Business for Britain was a well-funded and well-supported campaign group backed by some of the most successful business leaders in the country. We were building momentum and in 2015, after the Conservative election victory, we launched 'Change, or Go', our blueprint for life outside of the EU.

Lauren Fedor of *City AM* wrote:

A new report from business leaders is giving momentum to an increasingly well-organised group of euro-sceptics who stand to vote 'no' – in favour of the UK leaving the European Union.

'Change, or Go', a new report from the euro-sceptic Business for Britain campaign group, argues that the UK 'could prosper and gain influence outside of an unreformed European Union'.

The 1,000-page report, which is being serialised in the *Daily Telegraph*, counts Risk Capital Partners chairman Luke Johnson; Newton Investment Management chief executive Helena Morrissey; and Institute of Economic Affairs director general Mark Littlewood among its authors.

Matthew Elliott wrote about BfB in 2016:

The central objective of BfB was to demonstrate that the business community was divided on the EU and to combat the general assumption that all business leaders were fanatically pro-EU. A crucial element of this was the creation of our regional structure … Our strategy – based on an important piece of market research done for us by Dominic Cummings after the 2014 European Elections – was that if voters could see that local business people in their communities supported a Leave vote, this would counterbalance the slew of corporate suits who would sign up for the Remain campaign …

By August [2015], we had recruited BfB Chairmen for eight

of the English regions, as well as Wales and Scotland. They came down to London for media training ... and briefings from myself and Dom [Cummings] on our strategy for the referendum. Following the June European Council meeting, the BfB Board had agreed to form Vote Leave and our small office was buzzing with new recruits joining by the day ...

A key factor to the success of Vote Leave was [that] ... we were not London or SW1-centric.

[During the autumn of 2015, we] recruited regional PR firms to handle our press and the BfB Regional Chairmen and signatories were their first port of call for all media requests. We knew that the most powerful voice was local business owners reassuring voters that leaving the EU would not hinder them nor their jobs locally. Voters listened to [manufacturing firm] Ebac's John Elliott in Aycliffe when he said the EU project was flawed, or to British Hovercraft's Emma Pullen who saw first-hand how the EU hampered her business.

Over Christmas [2015], the campaign team worked hard on the regional launches which happened across the UK in the New Year. In the first two weeks of January [2016], we launched in Durham, Leeds, Nottingham, Norwich, London and Portsmouth, attracting a considerable amount of media coverage.

[By March 2016,] the designation document to become the official Leave campaign was being prepared with a full submission from BfB [and its 1,000 business leader signatories,] highlighting the UK-wide support from business. By this point we had been joined by John Longworth, who sacrificed his position at the British Chambers of Commerce to be able to speak honestly in the referendum debate ...

Over three years, [BfB] provided the foundations for Vote

Leave and provided a voice for business leaders in the referendum debate.

By the end of 2015, BfB had published its 'Change, or Go' booklet on life outside an unreformed European Union. We had built a large and well-organised infrastructure across the country from north to south. And the board of BfB had agreed to form Vote Leave and prepare for the imminent in/out referendum.

Matthew would be our CEO; Dominic Cummings would be our campaign director; and I would be treasurer and main board member, with other BfB board members joining the Vote Leave board. It was a formidable line-up of talent – one that would run a successful campaign and ultimately win the 2016 referendum.

Vote Leave was not created overnight; it evolved out of BfB and all the infrastructure, contacts and expertise that had been gathered over the previous two years. We were fit for purpose and ready for the mother of all battles. At that time, we did not know the date of the referendum but whenever it came, we would be prepared to fight for our cause. And the rest, as they say, is history.

In the general election held on 7 May 2015, David Cameron was the first Conservative leader to win an outright majority since John Major in 1992, twenty-three years before. The Tory leadership were feeling buoyant, and who could blame them? I know I was buoyant and happy that we had another Conservative government, but the Conservatives won this election because they offered a referendum on our membership of the EU in their manifesto. Feldman and his team ran a good campaign but ultimately the difference was down to offering a referendum. Outside of London, our focus groups were telling BfB that people had had enough of the EU.

At this time, I felt that the party should have been better informed about the way the country was leaning and people's concerns about staying in an unreformed European Union. If I had met Cameron and Feldman, which I tried to do, my impartial advice would have been not to call the referendum in early 2016 because they would be up against a formidable opponent (Vote Leave) that was well-funded, well-organised, and had been working on a Leave campaign for at least two years.

I would have said, 'As Prime Minister, stay neutral and kick the referendum into the long grass until late 2017 or even 2018 because the Remain campaign needs more time, even though it has more money than the Leave campaign.'

Since Britain was already a member of the EU, Remainers felt less need to do anything as it was the de facto position. Whereas the Leave camp felt they had something to fight for and so we got a campaign group together early. Our campaign would be a positive campaign whereas Remain could only have a defensive campaign, to defend their existing position.

Throughout my time with BfB and Vote Leave, I never thought Leave would lose. It was clear there was a pent-up desire to leave the EU around the country among the working classes, especially in the north-east, where traditional Labour voters were prepared to vote on a Conservative manifesto pledge. Indeed, many Labour voters were voting Conservative in the 2015 general election just to have a chance to vote in an EU referendum.

Even if I was wrong, it was going to be close. Cameron needed to give himself time but, unfortunately, after winning the 2010 (not outright) and 2015 general elections, and the AV and Scottish independence referendums, the EU referendum proved to be one campaign too many for him.

Chapter 55

DEFEAT SNATCHED FROM THE JAWS OF (ELECTION) VICTORY

In October 2015 I was on cordial terms with Andrew Feldman and David Cameron, so I attended the Carlton political fund-raising dinner for the Conservative Party, at the Dorchester Hotel in Park Lane. I was on a table of ten with people from Business for Britain, including Matthew Elliott.

At the dinner, I said to Matthew, 'Let's go and say hello to the chairman, Andrew Feldman,' as I wanted to talk to him about the EU referendum. So we both made our way to the chairman's table and started chatting to him.

I congratulated Andrew on the party's election victory and his part in that victory. But I said to him, 'Be careful over the referendum. There is a lot of upset in the country and it is not guaranteed that they will vote to remain.' I told him about BfB and what we were hearing and that this might not turn out the way the PM thought.

Then I said to Andrew, 'Matthew and I are ready to sit down with you and the PM to update you on what we are hearing. We need thirty minutes of your and the PM's time, it is important. If the PM is busy, we will see you on your own.'

I continued, 'We are not some Mickey Mouse outfit running out of somebody's back bedroom. We have a proper board, we have some well-known businesspeople as our supporters, and we are well-funded.

'We are gathering lots of knowledge that the party should hear, especially before the PM declares his and the party's intentions. The PM needs to hear what we have to say, and we will keep it brief. If you want, we will engage with you and the team at CCHQ, but it is important.'

I may have been a Brexiteer, but first and foremost I was a Conservative and whether we remained in or out of the EU I wanted a Conservative government. I wanted the party to stay in power, but I was worried about their position on the referendum, so I offered whatever help I could.

Andrew said he would think about it.

However, for whatever reason, he ignored our offer of help. It was free advice with no strings attached but we never heard back from him. I do not know why to this day. But it might have made the party and the PM think differently about the referendum. Matthew and I had lots of pedigree for winning a referendum and I felt the party should have taken us seriously.

I feel that if the party had known there was a real chance of the country voting to leave the EU, the PM might have delayed the referendum, to give them more time to think it through. The government could have had more time to assess the situation to work on a long-term referendum plan and strategy; and the Remain campaign would have had more momentum and it would have been better prepared.

As a Brexiteer, I am glad this didn't happen, but I felt duty-bound to inform the party about how people were thinking outside Westminster.

This is not hindsight thinking. I knew it was a risk calling a referendum so soon after winning the last election because of the feedback we received from our focus groups.

During the EU referendum campaigns, I never thought the polls reflected the true position, even though all the pollsters put us anywhere from one to twenty points behind. I always thought Leave would win the referendum and, before the campaigns got going, I was worried that the PM would make the wrong choice. Not so much over whether he was in favour of Remain or Leave, because you cannot change your beliefs, but because I felt there was an opportunity for him to remain neutral. He could have said something along the lines of, 'Boris Johnson is for Brexit and George Osborne is for Remain – whoever wins, I will implement the result. I gave the country the right to decide and, as PM, it will be my job to implement the result, whatever it is.'

In this scenario, everybody could have kept their jobs. David Cameron could have appointed a Brexit committee and he could have stayed as leader. The problem was that Cameron thought he had to take a side. I did not share this belief, especially as he had just won an outright majority in the 2015 election. At one point, I even thought the PM might come out in favour of Brexit as I had heard him on two occasions say that there was no bigger Eurosceptic in the Conservative Party than himself.

I still think Cameron should have been the referee between the Leave and Stay campaigns. I might be politically naïve to think this, but it happened before, when then Prime Minister Harold

Wilson stayed neutral during the 1975 referendum on membership of the European Economic Community.

I believe that the country liked and trusted David Cameron. If he had been the administrator of the referendum result, I am convinced there would not have been as much divisiveness as there was following the result.

After my conversation with Andrew Feldman at the Carlton political dinner, I remember thinking, 'There is no way he will contact us.' I said this to Matthew Elliott on the night, but Matthew said, 'Let's see.'

Andrew was still relishing the election victory and a job well done. Nevertheless, I feared he would carry on in a somewhat normal dysfunctional way. If anything, his position had grown stronger. For Andrew, it was business as usual and he would continue his dinner circuit ritual, collecting cheques and telling everybody how far he and the Prime Minister went back as friends.

Matthew and I were two credible people who had worked with the party on a previous successful campaign and we were offering free advice. I believe that not to follow up on the conversation with us was a failure on the part of the chairman. I know it was at a social event and it was not in a formal setting, but Andrew could have invited us into CCHQ to elaborate more on what we were seeing and hearing, if only to assess the situation.

Four months after this conversation, the PM announced on 20 February 2016 that the referendum date would be 23 June 2016. Within a month, Business for Britain had morphed into Vote Leave and in April 2016, Vote Leave won the nomination from the Electoral Commission to be the official Brexit campaign party with Matthew, myself and others at the helm. Two months later, on

24 June 2016, David Cameron resigned as Prime Minister having lost the EU referendum and Dominic Cummings, our campaign director, was punching the ceiling at Vote Leave HQ right opposite the Houses of Parliament.

I could have written 'I told you so', but that is not my style.

Chapter 56

A BRIEF HISTORY IN TIME

The day of the EU referendum, Thursday 23 June 2016, I woke up at 6 a.m. and checked Twitter to see what was going on. There was silence because it was voting day and the media were banned from reporting anything to do with the referendum by law.

The first thing I noticed was that it was chucking it down outside and I thought I would get soaked casting my vote across the road at the Dance Studios in Mayfair. Nevertheless, I was one of the first to cast my vote at around 7.05 a.m.

Ten minutes later I was in my car driving to the office and I spent the whole day watching the financial markets and the television, which were all benign. The work for Vote Leave was done and all we could do was wait for events to unfold.

When I got to the office, the pound was riding high at around $1.50 – it had already appreciated by about 10 per cent since Christmas as the markets predicted a Remain victory. Even the bookmakers, who generally get it right, were predicting a win for Remain.

Matthew Elliott was travelling up to Manchester for the official result declaration, which would be broadcast early the next morning, with Gisela Stuart, our chairperson. I declined to go as I wanted to be in the office to see how the financial markets reacted. I was worried that they would go crazy when/if Leave won.

The day passed quickly. In the evening, I was watching the 10 p.m. news with Fiona when the newscaster announced that polling stations were closed. The result was due around 4 a.m., so I decided to go to bed around 11 p.m. to get some sleep before events unfolded.

Just as I was going to switch off the television, somebody from YouGov came on to say that they were predicting a 52–48 victory for Remain. I immediately turned to Fiona and said, 'That's complete bollocks.'

During the day, I had been speaking to Matthew on the phone. We agreed that if we went into the referendum level in the polls, we would win. We even thought that if we were two points behind in the polls we would win. Our research told us that young people do not always vote, even if they take part in opinion polls, whereas our strong core voters were over thirty-five and they were more likely to vote.

Fiona asked me if I was staying up for the result and I said no, I needed to sleep because tomorrow could be a busy day in the office. So we both went to bed.

Before I fell asleep, my mind cast back to a seminal moment in the Vote Leave campaign. Dominic Cummings, our campaign director, had been thumping the table at one of our board meetings asking for money. The board had always taken the view that we would only spend what was in the bank and not a penny more.

On this occasion, about four weeks before the referendum, Dominic wanted to print forty million leaflets to send to every household around the country, but we didn't have enough money. The Electoral Commission paid for postage as part of our nomination grant, but we had to pay for the printing of the leaflets.

The government had spent £9 million on pro-Remain leaflets

and Dominic felt that this was our chance to get the Brexit point over to the public. A leaflet could be delivered to every household in the UK. Dominic said it was crucial that the leaflets were posted, and we all agreed with him. If they were not printed, we would lose the money for the stamps and miss a big opportunity. We didn't have much time to decide. But we had to find a way as we didn't have the money in the bank to pay for the leaflets.

The board proposed that we would call in all the pledges that hadn't been received – in effect, all the money that was pending. We would all hit the phones and try to get the money in ASAP. Dominic said that would be too late as we only had twenty-four hours to give the go-ahead to the printers. It was a tense moment for us all and Dominic put us all under lots of pressure. However, I came up with a solution.

We needed around £500,000, more or less, to print the leaflets. I asked our accountant, Antonia, what the total amount was we could expect from the Electoral Commission as our grant and she replied £600,000, not including the cost of the postage.

I said, 'Right, I will lend Vote Leave the £600,000 to get the leaflets printed but as soon as the Electoral Commission money arrives then it has to be used to repay my loan. I have already made substantial donations and there is enough money pledged to pay for our campaign. What we have here is a cashflow situation and I can help with that.'

The board applauded me, and we went ahead. Dominic gave the printers the green light and we sent out a leaflet to every household in the UK on why they should vote Leave.

In fact, I never actually had to lend Vote Leave the money because within a week we had received over £1 million in donations – my pledge was enough to get the leaflets printed. I had already given over £1 million to the campaign, mostly before nomination, so they knew I was good for the money. But without my commitment, we would not have got the leaflets printed. It was a pressure situation and a week later one of the board members said to me that it was a master stroke in how to get something done without having to pay for it. I agreed but then I thought, 'Hang on a minute, this campaign has cost me a packet.'

Once Vote Leave had become the official Leave campaign for the referendum, all donations over £5,000 had to be declared and made public. If you scan the Electoral Commission website, you will see that I donated approximately £300,000 to Vote Leave. But that does not take into account the money I donated to the campaign before the official nomination when donations did not have to be declared. In all, I contributed around £160,000 to Business for Britain and £1.2 million to Vote Leave.

Now, before all the Remainers get on their high horses and say these were illegal donations, they were not. They were given to campaign groups before and after nomination by the Electoral Commission. Tax was paid on all the donations and all donations were declared to HMRC. Everything was done within the rules set by the Electoral Commission and HMRC. I am a UK resident and domiciled in the UK.

On the morning of the referendum result day, 24 June, around 4 a.m., I woke up and Fiona was on her iPad checking the news. The light from her iPad lit up the darkened room. My first words to her were 'Has Vote Leave won yet?' and she replied, 'No, not yet, but Leave will win.'

I immediately kicked back the covers, got showered and shaved and made my way to the office, getting in around 5 a.m. It was a surreal moment because it reminded me of when I walked into the same office three years earlier after the *Sunday Times* story had broken and my face and the story were all over the television screens. Only this time, it was pictures of Cameron, and politicians discussing the referendum result – the UK had voted to leave the EU.

It felt like vindication and revenge for a fleeting moment, and I was very happy. However, there were more important issues to deal with as the financial markets were in meltdown. The pound was dropping, the Far East stock markets were dropping, and it was all doom and gloom as the world's financial markets reacted to an unexpected result. Well, unexpected by the financial markets, but not by myself and the Vote Leave team.

I stayed in the office until 9 a.m. when the London Stock Exchange opened, and the foreign exchange markets were busy selling the pound. Everything was now under control in the office as clients were closing their positions or buying at what they thought were oversold markets.

I left my car at the office and took the tube to Westminster. I arrived at Vote Leave HQ at Westminster Tower around 9.30 a.m. There were various MPs and campaign workers celebrating and patting each other on the back. Boris Johnson arrived with his team and there was going to be a press conference later when Gisela Stuart and Matthew Elliott got back from Manchester.

The press conference took place with Michael Gove, Gisela and Boris and I was in the wings with Matthew and Dominic. We said nothing and just watched Boris and the others delivering their speeches. Dominic had been shut in a room earlier with Boris and Michael to help them with their speeches.

I hung around HQ chatting and having my photo taken with various people including Dominic, Matthew, Boris and Michael.

It was a beautiful day in more ways than one with the sun shining through the windows of HQ. As the result sank in, we all felt a sense of relief and exhaustion but also a great sense of public duty.

At one stage, I was standing next to Boris as he watched his father, Stanley Johnson, giving an interview on television. Stanley had supported the Remain campaign. It was a surreal day in more ways than one.

Both sides ran strong, aggressive campaigns and spent lots of money, with the Remain campaign spending twice the amount of the Leave campaign. However, whatever the arguments, it was the people of the United Kingdom who decided whether they wanted to stay in or leave the EU. The two campaigns just laid out the arguments and the people decided.

The Vote Leave team made a major difference to the result because we ran a good campaign, but if people had wanted to stay in the EU, they would have ignored what we had to say and voted to remain. For me, it doesn't matter why people voted to leave the EU. What matters is their vote and their vote must be respected.

After the news conference I left to go back to my office. As I walked back to the tube station on that sunny morning, there were masses of people milling around Westminster with interview after interview on College Green opposite the Houses of Parliament. It was as if nobody could understand what had happened apart from the leader of the UK Independence Party, Nigel Farage, and his team, who were revelling in the result and trying to claim most of the credit for it.

I arrived back in my office just in time to see David Cameron walk out from No. 10 Downing Street to deliver his resignation speech. A few hours later Lord Feldman resigned as Conservative Party chairman.

As I watched the Prime Minister deliver his speech, it did make me think about the working-class boy off a Hackney council estate – whose mother was a cleaner and whose father was an alcoholic and who left school at fifteen without any qualifications – out-flanking two privileged muppets from Oxford University. That thought did make me smile.

Chapter 57

GIVING BACK

I often get asked to speak to young people about my upbringing and my success. I usually speak at schools or universities or youth events and the one bit of advice I like to give to them is to donate to charities if you become successful. I explain that when I was growing up the one thing that helped me to remain stable and happy was being in the Boy Scouts. The Scouts got me out of a hostile home environment and helped to get stability in my life.

The Scouts taught me life's skills like cooking, sewing and fending for myself, but above all independence. I loved scouting life including camping and competitions, like swimming galas and camping competitions against other districts. I loved camping especially as it was a change of environment from our estate to the green fields of Surrey and Essex. For me it was a different world.

I also enjoyed the challenge of learning how to do things like tying knots, making models for competitions or building a raft to paddle across a lake. On one big camping trip we even built a bridge across a small ravine for which I qualified for my pioneer badge.

There were so many aspects to the Scouts that I am grateful for because it allowed me to see a different world and meet people from all walks of life. I often say when speaking to students about my success that if it wasn't for the Boy Scouts I would not be here today.

I also like to explain to budding entrepreneurs that through charity you meet more business contacts than you would through normal business events. It's a great way to meet like-minded people who are also businesspeople. I tell them that through giving to charity I have met a lot of nice people who have become friends. Of course, I have also met lots of businesspeople. For example, through my charitable work I met Bill and Melinda Gates when Fiona and I had dinner with them in London. I would not have met them through business.

Also, giving to charity keeps you in touch with the real world. On one occasion I was at a Prince's Trust event in London with young people who were opening small businesses after receiving a business loan through the Trust. Most of the young people had been in prison and they were showcasing what they had achieved since they got support from the Prince's Trust.

The Prince of Wales himself attended the event and we strolled around the venue together because at that time I was the biggest private donor to the Trust and on their board of trustees. I had given their business programme in the region of £3 million.

As I passed one stall a young black girl called Gina came up to me and threw her arms around my neck and gave me a big hug. I felt slightly embarrassed and I said, 'Well done, keep up the good work.'

Her response was instant. She said, 'Mr Cruddas, forget all that, you don't know me, but I know you, because I know how generous you have been to the Prince's Trust.

'I was in prison because I did some bad things and I deserved to be in prison for what I did. However, the Prince's Trust helped me and because of people like you giving money to the Prince's Trust I was able to get my life back on track and get reunited with my two small children. Your donations have helped give me back my life.

'I just wanted to say thank you for helping me, through the Prince's Trust. It is amazing to think that successful people are prepared to give up their time and their money to help people like me.' She then started to cry because she was so happy to have her children back, and I got very emotional too.

For me it was a wonderful moment and one that I will remember for ever. Afterwards it crossed my mind that maybe all my business success was not about me and what I had achieved. Maybe it was because it meant I could help others that it jogged my heartstrings. I was proud of my achievements in business but what was more important was how I could give back to society following my business successes.

I felt compelled to do this as the Scouts had done so much for me and now, I was trying to help others out of difficult life situations. That is why when I am speaking to young budding entrepreneurs, I tell them to give back as much as they can.

Thank you, Gina. I hope the florist business is still going well and I hope you are well.

When Gina was speaking to me, I could relate to what she was saying. Although I had never been in trouble myself with the police, growing up was not easy. I had the Scouts to rescue me, but some people just get into bad situations before they can work out what life is all about. It reminded me to always keep my feet on the ground.

During this time, I was the biggest private donor to the Prince's Trust and the biggest donor to the Duke of Edinburgh's Award scheme, having given them around £3.5 million. I also helped many other charities and to facilitate my donations I set up the Peter Cruddas Foundation in 2006.

All donations to my foundation are made entirely by myself. I do not fundraise; I just pay into the foundation every year and we give the money away to good causes. Steve Cox, who runs the foundation for the trustees, travels up and down the country meeting people and dealing with donation requests which are then put in front of the trustees, who include Lord Young of Graffham, Martin Paisner, a prominent lawyer, and myself.

Incidentally, a recipient of a Prince's Trust business loan early on in their company's journey designed my foundation's logo for free. They said they didn't want my foundation to pay for it as they had been helped by the Prince's Trust to set up their own design company and it was their way of saying thank you. I love the logo because it is made up of a P and a C, my initials.

The foundation has helped and supported over 200 charities since 2006, as you will see if you go onto our website. These charities have supported so many different causes, but the foundation's focus is on helping young people. This is the cause closest to my heart because of my own personal situation growing up.

I have included my charitable work in this book as it makes me proud and it is something that is also part of my life's successes. I will continue giving to charity for the rest of my life.

Chapter 58

THE FINAL CHAPTER
– OR NOT?

I am often asked by people who have known me for a long time: when am I going to retire? It is a question I struggle to answer as I genuinely do not know.

I suppose it is a valid question. I am sixty-seven years old at the time of writing this book. I have been working since 1969 when I was fifteen years old, over fifty years. I have never been out of work and I have never claimed one day's benefits in my life. Both of my brothers are retired from driving black taxis, yet I carry on working.

The simple answer is that I like working. I have built an amazing company over thirty years and along the way I have picked up some good people who have supported and helped me for a long time. I have succession planning in the company and the systems I/we have put in place will ensure that the company remains profitable for years to come.

However, I still get a great buzz, from working especially as I started CMC Markets as my own company. I am in the office every morning before eight o'clock. I also feel that if I stop working my health will suffer because I need to maintain my routine and not take it easy too much. If I did, I would probably put on weight and I am sure my mind would not be so active. I think working keeps me youthful. I do not take days off and I like to walk around the office chatting to people. Working is fun so why would I stop something that I like?

A good friend of mine, Lord Young, who is eighty-nine years young, says that life is like a bicycle: if you stop pedalling you fall off. He is my inspiration to keep working because he looks amazing and is still as sharp as ever.

I also feel I still have a great deal to offer to the business as I am never short of ideas. A lot of them never materialise but it is fun challenging the young people I work with to come up with better ones. My ideas keep them thinking and they love the challenges that I present – well, most of the time, I think.

I also feel that over the years any business will face challenges. I believe that CMC Markets can benefit from my experience and should there be any dramatic events I am the best person equipped to deal with them and advise the team. This has happened on many occasions over the last thirty years. I like to think that the team lean on me when they are facing difficult issues.

I still own around 62 per cent of the company even though it is listed on the London Stock Exchange. Because of this, I want to protect my investment and make sure that the company keeps delivering for all the shareholders including my family and me.

I believe I will know instinctively when it is time to retire and when that day comes, if it comes, I will gladly hand over the business to the team.

I once did a small exercise and worked out on the back of an envelope that since I started work in 1969, I have contributed over £2 billion directly and indirectly to the British economy, mainly when I started CMC Markets. I have contributed to various governments around the world but mainly to the British government, through taxes paid by employees, employers' tax, capital gains tax, dividend tax, corporation tax, personal tax and through job creation. That's not bad and something I am very proud of. I am one of the top fifty taxpayers in Britain.

I have been asked to work for the Conservative Party on three or four occasions. I have been offered really good jobs and responsible positions. But for various reasons I have declined, mainly because of work commitments. However, I do want to work for the Conservative Party again in the future and I am a big supporter of the Prime Minister, Boris Johnson. We are both Brexiteers and worked together for Vote Leave.

Hopefully if a decent referendum is called over the next couple of years Matthew Elliott and I can team up again. However, I would not get involved in any Scottish referendum; that is for the Scottish people to decide and they would not appreciate a Sassenach poking his nose into affairs that are of no concern to him.

But this is not my final chapter as I intend to carry on working for the next ten years at least and, health permitting, longer. I do not want to stop pedalling. Who knows, I might even pen a sequel to this book.

But whatever happens I can look back on my life and say that it has been an epic journey and one of which I am very proud. I created a company and invented an industry. I created thousands of jobs and billions for the British economy. And I did it all without borrowing any money, without any other major shareholders and all from scratch.

I hope this book will help others to push on and do some great things and create their own company. If not, do with it what I did to Hussein Chalabi's financial chart book after the stock market crash of 1987. Chuck it in the bin and write your own book of life.

INDEX